PIVOT
OR DIE

ALSO BY GARY SHAPIRO

The Comeback: How Innovation Will Restore the American Dream

*Ninja Innovation: The Ten Killer Strategies of
the World's Most Successful Businesses*

Ninja Future: Secrets to Success in the New World of Innovation

PIVOT OR DIE

HOW LEADERS
THRIVE WHEN
EVERYTHING CHANGES

GARY SHAPIRO

WM

WILLIAM MORROW
An Imprint of HarperCollinsPublishers

HarperCollins books may be purchased for educational, business, or sales promotional use. For information, please email the Special Markets Department at SPsales@harpercollins.com.

FIRST EDITION

Designed by Kyle O'Brien

Library of Congress Cataloging-in-Publication Data

Names: Shapiro, Gary, author.
Title: Pivot or die : how leaders thrive when everything changes / Gary Shapiro.
Description: New York, NY : William Morrow, [2024] | Includes bibliographical references and index. | Summary: "From Gary Shapiro, New York Times bestselling author and head of CES and the Consumer Technology Association, a manifesto for today's top executives, entrepreneurs, and leaders: pivot or die"-- Provided by publisher.
Identifiers: LCCN 2024023835 (print) | LCCN 2024023836 (ebook) | ISBN 9780063374775 (hardcover) | ISBN 9780063374799 (ebook)
Subjects: LCSH: Leadership. | Entrepreneurship. | Businesspeople.
Classification: LCC HD57.7 .S47545 2024 (print) | LCC HD57.7 (ebook) | DDC 658.4/092--dc23/eng/20240612
LC record available at https://lccn.loc.gov/2024023835
LC ebook record available at https://lccn.loc.gov/2024023836

ISBN 978-0-06-337477-5

24 25 26 27 28 LBC 5 4 3 2 1

This book is dedicated to Drs. Edward and Jolanta Malinowski, who made the ultimate pivot: escaping communist Poland and coming to America to give their daughter—and my wife—Dr. Susan Malinowski a better life. Their sacrifice in leaving medical careers in Poland to start over in the United States inspired my wife to become a great retina surgeon and improve tens of thousands of lives.

May our nation continue to be a land of opportunity, attracting and welcoming the best and brightest from around the globe.

Contents

Foreword by Ed Bastian, CEO of Delta Airlines

There have been many "pivot or die" moments during my career. I was with Delta for the tragedy of 9/11 and when the company filed for bankruptcy protection in 2005. I became president just in time for the 2008 recession and oversaw the merger with Northwest Airlines in 2010. But 2020 was the hardest year of my life—both personally and professionally.

That January, I delivered a keynote address on the Future of Travel at CES 2020 in Las Vegas. I outlined my vision for what was to come for the travel industry, from robot exoskeletons that could handle heavy freight, to parallel reality that allows multiple customers to look at the same screen but each see their own flight information. The years ahead looked bright and exciting, and it was a long way from where Delta started as a crop-dusting service in 1925.

Of course, none of us knew that we were about to face a far different future of travel—or that it would happen so abruptly. There was no playbook for that incredibly harrowing first year of the COVID-19 pandemic. Delta went from $47 billion in revenue in 2019 to losing $100 million every day in spring 2020, as millions of customers canceled their business and leisure travel plans and hunkered down at home.

In addition, my mother, Mary—an enormous influence on my life and my closest friend—died that February. I felt like I had lost it all.

Pivoting isn't just about making the right business decisions. It's about mustering the courage to show up when there doesn't seem to be a way forward. It's about being honest about what you don't know, and having the confidence that you're going to get through. It took a lot of strength for me to realize the opportunity to guide Delta and its incredible team through its most pivotal period this century was a blessing, not a burden. A true privilege.

Now fast-forward to two years later. Gary had invited me back to CES, for the 2023 C Space keynote. I'm not sure he knew at the time what this invitation meant to me and to Delta. Not long before, many had written off our industry as permanently crippled by COVID. Gary's belief in our company and vision was a message to the world: In-person experiences are back. Travel is back. In short: We're back!

And if there's anyone with the experience and insight to talk about pivoting, it's Gary. CES has long been the place where businesses experiment and pivots start—and that's largely thanks to Gary and the platform he's created over more than thirty years. But *Pivot or Die* isn't just essential reading for fans of CES. It offers lessons for leaders and aspiring leaders across every industry, or even those who just want to make a change in their own lives.

At my company, operating in one of the most dynamic industries on the planet, we've taken those lessons to heart. Today Delta is the largest airline by revenue in the world. We fly more than 5,000 flights per day. We have the ability now to invest more resources than ever in anticipating the pivots of the future.

One of these, of course, is artificial intelligence (AI). "This is the age of the AI pivot," as Gary writes in this book. Delta has deeply embraced the technology pivot, and AI is already playing an important role. The challenge of the future will be figuring out how to use machine science as a predictive tool to help us make the best decisions at five hundred miles per hour.

Gary understands the nuance of the issue, and the importance of always putting the human factor first. "One special thing about humans," he writes, "is that we are the only species that can make conscious decisions. Only humans can imagine the future."

With technology advancing at this pace, we can't lose sight of the people behind it. That doesn't just mean people at the helm—the founders, the CEOs, the chairmen. Most of the greatest pivots of all time were made possible by the dedication and support of the larger workforce, the sometimes thousands of employees who buy into and advance a vision for change.

People are, truly, the heart of every business. That lesson is one of the most important I've learned in my career.

With that in mind, I want to share one of my favorite passages in *Pivot or Die*: "Sometimes . . . things that are totally out of our control go wrong. . . . It's how we pivot from those mistakes and setbacks that defines our future. Those who can't get over their failures move on, whether voluntarily or not, to less visible high-stakes careers. Those who learn from their setbacks find that failure can breed future success."

We all make mistakes. We'll never know what tomorrow may bring. Sometimes you can plan for change, and sometimes you can't. But Gary has it right in this book: the world is moving fast. So get ready to pivot, be courageous, and be humble. Or get out of the way.

Introduction

On Wednesday, January 22, 2020, I was sitting in an easy chair in my Detroit area home, finishing up some work and looking forward to a weekend getaway to Boyne Mountain in northern Michigan. Then, my wife arrived home from work with news that would dramatically reshape our lives.

Driving home, she'd heard a story on the radio: the Chinese government had quarantined the city of Wuhan to stop the spread of an unknown disease. While it's hard to imagine now, that story wasn't a top news item. In fact, it was buried behind a story on whether the Super Bowl should move to Saturday. But my wife, a practicing retinal surgeon and keen observer of health trends, knew that something big was coming.

My wife, Dr. Susan Malinowski (friends call her Mal), is the smartest person I know. As a child, she and her family emigrated to the United States from Poland. She went on to earn a joint BS/MD from the University of Michigan in only six years, specializing in ophthalmology with a subspecialty in retina surgery. She co-founded a successful vitamin company and invented a new, low-cost treatment for eye swelling. While she may not be an infectious disease specialist, she knows how to identify opportunities and manage risks.

"We've been to China. We know what this means," she told me that Friday. "It means the disease is out of control. If China has blockaded an entire city, it means this is a harmful and highly contagious disease. Plus, it's a new disease. This is serious."

While I felt out of my element, I trusted my wife and her instincts. I also started to think about the impact of a new disease (at that point few people were using the word "pandemic") on the business world. As president and CEO of the Consumer Technology Association (CTA), North America's largest technology trade association, I knew that large-scale illness could be one of the black swan scenarios that upend entire economies—not to mention trade shows like CES, the world's most powerful technology event, which CTA owns and produces. But as I spoke to friends and family in the days following, no one else seemed especially concerned about the looming threat of COVID.

Luckily, CTA's investment committee meeting was set to take place just a few days later. Mal had already been planning to join at the invitation of our chairman, John Shalam, the founder and chairman of Voxx International Corporation. After the group discussed the new virus and implications for Chinese manufacturing and supply chains, my wife asked to speak.

She moved up to the table of C-suite executives, including top leaders from companies like Amazon, HP, and Sony, and dropped a bombshell. She told the initially skeptical group that they were "in the Kübler-Ross stage of denial" and that COVID-19 would eventually infect and even kill people in every country in the world. As a medical professional, she knew that it would take at least a year to develop a vaccine, and she told the board to expect economic tumult and a roiling of stock markets. She predicted that COVID's spread would catalyze social unrest and asked the board to consider how a world turned upside down would impact business and investment strategies. Later, I learned that half of the executives at that boardroom table thought she was crazy, and the other half were terrified by what she said. Ultimately, her words prompted serious reflection on how CTA could and would respond to what then seemed unthinkable: a global pandemic that would reshape the lives and livelihoods of billions of people.

The COVID-19 pandemic initiated one of the biggest pivots in history—in technology, government, education, policy, trade, retail, and every sector that touches our lives. I experienced it firsthand when the Consumer Technology Association raced to support member companies struggling with supply chain challenges in 2020, and then as our team planned the world's first and largest digital tech show—CES 2021—and the largest in-person event post-COVID—CES 2022. I also had a front-row seat to the incredible pivots in technology, business, and government that came from the pandemic. It has been a wild ride—and we're still feeling its impact.

This is a book about pivoting—what it means, when to do it, and what happens when it goes wrong. In a complex and fast-paced world, the ability to process new information and act fast is important in nearly every facet of our lives. In some cases, that means investing in the partnerships and strategic alliances needed to meet the rapidly evolving demands of new technology developments and consumer desires. Other times, it means recognizing an opportunity and defying industry trends or the status quo to seize an advantage.

Over my more than forty-year career in the technology industry, I've had a front-row-center seat to changes in the tech world. I've seen groundbreaking new ideas come to life, including some that seemed groundbreaking at the time but eventually flopped. I've gotten to know tech industry founders and CEOs, and watched retailers like Blockbuster, Bed Bath & Beyond, Circuit City, Fry's, RadioShack, and Sears grow to dominate their industries—at least for a time—only to shrink as consumer needs and wants changed or challengers introduced better business models. I've seen major companies like Atari, Eastman Kodak, Monster, RCA, and Sega peak and then descend to licensed names.

On a more positive note, I've seen countless companies and the executives who lead them show that they have the foresight and the capacity to challenge staid business practices. In the face of rapidly changing technology and a rapidly evolving world, they've been able to avoid irrelevance and reinvent themselves.

As humans, we naturally resist change. We like the status quo. The present we live in seems more comfortable and safer than the unknowns of the future. In fact, for most of us it's actually hardwired into our brains. We owe that tendency to the amygdala, the part of our brain that interprets changes in our environment as a potential threat, triggering the infamous "fight or flight" reflex.

While it may have had an evolutionary advantage, this resistance to change often serves us badly in the modern world. Things change! And we either adapt, or we wither. If that's true for individuals, it's doubly true for businesses. In business, if you stand still and don't change, the odds are high that some competitor will make your products or services cheaper, better, or more interesting.

Failure can also be a powerful driver for pivoting. In the United States, we appreciate failure more (or, depending on how you think about it, stigmatize failure less) than most other countries, because we recognize that we learn more from our failures than we do our successes. The people who can do this with humility and curiosity are the ones who will succeed.

In two earlier books, I called these people "ninjas." Ninjas were ancient Japanese warriors who often won their battles despite being outmanned and outgunned. They used cunning, skills, and unconventional means to accomplish their objectives. They recruited warriors with different skills, worked as a team, and adjusted quickly to new conditions. When confronted with a problem, they had a remarkable ability to think fast and find a solution.

Today's ninjas don't just win on the battlefield. Ninjas are master pivoters. They focus on the big goal, and they're not wedded to the steps it takes to reach it; they're open to exploring multiple paths. They are passionate, committed, and motivated. They seek out those with diverse experiences and skills to build effective and impactful teams. Modern-day ninjas problem solve in the boardroom, innovate in sourcing and supply chains, and outmaneuver in the market.

Not every pivot works, and that's okay. During COVID, with air travel limited and hospitals in cities like New York soon overrun with patients, Mal had an idea for repurposing unused commercial airplanes with hospital-grade air-filtration systems as surplus hospital units. We floated the idea by Delta Air Lines CEO Ed Bastian, who liked it enough to assign an internal team to work on feasibility. We tapped connections at the American Hospital Association and elsewhere to explore the idea. Thankfully, more effective treatments for COVID meant that cities didn't need as many remote hospital facilities as predicted. But it was the "miss every shot you don't take" type of thinking we felt the nation needed to confront the breadth of the pandemic.

Of course, that kind of thinking isn't new. In the late 1970s, a man named Sheldon Adelson created a series of smaller businesses before hitting on his first big success with a Las Vegas business event for computer dealers. That tradeshow, COMDEX, quickly grew into the world's largest business event, which he later sold for almost $1 billion. He took that money, pivoted, and put it into an old hotel, remodeling the property into a huge hotel and convention center complex, now called the Venetian—one of the most popular venues on the Las Vegas strip. The Venetian, along with other hotels he built globally, made Shelly, as he was known to friends, one of the wealthiest people in America.

In this book, we'll explore pivots that reshaped the consumer technology industry and our world. Some worked, some didn't. Some you may have heard of; others have flown under the radar but introduced major shifts in our society. We'll explore the pivots that are underway in technology and business, and the political and policy pivots that are needed to protect the "secret sauce" that is American innovation.

I'll also share some of the pivots that shaped my thinking. I grew up with a black-and-white TV, a telephone that plugged into the wall, and one-dollar-per-minute phone charges for any call made to outside our county. I listened to music on vinyl discs. At the age of twelve, I chipped in with my brothers to buy my dad the most expensive gift we had ever given him—a huge, early-stage calculator. Fast-forward several decades, and tech has zoomed ahead. On a recent April Fools' Day, my own teenage son jumped onto the ChatGPT craze to prank me, using it to draft a fake email from a major airline CEO restoring my coveted elite frequent-flier status.

The transformations we're seeing today are a direct result of pivoting. While all of us benefit from the pivots happening constantly in the field of technology, I'm lucky enough to see it personally at CES. Each year brings some new magic—aha moments spurred on by discovery, serendipity, and connection. Businesses get a chance to put their products forward for feedback and critique, new products and services are unveiled for the first time, and new partnerships are forged. It's pivoting in real time!

After many decades walking the Las Vegas hallways of CES, one thing is clear: The future isn't just about what we can imagine, or what it takes to bring those ideas to life. It's about how we can adapt and adjust along the way.

CHAPTER 1

What Is Pivoting? The CES Story

A pivot is an intentional change in direction. Not more. Not less. It is not a change in who you are, a move away from your core beliefs, or an abandonment of your ethical principles.

Every pivot begins with a decision. We need to make good decisions to survive, both as individuals and as a species. What separates humans from other forms of life are the conscious decisions we make. Single-cell organisms do one thing well—they survive. More complex organisms, like reptiles, fish, and birds, make decisions based on instinct. Advanced animals adapt and learn, developing habits that enhance their survival instincts. Natural selection allows those who survive to bear offspring. These progenies have genes that increase the likelihood of their survival.

This cycle of life, repeated millions of times over centuries, passed on the most adaptive decision-making traits to every species, including humans. Of course, good genes don't help much in the face of big disruptors—including weather shifts like the Ice Age, or seismic or volcanic activity.

Visit the centuries-old city of Pompeii in Italy and you will see how a sudden volcanic eruption can devastate a city.

But the biggest, or at least the most probable, threats to species on Earth come from humans. We overhunt, overfish, overeat, fight, and engage in destructive behavior. As humans tamed fire, we also invented gunpowder, dynamite, and nuclear weapons. Dangerous weaponry is not limited to explosives. Viruses, bacteria, and chemicals created by humans make extinction-level events increasingly possible.

At the same time, human behavior is accelerating other existential threats—pollution and climate-altering emissions, growing use of limited fossil fuels, the spread of communicable diseases, and more. To bring things back to the tech sector, cyberattacks, cyberbullying, ransomware, misused artificial intelligence, and a laundry list of other concerns keep me and many others up at night.

All of these threats started with—and are perpetuated by—decisions.

Most decisions are inconsequential. But a few are life changing. People make decisions to sacrifice themselves for the good of their family or community. A soldier throws himself on an IED to protect his fellow soldiers. On September 11, 2001, passengers of Flight 93 intentionally crashed their plane into a field to protect those on the ground from terrorism.

In other cases, small decisions to pivot can have monumental consequences. Most initial COVID-related decisions were small. Eventually, as the virus's impact and spread became more obvious, the pivots became larger.

How CES Pivoted

The Consumer Technology Association is a nonprofit, and we serve an industry rather than any one company. More, there is no stock or equity—so most profits are plowed back into our mission to promote tech industry innovation. We do this through market research, public policy advocacy, and setting technology standards. (Without standards, electric plugs would not fit into outlets, radios and televisions would not get broadcast signals, and your devices could not plug into your computer ports.) And CES is the most high-profile way we promote innovation.

CES is an annual trade show owned and produced by the Consumer Technology Association. At CES each January, thousands of companies convene in Las Vegas to show off the latest and greatest technology to an audience of well over 100,000 media, buyers, investors, and innovators. Some of our attendees come with plans for partnership or acquisition. Others simply come to be inspired. It's the proving ground for break-through technologies and global innovators. It's where brands get business done and meet new partners, and where industry's sharpest minds take the stage to unveil their latest releases and boldest breakthroughs. While I've worked with CTA and CES in various capacities for more than forty years—including more than thirty as CEO—the show has a long and storied history that predates even me.

The first CES was held in New York City in 1967. It had 17,500 attendees, just a fraction of the more than 138,000 who traveled to CES 2024. It's a huge physical event, with exhibits sprawling across millions of square feet of space. In 2024, exhibits covered more than 2.5 million net square feet—an area larger than forty-three American football fields, or the Palace of Versailles, the Louvre Museum, and Buckingham Palace combined. It also delivers a massive boost to the Las Vegas economy, with an estimated economic impact of some $300 million each year as attendees flock to hotels, restaurants, and entertainment venues.

In July 2020, I announced a pivot to our first all-digital CES show, a full seven months before the event. At that point, COVID cases were surging, and the director of the National Institute of Allergy and Infectious Diseases, Dr. Anthony Fauci, had just testified that the US could see as many as 100,000 new cases of COVID a day. The US was two months into "Operation Warp Speed," a federal public-private partnership to speed up vaccine development, and while Moderna was just about to announce promising results in its early-stage trials, widely available vaccines were still many months away.

Leaning on advice from medical advisers, the physicians on our board, and my wife, Mal, it had long been clear to me and the CTA executive board who approved the decision that we could not responsibly host CES 2021 as an in-person event. We wanted to give our exhibitors and attendees as much time as possible to adjust. After all, CES isn't built in a day. (For those less familiar with the trade show world, the planning and execution of the big brand showcases—and even the smaller-scale booths hosted by smaller companies—happen many months in advance.) Despite what we felt was both a responsible and practical decision, we immediately faced questions and even criticism from other event producers who thought our pivot was premature. But we stayed steadfast in our plans.

To put this in perspective, canceling the physical presence of CES 2021—which also meant investing in an all-digital presence for the show that year and creating a fair refund policy for companies that had already committed to physical exhibit space—cost CTA millions of dollars in expenses and in lost revenue. It meant forgoing an opportunity to bring together thousands of exhibitors, members of the media, and executives from around the globe. It was not a decision I took lightly.

What's more, the huge drop in revenue meant that CTA had to cut expenses. Along with so many other CEOs at that time, I had to make an extremely difficult and painful decision—to lay off employees. In one terrible day, we lost 10 percent of our staff.

At the same time, we were focused on pivoting to reinvent CES as the world's premier digital innovation event. At that point, a digital event of that size was unprecedented. We had no idea how the exhibitors we worked with would react. We had no idea whether a digital CES would, or could, have the same impact. Would people show up? If they did, would they find that the wonder and serendipity of CES translated to a virtual platform?

Planning CES 2021 required a totally reimagined experience. We had to create an event that let exhibitors, media, thought leaders, and executives connect in ways that were both safe and meaningful. We knew we couldn't re-create the beauty and magic of Las Vegas or the five-sense experience that comes from being on the show floor. We were painfully aware of the hit to the Las Vegas economy when the show moved online—estimated at nearly $300 million. But we saw it as an opportunity to do something that had never been done before.

We had to pivot, as a team, from producing the world's biggest physical business event to creating the world's coolest online digital event. More, we had to do it quickly and present an experience consistent with the CES brand. After soldiering through crises at previous CES shows, our team was confident that we could handle anything. But our Las Vegas expertise revolved around floor space, hanging signs, union labor, busing, and the many other logistical questions and quandaries that go into producing the massive physical CES. This was different.

Karen Chupka, then our CES show lead, had an inspired idea: along with the move to an all-digital show, we could shift the show a week later without causing any problems with hotel or convention center arrangements or travel plans. In January 2021, our CES audience was at home anyway, and the shift bought us extra time to explore the possibilities of a purely digital platform.

That decision proved prescient, given the challenge of finding a platform to host the first all-digital CES in our history. Even before the pandemic, we'd seen dozens of demos from software and digital platform vendors, pitching us on the idea of taking CES digital. But in the pre-pandemic world, we were skeptical that our executive audience wanted to create avatars and explore virtual exhibits.

It took months to finalize a deal, as we negotiated with platforms unfamiliar with contracting for an event that involved so many exhibitors and the many features we knew would be needed to put on the show. By the summer, we'd decided to team up with Microsoft for its Teams platform, technical and cybersecurity expertise, global scale, and experience in creating compelling digital content. With Microsoft technology, CES 2021 attendees were able to build profiles and select areas of interest for a tailored event experience, complete with content recommendations. Before the show, we had over 70,000 people register and opt in for a "networking experience"—a sign that people were hungry for connection and community, even if that meant logging in from home.

Ironically, while the show was digital, our partnership with Microsoft required frequent trips to its headquarters in Redmond, Washington. Looking back, the trips themselves—taken at the height of COVID—were somewhat surreal. Our team traveled on near-empty airplanes to desolate airports. I later learned that the visible security presence at our hotel wasn't a sign of some highly private celebrity staying on-site, but the hotel's dual function as a quarantine site for COVID patients. I ate too much Chinese takeout and tried to keep my eyes on the prize: a well-executed CES.

The Microsoft team members were consummate professionals and did everything in their power to make things run smoothly. During our December 2020 visit, as we recorded our keynote remarks and other presentations, Microsoft's campus felt like the site of a Hollywood production, complete with beautiful stage settings, multiple cameras, directors, and producers.

Everything seemed perfect, until nature threw a curveball our way. When we returned to Redmond in January for the CES live event, full of anxiety and anticipation, we found howling wind and rain. On January 11, the morning of the first digital CES in history, we left the hotel before six a.m. for the fifteen-minute Uber drive to the Microsoft campus; on the way we saw downed tree limbs and power outages. On arrival, we learned that Microsoft was also experiencing a historic first—the first power outage in its history. Thankfully, the foresight of Microsoft's campus planners saved the day as backup generators hummed to life and saved our digital event. Sometimes, even the best pivots can't beat advance planning and built-in redundancy.

Ultimately, CES 2021 was a triumph. Neither our team nor our various audiences felt the all-digital experience could match the "absolutely overwhelming spectacle of technology and humanity" that comes from wandering our CES Las Vegas convention center halls.[1] But the show still delivered incredible new technology and tantalizing hints into the technology trends animating the industry. We were thrilled when, months later, *Trade Show Executive* recognized CES 2021 with the Gold 100 Grand Award for best digital event.

CES 2021 had 1,000 virtual exhibits, 150,000 visitors, and 100 programming hours. The show featured rollable phones, transparent screens, sanitizing robots, and vacuum cleaners that could throw away their own waste. Amid a rush to upgrade home technology, CES showed faster-than-ever laptops, high-end headphones, and 8K TVs making the leap from niche technology to the mass market—outpacing even the content available. We saw a big move toward product sustainability—a trend I'll discuss later—with devices like Chipolo's ONE Ocean tracker, built from fishing nets, trawls, and ropes collected in shallow ocean waters, and Panasonic's low-cobalt batteries earning media praise. And in a sign of the times, Razer's Project Hazel gaming "smart mask" concept featured both customizable LED lights and a reusable N95-grade filter. As CNET put it, while "flashy three-story booths and auditoriums full of tech nerds were replaced by highly produced livestreams and virtual pitches from executives,"[2] in the end, "it was still CES." Our pivot to the digital world was a success, and our entire team breathed a sigh of well-deserved relief.

While CES 2021 met our brand and customer goals, there was no denying the tough hit financially. We were about as generous as we could possibly be to our exhibitors and incurred a lot of our own costs. We were mindful that, as an industry, we were very lucky—first, because the technology sector as a whole prospered and grew during the pandemic, and second, because our show is held in January, which gave us time to pivot after the virus hit the US.

Of course, as anyone who helped navigate a business through the COVID pandemic can attest, one pivot isn't always enough. We pivoted again when we decided to make CES 2022 a hybrid event—returning to our home in Las Vegas for an in-person show, bolstered by a strong digital presence. The show was the first in-person event of that size since COVID, and it didn't come without criticism. Some people thought it was simply too soon to return to in-person events, with COVID still infecting millions each day globally.

More, some still wrongly blamed CES for bringing COVID to the United States. In spring 2020, a major US public broadcaster had run a national radio piece with an accompanying article speculating that CES was the super spreader event that introduced COVID-19 to the United States. The story, based on an account from just one CES attendee, was initially passed over by several media companies. But once published, it was picked up by scores of media.

I was horrified by the allegation. The story had several inconsistencies, not least of which was the time line: the person making these allegations was at CES for less than twenty-four hours and reported symptoms upon leaving the show. Even more significant, CES 2020 was in early January and COVID-19 cases were not reported anywhere in the US until later in the month, with no cases reported in Las Vegas until March. While the editor ultimately agreed to revise parts of the written story and add context from reputable medical experts, the sensational claims in the original story received vastly more global attention than the revision. Even the CES attendee pushing the story told media he didn't fault CES and that he would consider attending future shows. But the harm had been done. Even as a seasoned trade show veteran, the incident both scarred and scared me. As Warren Buffett once said, "It takes 20 years to build a reputation and five minutes to ruin it." That's especially true in our headline-driven, clickbait environment.

That reality was top of mind as we planned for CES 2022. We sought input on measures to reduce the spread of airborne infections from many sources including volunteer doctors and an outside medical consultant specializing in events. Based on their views, we required all participants to be COVID vaccinated and masked. We widened many aisles, created one-way corridors in busy areas, and offered Abbott BinaxNOW COVID tests to all attendees. We also created protocols to deal safely with those testing positive on-site. While these choices may seem obvious, especially in retrospect, each required careful discussions within our leadership team, given the polarized and politicized views on masking and vaccination.

Things looked great—until they didn't. Around Thanksgiving 2021, the Omicron variant began to spread around the world, prompting some major exhibitors to cancel or scale down their presence in the last weeks of December. The press amplified the big-name cancellations, putting pressure on us to cancel our physical event. We weighed the evidence and decided to proceed with CES, although we did shorten it by a day. What persuaded us to stay the course was the recognition that so many companies, especially startups and smaller tech companies, rely heavily on CES for much of their annual business. I was also moved by our board discussions as well as private input from the CEOs of a few Fortune 500 companies, including Qualcomm's Cristiano Amon and Abbott's Robert Ford, who urged us to go forward on principle. The nation needed leadership in learning to live with COVID.

The tough decision to go forward, by almost all accounts, turned out to be the right decision. While the show was smaller—attracting around 44,000 in-person attendees and featuring just 1.27 million net square feet of exhibit space—both exhibitors and attendees were thankful and joyous. Many of the smaller companies participating told us that this CES was a great opportunity for them to grab the spotlight and connect with buyers and media. We also saw success based on the principled leadership position we took, with the US Travel Association lauding CES as "a model for how business trade events can take place."

At CES 2023, we built on this success and focused on reducing transmissible illness as a whole. We consciously shifted to a more touchless environment. We strongly recommended but did not require vaccines, including flu shots. We kept many facility doors and even a few loading dock doors open. We hired eighty greeters to help welcome and open doors for arriving attendees. And we had remarkably few positive cases and near-zero social media chatter about illness. Afterward, we surveyed our attendees and found that fewer than 10 percent reported any type of sickness in Las Vegas or within three days of returning home. That's especially amazing considering the scale of the show: nearly 120,000 attendees and more than 3,200 exhibitors.

Pivoting and Resiliency

Some of the best pivots—most of them, I would argue—come from the need for resiliency. Hosting CES 2021 virtually wasn't ideal, but we learned lessons on creativity in using new technology and working with exhibitors that drove our planning for CES 2022 and beyond.

Our all-digital CES wasn't my first hard-won lesson in resilience. In 2017, CTA's executive board met at a new hotel in Napa Valley. It had beautiful rooms with wonderful views, electric blackout shades, and even a high-tech toilet that raised its cover as soon as you entered your bathroom.

The final night of our stay, wind gusts buffeted the valley and knocked out the area's electricity. In the wee hours, the hallway emergency light sputtered on periodically, sirens followed, and few of us could sleep. The rooms were pitch black, and the heavy electric-powered blinds could not be opened. The room lights were useless, the landline hotel telephones were dead, and our smartphones soon became unusable for anything other than their power-sucking flashlight function.

Tired guests gathered in common areas and soon learned that it wasn't just their rooms that had turned dark and unwelcoming. Fires were spreading nearby, and there was talk of evacuating the hotel. But there also was word of long lines of bumper-to-bumper traffic and a concern the fire was approaching the main roads. We were urged to pack. This presented a special challenge to me personally as my suitcase was on the patio outside our room, which could only be reached by raising the heavy, electronically controlled blackout shades.

As the hotel put out a cold buffet breakfast outside and delivered candles to each room, we decided to accelerate our meeting time. In a sunlit room without electricity, phone connectivity, and coffee, we spent the next couple of hours discussing a vital and substantive topic. Without the distraction of connected smartphones, we had our group's full attention and soon concluded an important and productive meeting.

I found the experience transformational in my thinking. We assume the availability of basics like water, electricity, and a telephone signal. Yet our society, homes, and lives are increasingly vulnerable due to real changes in our environment and dependence on technology.

Increasingly freaky weather, electricity outages, cyberintrusions, nuclear threats, looming trade wars, and dependence on an array of technologies means we need to start thinking differently. We need to start considering risks and balancing them with prudent investments. We need to focus on the resiliency of the essentials in our lives.

This book is all about pivoting—in technology, in business, in government, and in our personal lives. We're going to talk about the four types of pivots, which will overlap in places but will provide a foundation for understanding how to steer your business (and yourself) through challenging waters and find success in a rapidly changing world. We're going to look at case studies of companies and organizations that have and haven't pivoted well. Some of them have changed the course of history or improved the lives of millions of people. Some of them have simply delivered connection, entertainment, or delight. Along the way, you'll hear how these pivots can inform how you should think about pivoting in your own organization and even in your own life.

The Four Types of Pivots

The Startup Pivot

Most successful startups have to pivot at one point or another to find success. In a survey by Wilbur Labs, a San Francisco–based startup studio, 40 percent of founders reported pivoting to avoid failure. And that's just the percentage willing and self-aware enough to admit to it! Pivots included adapting business plans, improving products, diversifying revenue streams, and rebranding. What's more, the study found that "founders willing to pivot tend to raise their odds of success."[3]

The best startup pivots are a combination of rational and gut decisions. Taking an analytic and thoughtful approach makes sense, by definition. You think carefully. You consult others with relevant knowledge, those you trust and those who have a stake in the outcome. You define important factors. You create lists of pros and cons and weigh them against one another. With ChatGPT and other AI programs and apps, you can even get some tech-driven guidance on which option is best.

Rational decision-making is what most businesses do. They survey existing and potential customers, show them prototypes, and get input. Indeed, we facilitate this process at CES each January in Las Vegas, where companies introduce thousands of new ideas, prototypes, products, and services. In fact, this is what our startup area Eureka Park is expressly designed to do: expose entrepreneurs' innovative ideas to a global audience of tens of thousands. I counsel Eureka Park exhibitors that it will be like drinking from a fire hose over four days as they get reactions and feedback from what can feel like an endless stream of potential partners, customers, and investors.

I promise them that the idea or innovation they bring to Las Vegas will most likely shift based on the input they receive from the people stopping by their booth and engaging with them. In fact, if the experience *doesn't* give you new ideas and perspectives, you might just be doing it wrong. Each year, close to 100 percent of Eureka Park exhibitors responding to our post-CES survey tell us they're satisfied with their CES experience. They go on to adjust their planning and make decisions about building, marketing, and selling their products and services.

Rational decisions are usually good ones. They prove that careful work, written strategies, and a lot of research can help improve the odds of success. With data and metrics now available for nearly anything, it's also far easier to make data-driven decisions, and a growing number of CEOs and C-suite executives have declared themselves data obsessed. The downside of rational decisions is that they take time. Rational decision-making may slow down action while gutsier people act.

That's why rational decisions need to be counterbalanced by gut decisions. The beauty of a gut decision is that—when the stars align—it just feels right. The disadvantage is that these decisions can sometimes fly in the face of logic, facts, and reason. In fact, they can be precisely the opposite of the rational decision I outlined above. People trying to sell you something know that potential customers make decisions based on how they feel. Good salespeople try to form a bond, a strand beginning a relationship so you'll grow to like and trust them. The best ones ask questions, helping to keep you so focused on your response that you forget to think about whether you're actually interested in the product or service. Salespeople want you to think you are making a rational decision. But I'm sure I'm not alone in realizing too late that I've bought a product I didn't really need or want. Why? I had a gut feeling about the salesperson and the product.

People who go with their gut often beat the odds and make a wise decision. In fact, studies show that melding gut instinct with analytical thinking can help people make decisions both faster and better.[4] That's even more true for the overthinkers, or people facing "best of the bad options" decisions. Gut pivots can help people veer from the status quo and hit it big—or not. That's especially true for startups, whose founders nearly always need to rely at times on gut instincts, since they have limited business history to go on.

How do you balance rational and gut decision-making? A gut check is always a good idea. Choose someone you trust whose interests align. Listen. Don't argue. Delay action for a moment. Try to see if objective rational decision-making matches your gut. Make sure you're aligned with your key values. Then act accordingly.

The Forced Pivot

Forced pivots happen when outside forces, from global pandemics and natural disasters to government regulation and supply chains, change the environment in which a company manufactures, sells, profits, or functions. In forced pivots, companies often have few good choices; sometimes, it's simply a choice between pivoting or shutting down. The most dramatic example in recent years is the COVID pandemic, which introduced forced pivots to companies across nearly every industry.

But forced pivots often have unexpected positive results. When the COVID pandemic shut down global semiconductor chip supply chains, technology companies reconfigured their devices and saved money. Others reassessed their supply chains completely, with some deciding to shift manufacturing hubs to new locations. Car companies reallocated auto inventory, focused on building the most in-demand models, and removed convenience features that could not be supported with the chips available. Car buyers in Florida, for example, probably don't need heated steering wheels or seat warmers.

Forced pivots during the COVID pandemic also delivered another important lesson: the "butts in seats" mentality common in the corporate world didn't always serve either companies or employees well. Many white-collar businesses have shifted to a permanent hybrid work model, allowing for more flexible work arrangements, less commuting, and greater job satisfaction. In most cases, these arrangements deliver just as much productivity!

As a general rule, pivots foster innovation and creative thinking within an organization. That's especially true of forced pivots, where do-or-die situations foster an all-hands-on-deck mentality and reward out-of-the-box ideas. Employees at all levels must come together to collaborate, experiment, and create, and people from different backgrounds and disciplines can bring their unique expertise to the table.

Forced pivots can also prompt companies to double down on technology innovations that streamline work and make employees more productive. While I don't think technology is the solution to every problem, there is enormous untapped opportunity for businesses to embrace these innovations and integrate them into their business models.

Ultimately, forced pivots speak to my favorite maxim: Innovate or Die. I believe so strongly in this concept that it's written in a huge font on the wall of CTA's Innovation House in Washington, DC. That's also the inspiration for the title of this book.

The Failure Pivot

Failure isn't a bad thing. In fact, many successful pivots are prompted by failures. More than perhaps any other culture, Americans have come to embrace failure as a learning opportunity. Personally, I find that some of my best employees are those who have tried, failed, and learned from the experience.

Success can breed complacency, but losses and mistakes teach humility, creativity, and adaptability—as long as we first look backward and learn from our mistakes. I've learned from my many years in the tech industry, as well as my own personal failures, that failure fuels ingenuity. The very act of thinking differently, of problem-solving, sharpens the part of our brain that helps us become more thoughtful and imaginative—two traits that are critical for success.

Reflecting on the benefits of failure can also be a comforting thought amid the red-hot disappointment of mishaps and fiascos. "At least I learned something" and "Someday I will think this was a good thing" are the mantras I've often repeated to deal with the emotional sting of failure.

In many ways, America was built by leaders who successfully executed pivots from failure. Think of Henry Ford, whose first two auto ventures failed for lack of funding. Or Thomas Edison, who famously proclaimed that he "[had] not failed 10,000 times . . . but succeeded in proving that those 10,000 ways will not work." Even Walt Disney was once fired from a newspaper job for a lack of creativity. Beauty supplier Avon first sold books. Chewing gum magnate Wrigley sold soap. Berkshire Hathaway sold textiles before homes and insurance. Tiffany & Co. sold stationery.

Visionary leaders use a combination of trends, research, and instinct to forecast the future and know when to pivot ahead of time. You pivot because if you don't, you'll fail—or at the very least, you won't succeed.

The Success Pivot

We're used to thinking of pivots as the result of a failure, but that's not always the case. Sometimes, companies pivot on the back of success. These companies don't rest on their laurels. They build on existing achievements and know-how to take advantage of new opportunities. Rationally, that should make success pivots the easiest ones to execute, but often it's just the opposite: people tend to like the status quo, especially when that status quo is delivering accolades and strong profits.

In the face of an existential crisis like the scenarios that often precede a forced or failure pivot, the need to adapt is obvious. In most success pivots, that's less true. They require leaders with the vision not just to see what's successful *now*, but what will be successful in a year, five years, ten years, or even further down the road. Speaking at the Economic Club of Washington, DC, in 2018, Jeff Bezos highlighted one of the best-known examples: Amazon's move into cloud computing with Amazon Web Services (AWS). While Bezos felt the opportunity was obvious and expected other big companies to follow quickly, it took years before AWS had major competitors.

The reality is that many people struggle with this sort of vision, though I think those who have it are more common in the fast-paced technology industry. Consider that in the financial world only 20 percent of mutual fund managers beat market indices.[5] In the medical field, peer-reviewed journals tend to publish a small coterie of experts from well-known institutions pursuing traditional studies and treatments. How do breakthrough ideas and results emerge in these constricting environments?

Often, a pivot from success requires betting on an outsider with a new approach. Breakthroughs and new ideas often come from outsiders who have a totally different perspective and see an opportunity. Outsiders are hungry, eager to try a new approach and implement new ideas. No wonder some 80 percent of American tech unicorns (new companies with a market valuation over $1 billion) are founded by immigrants or have immigrants in key leadership roles.[6] Betting on outsiders can sometimes mean bringing them into the organization, one of the reasons that big companies often have venture capital units or actively seek opportunities to acquire promising startups. Success pivots can also be driven by collaborations between companies, sometimes even companies in direct competition with one another!

Other times, it means bucking tradition and listening to a wider variety of voices within your organization. In a 1994 letter to then-president Bill Clinton, former president Richard Nixon warned about the dangers of relying on counsel from senior leaders who "are more interested in covering their asses than protecting yours." Nixon encouraged Clinton to embrace big and bold plays on the world stage, reflecting that some of his best decisions—including his landmark 1972 visit to China—were made over the objections of career foreign service officers. The moral? Don't always listen to advisers, whose job it is to play it safe!

That's especially true in the tech world, where investing in bold ideas is the key to long-term success. The status quo is made to be broken, and status quo companies will be upended by startups and others willing to challenge business models, even those that still seem to work.

In the next chapter, I'll take you on a tour through the technology industry for case studies of pivots that have reshaped not just the industry, but the world more broadly. While pivots certainly aren't unique to the technology industry, I'll share why they're so common, and how that approach has been more broadly adopted by business leaders in a world where every company is a tech company—or at least is tech adjacent.

We'll then go into greater depth on the four types of pivots—the Startup Pivot, the Forced Pivot, the Failure Pivot, and the Success Pivot—and the circumstances or skills that make each possible. In most of these pivots, there's some overlap. Startup pivots can build on prior success or connections forged by their founders. Forced pivots can sometimes be executed just before a venture falls into failure pivot territory. But as you'll see in the following case studies, each of which I explore in its own chapter, each type of pivot does offer unique lessons on how to change your mindset as a leader and innovator and steer your business through challenging waters.

After a long career in the technology industry, I divide people into two basic categories: the doers and the talkers. You can learn from the talkers, but they get little done. But the doers? They're the ones who make things happen. They aren't afraid to make decisions, and they aren't afraid to pivot.

Which one are you?

CHAPTER 2

Pivotal Shifts in the Tech Industry

n 2017, entrepreneur and venture capitalist Marc Andreessen coined the terms "fast sectors" and "slow sectors." Fast sectors, he noted, benefit from falling prices and less regulation; slow sectors are characterized by rising prices and more regulation.

Consumer technology is a fast sector. So are industries like media, retail, and food. Typically, eldercare, childcare, healthcare, education, construction, banking, and government are slow sectors. What makes a fast sector? In my experience, fast sectors attract and reward great pivoters.

Dissecting how and why tech leaders are, overall, such great pivoters can help us understand the concept of pivoting in general. As Andreessen put it in a March 2023 blog post, "We are heading into a world where a flat-screen TV that covers your entire wall costs $100, and a four-year college degree costs $1 million."[1]

This doesn't mean that *all* tech companies are fast, and *all* healthcare companies and educational institutions are slow. I can think of hundreds that aren't! But it's notable that the most successful companies across every sector are the ones who tend to *see themselves as "tech companies,"* introducing technology tools to shake up stagnant industries. That's why we have terms like "health tech," "fintech," "edtech," and "agtech." It's a testament to the power of technology to drive change. The ones who embrace innovation and can quickly pivot when something doesn't work are the ones who succeed in the long run. Being "fast" means being agile.

Still, even the most ambitious tech adopters sometimes find themselves stumbling into the red tape of regulation. As Andreessen put it, "technological innovation in those [slow] sectors is virtually forbidden." Consider the financial compliance industry. Economist Gary M. Shiffman, the founder of tech company Giant Oak (which builds big data tools to combat criminal activities), notes that financial compliance firms spend more than $25 billion a year combating money laundering but counter less than 1 percent of the problem.[2] Most banks are still using technology that's decades old—despite the emergence of new AI solutions—while money launderers are using technology that's state-of-the-art. (This is beginning to change, as companies like NASDAQ and FinClusive work with banks to use the power of blockchain to reduce financial fraud and provide digitally verifiable identity credentials.)

Contrast that with the consumer technology sector. Twenty years ago, a high-end TV retailed for over $2,000. Now, consumers buying new TVs are getting 4K (or even 8K!) Ultra HD smart TVs for a few hundred dollars. You can buy TVs that fold up, roll up, or look like art on your wall. At CES 2024, we even saw the debut of fully transparent OLED screens. This same story is true for a wide range of technology products, as competitors jump in and prices fall.

In this chapter, we'll talk about how the tech industry overlaps with every other industry imaginable, rewarding innovators in an ever-greater number of industries and pushing them into the "fast" lane. It starts with the simple fact that nearly every organization in the world now relies on the internet, but goes much further. Machine learning is helping us process and glean insights from the huge amounts of data we all generate. AI is increasingly integrated into our software and hardware to make workers more efficient and accurate. These tools aren't just being deployed across the private sector. They're also increasingly adopted by our government. In fact, as I'll share in this chapter, by embracing technology solutions, the government has at times pioneered major tech pivots.

Who Invented the Pivot?

The basic idea of pivoting has been around for centuries. The umbrella was invented over four thousand years ago in China as a device to protect from the sun, not the rain. Coca-Cola was originally created as a way to counter morphine addiction. Play-Doh was invented in the 1930s to clean the residue that coal heaters left on walls; when oil and gas heating replaced coal, the company changed its business model to arts and crafts.

But it was the technology industry that really invented the modern-day pivot.

Many of today's big consumer technology giants didn't start in consumer technology at all. Nokia began as a paper mill in Finland, with products that ranged from rubber boots to military equipment to aluminum before focusing on telecommunications equipment in the 1990s. Samsung was founded to export dried fish and flour from Korea to China, then sold insurance and textiles before moving into electronics. Panasonic started with bicycles, and despite a pivot out of that market and into many other consumer products in the United States, still makes high-quality bicycles for the Japanese market. Nintendo began as a playing cards manufacturer, and tried out the taxi business, a TV network, and even a venture into romance—running some of Japan's famed "love hotels" and producing the Love Tester, a device that claimed to measure a couple's compatibility—

before transforming into one of the world's biggest names in gaming. YouTube was created as a video dating site, with the name and logo trademarked on Valentine's Day.

Nearly every name in the "startups who made it big" category has a pivot as part of their origin story. Before they became some of the biggest, most successful, and most used platforms in the world, PayPal, Airbnb, X (formerly Twitter), Groupon, Instagram, Netflix, and Slack all pivoted their business models.

Amazon started as an online bookseller, operating from the Bellevue, Washington, garage of Jeff Bezos's parents. I thought it was a cool idea, and in the early 1990s I invited Jeff to speak at our association meeting. I was flabbergasted when he pulled out an early Kindle and told us this device was the future of book delivery. Now, with a market cap exceeding $1 trillion, he proved that creating your own competition, pivoting your business to beat the competition, and constantly reinventing your business (consider Amazon Prime, AWS, Whole Foods, and more) can ensure not only survival but growth.

Jeff Bezos's trick is early pivoting. He moved quickly, not just responding to change but leading it. He created a culture welcoming change. When Amazon used the cloud to host its online activities, it figured out that it could sell cloud services some three years before any other competitor did, gaining a huge and still unsurpassed competitive advantage.

Why are pivots so common in technology? It's because competition, while present in every business sector, may be fiercer here than any other. Companies that have flourished recognized that they must pivot or die. They weren't wedded to one idea. They seized the opportunity. Along the way, they changed the way we use and relate to the technology products we use every day.

■ ■ ■

The Commercialization of the Internet

It's hard to imagine the internet without someone trying to sell you something. Ads sit at the top of your Gmail inbox and clog your spam folder. Sidebar ads clutter web pages. You can't read a news article online without closing an ad first. But it wasn't always that way. Back in the 1980s, the National Science Foundation (NSF), whose supercomputers powered one of the first networks in the United States, saw the internet as "an open commons, not to be undone by greed or commercialization."[3] In fact, until 1991, commercial enterprise on the internet was banned, and the NSF's "fair use" rules barred "extensive use for private or personal business."

But no matter how noble an internet for the common good seemed, it came with a problem: in the early 1990s, telecom companies had no idea how they could make money. In short, they needed to find a pivot.

In 1994, *Wired* magazine ran a digital publication called Hotwired. Needing to generate revenue, they came up with the idea to set aside portions of the website to sell space to advertisers. They called them "banner ads." One of the first ads belonged to AT&T, which paid $30,000 for a banner ad that ran for three months. The ad got an astonishing click-through rate of 44 percent—a number that will shock modern-day marketing professionals and would be nearly impossible to achieve now.[4]

In 1995, Netscape, founded by Jim Clark and Marc Andreessen, offered the first opportunity for the average consumer to connect to the emerging World Wide Web, with its web browser, Navigator. Netscape also created push technology, which allowed websites to send updates on things like weather, stocks, and news directly to a user's desktop. But businesses quickly recognized the ability of push technology to deliver ads to users.

When Jim Gilmore became the governor of Virginia in 1998, he made Don Upson the nation's first state cabinet-level secretary of technology. Don created a Commission on Information Technology to establish rules governing business on the internet. He put on the commission top technology-oriented state and congressional legislators from both parties, the president of Virginia Commonwealth University, and tech leaders like AOL founder Steve Case. I landed on the commission as well, thanks to my work at CTA but also the fact that Don was my law school housemate and close friend.

Don tasked us with developing a set of recommendations that could form the basis for legislation. For all of us, the stakes were clear: we needed to preserve the internet's flexibility, openness, and ability to serve as a platform for all, while recognizing the need for guardrails that would build trust for people doing business online. We were also aware of proposals in our backyard that were pushing for exactly the kind of clampdown on internet access we feared. Earlier that year in Loudoun County, Virginia, the county library board had enacted a new policy requiring the use of filtering software on all computers for its patrons. The software ended up blocking a huge array of constitutionally protected and in many cases innocuous websites, including state tax forms, the Yale Graduate Biology Program, and even a Beanie Babies website. It was ultimately ruled unconstitutional, but the issue highlighted the challenge of trust online.

We soon agreed on a set of guiding principles, calling for, among other things, the government to avoid undue restrictions on internet commerce, lift restrictions on encryption, and resist the temptation to apply tax policy to the internet in a manner that would hinder growth. Building on this framework, we agreed on the foundation for legislation to allow online contracts and electronic signatures, and resolve a range of roadblocks. The state legislature quickly passed these recommendations, and in March 1999, Governor Gilmore signed the measures, which he called "the first comprehensive set of state Internet regulations," into law.

Virginia's example prompted other states to follow and soon Don and I found ourselves traveling abroad to the Middle East, Europe, and elsewhere to explain the impact of our template to leaders in other countries.

We must have been persuasive, because the world followed Virginia's example. You have surely benefited from the result: commercialization of the internet has exploded over the past two and a half decades. As governments pivoted, millions of people saw the benefits.

Pivoters like Hotwired and Netscape were smart. They needed more revenue to sustain their businesses. And while ads might be annoying, they're also critical to the now-booming industry of e-commerce. Forward-looking policymakers coupled with visionary tech leaders opened the door to a plethora of internet functions that make the internet as we know it today—free, open, and vibrant—possible.

From IMs to Avatars

The internet enabled most of the incredible technology we see today. In 2004, serial entrepreneur Eric Ries was frustrated when startup ideas that seemed so great on paper fizzled out in practice. After multiple attempts, he knew that the problem wasn't his startups' ability to create products that functioned well. It was that not enough people wanted to buy his products in the first place.[5]

One of his ideas was to create a social network around instant messaging. The potential upside was huge—but so were the obstacles. People were already comfortable with their IM platforms, and to make it work, Ries would have to get entire networks of friends and acquaintances to join en masse. So when he co-founded a new social media startup, IMVU, he sought feedback early and often, and took inspiration from Japan's lean manufacturing systems, made famous in the 1950s and '60s by Toyota.

That instinct to seek feedback was the right one. His initial concept focused on instant messaging wasn't going to work. Instead, Ries pivoted to another kind of social platform: a virtual, 3D world where users could create avatars and buy virtual goods—blurring the line between social networking and gaming. Importantly, they could connect their existing IM accounts to IMVU, lowering the barrier to entry for new users. When the company officially launched to iOS and Android in 2014 it was an immediate hit, attracting six million active users in its first year. Since then, the platform has grown to more than 50 million users globally and raised more than $77 million from five rounds of funding. IMVU is now the world's largest social metaverse platform, with 700,000 daily active users across some 120 countries.[6]

In a 2009 blog post, Reis shared his recipe for success, urging entrepreneurs to be willing to "pivot from one vision to the next." Some startups, he noted, "avoid getting customer feedback [because] they are afraid that if early reactions are negative, they'll be 'forced' to abandon their vision." That, Reis declared, was precisely the wrong approach. Startups need feedback "to find out whether [their] vision is compatible with reality or is a delusion."[7] Those ideas coalesced into a 2011 book, *The Lean Startup*, in which Reis set out his philosophy for a broader segment of businesses. The book, which goes into depth on a variety of strategic shifts, makes a strong case for the importance of pivoting. According to Reis, "pivots are a permanent fact of life for any growing business. . . . Even after a company achieves initial success, it must continue to pivot."[8] Hear, hear!

The book was a huge success, selling over two million copies worldwide and generating translations into more than thirty languages. It's still considered a must-read for entrepreneurs, and its emphasis on building a minimum viable product (MVP) to test hypotheses and gather feedback has influenced startup culture worldwide. It also made "pivot" into a buzzword, first for Silicon Valley entrepreneurs but ultimately for the business world as a whole. In 2011, the pivot became such a popular concept that *Harvard Business Review* dubbed it "geek-ese for 'this isn't working: let's change it up.'"[9]

This success also helped engineer something of a personal pivot for

Reis—into a celebrated author, speaker, and guru for business and product strategy. While IMVU still exists as a privately owned company, making some $60 million in annual revenue, Reis left the company in 2008. He is now a celebrated and sought-after commentator and advice-dispenser for startups and big companies alike. That's the power of a good pivot!

The One-Man Helicopter

The US military might be known for its bureaucracy, but it's also a prolific technology innovator. The defense industry often pioneers new technology, trading on a significant federal budget allocation and senior leaders focused on developing the future technology that allows the United States to stay one step ahead of global adversaries. In fact, more than a dozen US government agencies and departments exhibited at CES 2024, and many more sent representatives to walk the show floor looking for innovations that could support their missions. Of course, that focus on innovation isn't new.

In the early 1950s, Charles Zimmerman, an aeronautical engineer, developed a one-man flying machine. The pilot stood on a platform, with rotors mounted on the underside of the aircraft, and steered the machine simply by shifting his weight. It was known as an aerocycle, and the US Army took a keen interest. An early test program ran more than 150 flights lasting up to 43 minutes.

The appeal of the aircraft was its ease of use. Early testing supported the idea that untrained soldiers could learn to operate the aerocycle in under twenty minutes. But as testing went on, it became clear that flying the machine was more difficult than initially expected. In several early flights, the contrarotating rotors collided, sending the aircraft crashing back to earth. The Army couldn't find a solution, and they abandoned the project.

Yet the US military held on to the idea of an easily operated, low-flying aircraft, and eventually recognized that the problem might just be the pilot.

More than a decade later, during the Vietnam War, the military began using unmanned aerial vehicles (UAVs) for reconnaissance. They were also used as decoys in combat, to launch missiles against fixed targets, and to drop leaflets for psychological operations. Fast-forward fifty years and they've taken on a new role in modern life. If you've never heard the term UAV, here's one that might be more familiar: drones. Despite its failures, Zimmerman's one-man helicopter took the first ascent toward the drone age.[10]

Today, drones remain an important component of our military, with drone operators popularly known as the "chair force." Instead of the Marines, it's often drones that go into conflict areas first. In fact, in Ukraine, a drone and its operator successfully negotiated a Russian soldier's surrender in 2023.[11] Drones also play important roles closer to home. Firefighters use them to evaluate the size, heat, and spread of a fire and to locate people who may be trapped. Amazon, Walmart, and other drone operators offer last-mile drone delivery services. Drones are now window cleaners for skyscrapers and other tall buildings. Rescuers use them to locate lost hikers. They're also changing the future of agriculture around the world, pollinating crops, fertilizing fields, and finding dry areas using thermography. All because the military took an old idea off the shelf and applied it in a different way.

From Trains to Credit Cards

In 1850, three express transport companies merged to create a corporation they called American Express, based in Buffalo, New York. Employees known as "expressmen" carried packages on trains from one city to another. They also traveled by wagon, stagecoach, horses, and boats, carrying packages in canvas and leather messenger bags, sometimes over rough or nonexistent roads. During the Civil War, American Express became highly profitable, distributing huge dividends to its shareholders as it shipped supplies to Army depots and packages to Confederate cities taken by Union forces.

American Express's foray into finance started early. In 1857, while it was still growing to become an express mail behemoth, the company launched a money order business to compete with the United States Post Office. In 1891, when executives found they were having a hard time moving cash abroad, the company launched the American Express Travelers Cheque to replace the letters of credit that travelers traditionally carried with them. In 1958, it issued its first credit card—in cardboard!

It's a good thing the company didn't stick with transport! In 1917, in the midst of World War I, the United States suffered a severe coal shortage. All contracts between express companies and railroads were nullified, and President Woodrow Wilson consolidated all domestic express operations as part of the war effort. Transport essentially became the business of the government. Shut out of the package business, American Express shifted completely to financial services.

Today, American Express is a leader in digital payments and banking technology. The company spent roughly $5.2 billion in 2022 on digital transformation, investing in everything from AI to cybersecurity and cloud tech.[12] That investment and pivot to digital paid off. In the 2022 Berkshire Hathaway annual report, Warren Buffett highlighted American Express as a company that has the pulse of American consumers.

But American Express isn't the only example of the blurred lines between technology and government—for better or worse.

Airplane Mode: The Threat That Wasn't Really a Threat

In February 1993, *Time* magazine ran a story about a DC-10 flying into JFK airport that, in the reporter's telling, "almost crashed when a passenger in first class turned on his portable compact disc player."[13] In the story, the reporter suggested that technology like cassette players, tape recorders, and laptop computers could put aircraft at risk, citing "a stack of pilot reports" that ostensibly linked "anomalies" in flight to a wide variety of electronic devices, ranging from laptop computers to Nintendo Game Boys.

Shortly after reading the article, I made a trip to Federal Aviation Administration (FAA) headquarters in downtown Washington, DC, to do some digging. I thought the issue seemed overhyped—particularly in the case of devices like laptops, portable audio equipment, and mobile game devices that have limited ability to extend signals. At the same time, I knew a media firestorm around "dangerous" electronics could be bad not just for work productivity and stress reduction while flying, but for the many consumer electronics companies whose products would be unfairly banned from thousands of flights.

After all, there was precedent. In the early 1960s, the Radio Technical Committee for Aeronautics convened to develop recommendations on communications, navigation, surveillance, and air traffic management . . . in response to concerns around the use of portable electric razors on airlines. (The committee ultimately ruled the razors safe.)

Then, in 1988, Pan Am Flight 103 exploded over Lockerbie, Scotland. The official inquiry determined that a bomb had been placed in a radio cassette recorder, and the US government rushed to ban all portable electronics technology on airplanes. Passengers accustomed to listening to music on their Walkmans or doing work on the first laptop computers suddenly found themselves out of luck. On behalf of CTA's predecessor organization, I urged Washington officials to reconsider. An explosive device, after all, could just as easily be placed in a perfume bottle or book as it could in an electronic device. Thankfully, the ban was lifted just a few weeks later.

With that history in mind, I set to work researching claims of a link between technology and reported flight anomalies. I'm no expert, but it didn't take long to find that my hunch was correct: the overwhelming majority of airplane "incident" reports involving tech products had nothing to do with navigation or airplane operational concerns. Some references to technology were even positive (for instance, a cell phone used to get help in an emergency). While I could understand theoretical concerns around "emitting devices" like cell phones interfering with a plane's navigational equipment, ten years of incident reports showed no upward tick in the number of incident reports involving tech products despite their growing popularity. In the years since, there have been fewer than one hundred anecdotal reports, from millions of flights flown.[14]

Luckily, the FAA seemed to agree with my assessment. Tony Broderick, a longtime and widely recognized safety executive at the FAA, told the *Washington Post* that he was "baffled by the whole thing" and saw "no technical basis for what has been reported." After all, he said, "what's the mechanism by which a DC-10 could be taken over by a lunatic CD?"[15]

I breathed a sigh of relief and considered the issue closed . . . until several months later when a *New York Times* front-page story brought the allegations back to life. The *New York Times* coverage made the evidence-light story important news, and I ended up making a guest turn on major TV networks that evening in an attempt to deflate the panicked reports.

These negative headlines prompted another wave of public hand-wringing and a different kind of pivot: the forced pivot. While FAA officials and airplane makers clearly believed that electronics posed little threat to airplanes, airlines were calling for restrictions to calm worried passengers. Some, like Northwest Airlines—since acquired by Delta—imposed their own restrictions without waiting for FAA action. Ultimately, the agency issued guidance allowing airlines to make their own rules about most electronic devices. There was one exception: a requirement, linked more to physical safety than interference concerns, prohibiting the use of larger devices on planes during takeoff or landing.[16]

Device restrictions until 10,000 feet of altitude became the status quo for years, but the reality was the passengers were still using their devices almost constantly on planes. (Those, like me, who have been flying for decades may also remember the pay-for-use satellite phones built into the back of some airplane seats for in-flight calls.) The restrictions made little sense. Doug Johnson, CTA's vice president for tech policy, had an idea for a new pivot that could solve the issue. He convened airplane makers, airline executives, and device makers, and the group agreed to create "airplane mode," a simple approach that would disable potentially harmful signals coming from devices.

It wasn't a perfectly rational pivot; there's still little evidence that the signals coming from our cell phones have any impact on a plane's operations. But it showed the power of the technology community to come together to solve problems—even those problems that may have been more media hype than reality.

When Work and Play Collide

In 2009, Stewart Butterfield was eager to get into the online video gaming space. He had been part of the team that built the photo-sharing app Flickr, which had become enormously successful and had been sold to Yahoo! in 2005. Now he wanted to try his hand at something else.

Butterfield had the idea for a massive multiplayer online role-playing game (MMORPG) he called Glitch. He envisioned a collaborative game that didn't involve combat or conflict. Instead, players would talk to each other and work together to complete tasks and go on quests. He got together members of the original Flickr team and rounded up more than $17 million in funding.

But while the idea generated excitement among the new team members, it never got off the ground. After sinking $10 million into development, Butterfield realized Glitch was never going to succeed in the market. Early versions of the game weren't attracting a large enough audience. The game was too unique. Players—used to combat games—didn't understand the absurdity and whimsy of Glitch.[17]

But Butterfield still had $7 million left of funding. He used it to take the Glitch team's internal communications tool and turn it into his next venture.

And so Slack was born.

Characters from Glitch became Slack emojis. The whimsical vibe of Glitch became the words of encouragement when Slack users finish reading all their messages. And the Glitch guide, called Pet Rock, became Slackbot.

In 2020, Slack was acquired by Salesforce for $27 billion. And that's how a failed video game became one of the most successful work tools of all time.

Accessibility Tech

Nowhere are tech pivots more rewarding to me than when they end up empowering the lives of people in direct and tangible ways. One of my favorite examples comes from the world of accessibility technology and audio-based navigation.

For many people, failing eyesight means an increasingly limited life. Some 60 percent of blind people never go out alone after they are first diagnosed. The growth of indoor location technology, beginning in the early 2000s and accelerating today, has provided an answer. Smartphones and the increasingly sophisticated sensors embedded inside them can measure movement, direction, and elevation.

Waymap co-founder and CEO Tom Pey is one of the pioneers paving the way. Supported by philanthropic funding from organizations including Google.org and our own Consumer Technology Association Foundation, Pey and the Waymap team launched a new audio-based navigation app in spring 2022. Prior to the launch, the team had conducted thousands of interviews with prospective users from London to Hong Kong to Madrid. They'd done a deep dive into existing surveys and collaborated with industry partners like Verizon and T-Mobile and stakeholders from the disability community. Pey himself brought multiple decades of experience in audio-based navigation technology.

Even so, Pey almost immediately discovered a need to pivot in the new company's approach. To be successful, he realized, Waymap couldn't just produce a "disability app." It needed to be an app that could "take anyone anywhere," both to be commercially viable and to build a community of people without disabilities "lending their steps" to help trace routes. The R&D process produced more pivots. As Pey put it, "We started out believing that we could give instructions in a particular way, and we found that was inflexible. So we changed that. . . . We also found that the original algorithm we had was far too rigid . . . it has been a whirlwind of learning."

The pivots paid off. Waymap trials have expanded to cities across the globe, from Singapore to Brisbane, from Liverpool to Los Angeles. As of 2024, the app is rolling out across the Greater Washington, DC, area, with an expected user base in the hundreds of thousands by the end of the year.

Closed Captioning

Unfortunately, not every effort to make technology more accessible is a good one. Right around the time I became head of CTA in 1991, we faced a conundrum: a bill was rushing through Congress, mandating that TV makers use a proprietary chip to allow captioning for hearing impaired people at the push of a button. We opposed the bill on principle. Government regulations, when needed, should focus on desired outcomes rather than specific technologies. At the time, we also estimated that the proprietary technology would raise the cost of television sets by nearly $50, not welcome in an industry with razor-thin margins.[18]

But much like our conversations around airplane mode and the potential for crashes a few years later, we knew that principled arguments—

no matter how correct—seldom won out against emotional appeals. And ultimately, neither CTA nor our industry partners wanted to stand in the way of more accessible options for people with hearing impairments. At the time, studies suggested that only 10 percent of people with hearing problems had access to closed captioning, which was only available through the purchase of pricey "decoder" equipment.[19] TV set manufacturers were just concerned that Congress was essentially designing TV sets by fiat, potentially inhibiting future innovation.

I told key legislators we would stop opposing the bill if they changed the design requirement to be technology neutral, focused on a requirement that sets be able to display captioning. We also insisted the bill allow flexibility on how those captions were displayed. The bill was changed, passed Congress, and signed by President George H. W. Bush later that year. Those pivots, while seemingly small, created common ground between industry and disability advocates, and made television entertainment more accessible for millions of Americans.

As television makers developed and deployed their own designs, the marketplace took over in ways legislators had not anticipated. As Representative Ed Markey put it in a 2010 retrospective on the Americans with Disabilities Act, "captions now are used in immigrant households to learn English and watched in sports bars and on treadmills across our country."[20] Thanks in part to CTA advocacy, use of closed captioning—including an increasingly robust selection of colors, fonts, contrasts, and text locations— has spread far beyond our homes and the hearing-impaired community to restaurants, health clubs, stadiums, and airports. CTA leaned in, documenting the approach to closed captioning in industry standards that were recognized with two technical Emmy awards.

At the time, we were focused and intentional in our strategy—turning the lemons of a legislative challenge into lemonade. We kicked off a media tour focused on the benefits of captioning for kids learning how to spell and spouses who could sleep while their partner watched a silent but captioned TV. I am proud that a few decades later, half of Americans—nearly all of whom do not have hearing challenges—would report watching content with subtitles "most of the time."[21] Incredibly, that figure rises to 70 percent for Gen Z, the latest generation of content consumers.

The result: almost everybody won. I will never forget celebrating the law's passage at Gallaudet University, founded for the education of deaf and hard of hearing people. I was overwhelmed with enthusiasm as we all applauded by waving our hands above our heads. Set makers won as they did not have to pay for unnecessary patent licenses. Production efficiencies, intense competition, and expiring patents brought lower prices. Consumers won with greater TV set functionality and more affordable TV set prices. Politicians helped the hearing impaired. The only loser was the patent owner urging Congress to mandate its technology—a company that learned the hard way that advocating for mandates can expose the weakness of your competitive service.

In Tech, Mandates Aren't the Answer

I'd like to say that this several-decades-old lesson prompted a sea change in the way our government approaches technology mandates. But sadly, it seems to be a battle that needs to be waged every few years.

Back in 2010, I warned legislators about provisions in the Twenty-First Century Communications and Video Accessibility Act, designed to allow people with disabilities to access broadband, digital, and mobile innovations. Sounds good, right? Technology plays a big and important role in giving people with disabilities more access to the tools they need to survive and thrive in an increasingly complex world. But in this case, the bill as originally drafted granted the government sweeping powers to mandate the features and design of every phone, computer, or internet-connected device with a screen. Simply put, the proposal required every device to be usable by *any* person with *any* disability.

Just on social justice merits, the bill faced an immediate snag. If manufacturers were required to load every device with dozens of accessibility features, some of which may conflict with each other and all of which will add cost and complexity, what would happen to the most affordable products intended for consumers with low incomes? The troubling answer: they would become more expensive because of features most people wouldn't use or need. The legislation would also thrust the federal government into the product design business, an uncomfortable position for regulatory agencies largely staffed by nontechnical experts.

I expressed my concerns about the legislation in an opinion piece for the *Washington Times*, titled (by the op-ed editor) "Dems Want to Redesign Your iPhone." It ran the day I was set to testify at a congressional hearing on the issue, and it made proponents of the bill, including Speaker Nancy Pelosi, furious. The committee chairman pushing the legislation, Representative Markey, lashed out at me for daring to suggest modifications to his proposal and asked one of the other witnesses, a blind veteran testifying on behalf of the bill, for his thoughts. On this count, Markey miscalculated: the veteran seemed swayed by my testimony and said so. He wasn't alone: two other legislators on the committee spoke movingly in defense of both me and an entire industry working hard to offer creative solutions to making technology more accessible.

While individuals with disabilities need and deserve access to the newest communications technologies, we knew that free-market competition was already working to make it happen. For example, in a throwback to our 1990 negotiations, the new legislation would require every single remote control to have a closed caption button. However, a product search on Amazon showed at least twenty remote controls on the market that already offer that feature, one priced as low as $5.[22]

The process ended with a victory: we got the proposal changed so devices did not have to include every available accessibility feature and the marketplace could deliver a variety of different products to meet various needs. Innovation won, and today thousands of devices and smartphone applications help people with varying abilities watch TV—and perform hundreds of other tasks.

Innovation Changing Our World

New pivots and new innovations aren't just opening new doors for people with disabilities. Technology advances are reshaping the relationship we all have to the world around us. AI is increasingly driving the algorithms that feed us content, providing increasingly personalized medical support and serving as assistants in the workplace. Blockchain is shaking up financial systems and may even change the way we one day vote. Augmented and virtual reality is reshaping not just the gaming experience, but our classrooms and factories. And a broad range of connected devices is changing the "at-home" experience.

The innovations in these spaces are incredible and sometimes mind-boggling. Just a few years ago I wrote *Ninja Future* in which I traced shifts and changes in the technology world. In some cases, the technologies cataloged in that book already seem like old news, replaced by even more thrilling innovations. Later in this book I take a look at emerging technologies that are reshaping the way we live, work, connect, and learn *right now*. Just as people and businesses can pivot, technology itself is in a near-constant state of pivoting and transformation. Some technologies—like generative AI, which burst into public view in late 2022—are still near the beginning of their pivot, as industries learn and adapt to what the technology can do. Others, like the metaverse, have forced some second pivots as early hype gave way to more tempered expectations around its real-world applications.

These pivots aren't just changing the world of technology—they're changing what's possible and what's next.

CHAPTER 3

The Startup Pivot

I n 2011, Jamie Siminoff was working out of his garage in the Pacific Palisades. He was a serial entrepreneur, but big success had eluded him. He had failed with a product called Body Mint, a vitamin supplement that used chlorophyll to eliminate body odor but had the unfortunate side effect of turning users' stools green. He'd had moderate success with a voicemail-to-text transcription software sold in 2009, netting him $1 million. It was no small sum, but he felt he hadn't had a great enough impact. He was still searching for his "big idea."

He came up with his next product, a Wi-Fi connected video doorbell, when his wife said she couldn't hear the doorbell when she was outside or in the back of their Los Angeles home. Jamie called his doorbell DoorBot and drained his savings to order five thousand of his new design from a factory in Taiwan. Then he got what he thought was his big break: a spot on the hit TV show *Shark Tank*.

But when pitch day arrived, none of the sharks opted to invest in his product. They liked it—they just didn't like it enough. "I think it's a great business," Mark Cuban told him. "I think you'll be successful. It will be worth $20 million. I just can't invest in something that's not going to be $70 million someday."[1]

The publicity from the show resulted in new orders, but he was still barely making ends meet. He would wake up in the middle of the night in tears, terrified he wouldn't be able to support his wife and baby daughter.

Customer reviews poured in—and they weren't good. People complained that DoorBot's picture quality was poor, its sound was muffled, and the Wi-Fi connection kept cutting out.

So Jamie pivoted. He collaborated with Foxconn, a large Chinese iPhone manufacturer, to redesign the product. He put his email address on every box, so he could personally respond to complaints. Then, he made one more key pivot: he changed the product name to Ring. This was huge not just as a marketing decision (we can all agree that the new name has a certain *ring* to it), but because of what it represented. From the beginning, the doorbell had been a product of convenience—knowing when that delivery person is at your door, even when you're in the backyard. But the name Ring signified something else. It signified a ring of security around a customer's house. His doorbell went from a product of convenience to a product of necessity. It became a security product to ward off intruders.

Ring first exhibited at CES 2011, when Jamie brought a card table to the show to display his product. His creativity, vision, and problem-solving technology inspired confidence in dozens of retailers and media. CES helped him make deals to get Ring into Walmart and Target, and that's when Ring really started gaining traction.[2]

Later that year, billionaire Richard Branson invested in Ring. In 2016, Jamie partnered with the Los Angeles Police Department to give away forty doorbells in Wilshire Park, a middle-class LA neighborhood. Burglaries in the area fell by 55 percent within six months, according to the LAPD.[3] In 2018, Ring sold to Amazon for more than a billion dollars. More importantly to Jamie, it has helped reduce and solve crimes across the country. Ring partners with thousands of police departments in the US. In 2019, Ring famously led to the safe rescue of a young girl who was kidnapped in Fort Worth while out walking with her mother.

Ring is now the largest company ever to have appeared on Shark Tank. And despite his initial rejection, Jamie was invited back to the show—this time as a "Shark" investor for the 2018 season.[4]

Why Startup Pivots Matter

New businesses are critical to any economy. They catalyze innovation and shake up industries. Globally, startups add trillions of dollars to our collective GDP[5] (to put it in context, that's about the GDP of countries like the UK, France, or Brazil) and attract billions in venture capital funding.[6] Here in the United States, a 2023 report from the Small Business Administration found that small businesses create 44 percent of economic activity and employ nearly half of workers in the private sector.[7]

Tech startups have an especially outsized impact. Technology-based startups account for 3.8 percent of the total firms in the United States, pay 8.1 percent of wages, and generate an eye-popping 27.2 percent of US exports. Because tech sector jobs are often export-oriented, a single job in the technology sector can generate another five jobs in related industries.[8]

Sometimes newness itself is the advantage. New companies aren't bound by the expected or ingrained way of doing things that bigger, more established organizations so often are. By necessity, they're in constant experimentation mode to invent and hone new products and business ideas. In a 2018 paper, researchers from the National Bureau of Economic Research found that more than 25 percent of aggregate US growth from innovation is created by firms entering new markets.[9]

In fact, when budding entrepreneurs come to me for advice about a prospective new venture, I tell them to avoid going into "stealth mode"—an approach to startup operations that prioritizes secrecy. Why? The reality is that while there are many great ideas, few have the capital, moxy, experience, ability, and drive to turn their vision into reality. Founders need feedback early and often to help hone their concept and figure out what value-add or differentiator their product is actually providing. Failure isn't a bad thing, especially in the startup community, so entrepreneurs should be willing to fail, adapt, and—most importantly—pivot.

So, to execute a startup pivot, besides passion and creativity and the obvious traits, you need to have a willingness to fail. You need to be open to feedback or collaboration. You need to know when and how to hire the right people, and sometimes make tough decisions if you discover down the road that their skills aren't aligned with your mission. Ultimately, you need to have a vision that's flexible.

Eureka Park: The CES Startup Pivot

I vividly recall the first meeting of the CTA governing board I attended, even before I joined CTA as a full-time employee. In a conversation on raising rates for CES exhibitors, then-CTA chairman of the board and Panasonic CEO Ray Gates laid down a bedrock principle: CES should be accessible to anyone with a technology idea or product, whether they were working in an advanced lab or R&D center or innovating from their kitchen, basement, or garage. I relay that story to our staff every year. I want them to empathize with and understand that many entrepreneurs rely on credit cards to exhibit or pack their wares into their own cars and drive across the country (or even across borders) to reach Las Vegas.

But while favoring startups has been in our organizational DNA for over forty years, in the early 2010s we recognized that costs for exhibiting at CES were a barrier to participation by many of the startups we hoped to attract. As we focused on expanding the show's global footprint, we also realized the potential to tap into the growing international startup scene. With the world emerging from the 2008 recession, countries were building and developing programs to support tech startups as a key pillar for economic growth. We were watching in real time as startup ecosystems expanded around the globe, from Algiers and Amsterdam to Mumbai and Shanghai to Toronto and Tel Aviv—and dozens of other new and growing technology hubs.

The world of startups was changing, and our show had to change along with it. With that in mind, we created a new area of the show just for startups, dubbed Eureka Park. The catchy name, coined by CTA's senior vice president for research and standards Brian Markwalter, reflects the problem-solving momentum driving many entrepreneurs.

The initial goal for the new area of the show was thirty companies. As it turned out, that goal wildly underestimated the demand by startups to show their innovations to a global audience. At CES 2012, we hosted just over a hundred startups. Just over a decade later at CES 2024, over thirteen hundred entrepreneurs showcased their ideas in Eureka Park, and were the stars of CES. Attendees flock to Eureka Park every year because they love the creativity, enthusiasm, excitement, and personal stories of the entrepreneurs. I personally look at Eureka Park as proof that humanity *can and will* solve big problems!

Eureka Park helps entrepreneurs find mentors, get media attention, and connect with investors. Investors look to Eureka Park for their next unicorn. As a result, startups at CES have raised more than $16 billion in venture capital since 2012.

We make Eureka Park accessible for anyone with an idea. We supply almost everything, from electrical hookups to wastebaskets. Entrepreneurs just need to show up with a product and a sign. We also subsidize it, so that anyone with a few thousand dollars and an idea can get global exposure. We tell Eureka Park exhibitors to wear comfortable shoes and keep drinking water, but more important: we tell all our startup entrepreneurs to be prepared to pivot.

The worst thing an entrepreneur can do is show up to Eureka Park thinking they have a "perfect" prototype, model, website, or service. If they do, they're less likely to listen to the feedback of global media, buyers, investors, and executives. The ones who come *only* looking for investment—and not for advice—are less likely to succeed. Many Eureka Park exhibitors leave with a totally different concept of what their product or service is than when they began a few days earlier at CES—and that's the whole point.

The Lock That Didn't Work

Robbie Cabral debuted his invention BenjiLock, the world's first traditional rechargeable padlock with fingerprint technology, at CES 2017. A hybrid product, BenjiLock can support ten fingerprints and can also be opened using a traditional key. It was innovative and impressive enough to win an Innovation Award at CES that year.

At the time, it was just a prototype. Later, Robbie told me that the lock itself barely worked when he brought it to that year's show. But he didn't let that stop him. His main goal as a Eureka Park exhibitor at CES was, he said, "the chance to learn from a blend of hardworking entrepreneurs, businesses, startups, media, and emerging technologies." He also participated in a *Shark Tank* casting call at CES and later appeared on the show, generating interest from all the "sharks" and ultimately accepting a deal from Canadian businessman Kevin O'Leary.

The BenjiLock idea itself was the product of a major life pivot for Robbie. An immigrant to the US from the Dominican Republic, he did everything from janitorial work to housekeeping and catering to make a living. On the same day his daughter Livia was born, he was laid off from his job.

It was the darkest time in his life. He decided to focus on raising his kids as a stay-at-home dad and started going to the gym to lose weight. His time in the gym locker room sparked the idea for BenjiLock, which offered a far better experience for gym-goers than the classic but finicky combination lock. While Robbie had no technology or engineering background, that didn't stop him. Once he had a patent, he signed up for CES, and the rest is history.

A year after his initial success, Robbie returned to CES in 2018 with a smaller version of his lock, BenjiLock Mini, which won a second Innovation Award. BenjiLock ultimately got deals with retailers Ace Hardware, Amazon, QVC, and Walmart.

What About Failure?

I'll be the first to acknowledge that building and scaling a new company is a major challenge. I've seen many startups fail—and even in a boom cycle, some *75 percent of startups* will fail to return investors' capital. According to the Small Business Administration, only half of all small businesses last five years or longer.[10] And that number can scare off a lot of smart, visionary people. But I've also learned those that succeed all have one thing in common: the ability and willingness to embrace change and transform their business. It's not about coming up with "the" great idea in round one. It's about pivoting, sometimes over and over, to round ten and beyond.

And let's not forget that tech founders are used to tackling seemingly impossible challenges. Our industry is meant to hack its way out of problems. Startup founders have a "ninja mindset" that allows them to navigate a volatile market environment, understand what their customers want, and capitalize on opportunities at lightning speed.

Tough economic times can actually be a differentiator for savvy start-ups. Several of today's most recognizable tech platforms—like Slack, WhatsApp, and Instagram—launched in the aftermath of the 2008–2009 recession, which forced innovators and entrepreneurs to take risks and adapt their business models. Robert Workman, the founder of Goal Zero, launched his company's first product, a portable solar-powered generator, in 2008. The company has since deployed its products across the globe, bringing light and power to villages in Africa, South Asia, and the Caribbean, as well as areas of the US living without power after natural disasters. As of January 2024, there were more than twelve hundred unicorn companies (that is, a startup valued at over $1 billion) around the world.[11] The US has more than half of them.[12]

It's natural for startups to be cautious, especially when times get tough. But being too cautious can mean missed opportunities to grow your business and propel life-changing technologies forward. I often think back to the leadup to CES 2022, as we prepared to return for an in-person event after going virtual in 2021. While some companies chose not to join us, I knew that many founders max out their credit cards just to get to Las Vegas, and that opportunities for exposure and connections at the show could make or break their business. Despite lighter attendance, CES 2022 was chock-full of innovation and buzzing with optimism and excitement, and cancellations by some of the traditional exhibitors created opportunities for small companies to shine. One small company leader thanked me "on behalf of startups" and innovators trying to "break into the industry," while another company executive—this one a large multinational looking for potential partnerships and acquisitions—told me it was phenomenal for them for partnering and investing as it was "the show of small and medium-sized companies." Startups found huge success by embracing a challenging environment and learning to pivot fast.

It isn't luck that gets entrepreneurs to the top. And it's not just having a good idea. Many of the entrepreneurs behind CES's most promising recent startups share traits that have helped them navigate the obstacles of creating a new business—traits that help them know when and how to pivot. Here are four that I see over and over again in the companies that rise to the top at, and after, CES:

1. Curiosity

Don't be afraid to look stupid. Asking questions is a life skill that's worth practicing every day. Entrepreneur Fedora Lee painfully watched his father begin suffering from hearing loss. He asked a lot of questions about his father's condition, and eventually landed on the biggest one: "Could there be alternatives to hearing aids?" In 2019, he founded Nuguna, a neckband and safety device for the hearing impaired. It looks like your typical neckband-style Bluetooth headphone set, but its built-in microphone recognizes ambient sound and can tell the direction of the noise by vibrating.

2. Assertiveness

The "experts" aren't always right. You have to trust your own instincts and judgment. Take Anna Skaya, the founder of Basepaws, which developed the first consumer genetics test for cats. "Coming to the show," she said, "I knew people would call us the crazy cat company, but I don't mind being the crazy cat lady." Instead, she brought along her cat to help her out in the booth. People loved taking pictures with the Basepaws cat, and the unique presentation earned Basepaws media coverage in media outlets like CNET and *Fortune*, which called it "CES's strangest new product."[13]

3. Resilience

Resilience—the ability to withstand and recover from challenges—may be the tech industry's latest buzzword, but we've been talking about it for years. In fact, we had a "resilience"-focused area on the show floor at CES 2019, and I wrote about diversity and resilience at length in my 2019 book, *Ninja Future*. For entrepreneurs, experiencing failure can be one of the toughest events to recover from. I particularly love the perspective of one Eureka Park participant—Chandra Devam—on failure as a learning experience: "We don't have failures," she told me, "just lessons for future successes."

It didn't happen overnight, but Devam eventually sold her startup, Drift, to Apple. Then she founded Aris MD, which uses virtual reality to overlay diagnostic images such as MRIs onto the patient during surgery, giving the surgeon a guided map of a patient's pathology or injury.

4. Commitment

Commitment and passion go hand in hand. You must have a dedication to your mission. Dayu Yang, co-founder and CEO of Pillar Learning, created Codi, a robot for kids, after finding that a lot of parents, inundated with choices, decided to take a step back from using technology with their kids. There were a lot of bumps in the road, but his belief that technology can do wonders for children's imaginations—if done correctly—drove him forward despite the challenges. Codi's inventors eventually landed a deal on Shark Tank.

■ ■ ■

Startups Need a Good Innovation Environment

Sadly, it's not enough to have resilience and passion. American entrepreneurs also benefit from a strong innovation environment. While many large companies are growing, almost every state has experienced a drop in the number of new small businesses in recent years, according to CTA's Innovation Scorecard—a biannual ranking of all fifty states on their openness to innovation.

One likely reason is that stifling bureaucracy and an unfriendly legal environment are hamstringing today's startups and small businesses. Higher taxes leave less money for investment. Old laws can choke the next revolutionary consumer technology products, such as drones or self-driving vehicles. Outdated immigration laws limit companies from finding the right employees and discourage immigrant entrepreneurs. Another, more recent problem for startups is the Federal Trade Commission's efforts to discourage big companies from acquiring smaller ones—an issue I'll discuss in greater depth in Chapter 8.

Our nation needs new small businesses, which generate two-thirds of all net new jobs.[14] But absent the right policies, many small businesses are never created or can't survive, even if they're creating products or services people love. Tariffs on imported goods from China, imposed by the Trump administration and maintained by the Biden administration, offer an example of precisely the wrong approach. While designed to punish China for unfair trade practices, they actually punished American businesses—who have paid over $30 billion in extra Section 301 tariffs—and the consumers who paid higher prices.

Here's how those tariffs impacted one company, Brilliant, which created a new kind of smart home control that gives homeowners touch and voice control over all their smart devices from anywhere in their home.

For three years before launch, its team of thirty iterated on their idea, raised capital, and built an ecosystem of partners.

Just two months from their 2019 launch, the Brilliant team learned that their products were caught up in Section 301 tariffs—10 percent tariffs on $200 billion worth of products imported into the US from China. This despite the fact that Brilliant's smart home product is designed entirely in the United States. But like many consumer electronics products, the company was sourcing its components from China, where the electronics supply chain was based.

Brilliant was forced to raise its prices. Then the tariff rate was abruptly increased to 25 percent. Company leaders felt they could not raise prices further without pricing themselves out of the market, so they had little choice but to absorb the price increase.

Technology startups generally lose money as they establish their business, because everything is more expensive for a startup than it is for a large company operating at scale. The initial objective is not to make money, but rather to prove that a product can ultimately be profitably scaled. (That's why access to venture capital funding is often so critical for early-stage startups.) But government-imposed obstacles like tariffs often mean that a startup has to take on more investment to keep it afloat. Startups that are on shakier ground may run out of capital before they have a chance to prove themselves. While Brilliant managed to survive fallout from the tariffs, many hundreds if not thousands of otherwise promising startups couldn't absorb the huge cost increases—and failed.

CHAPTER 4

The Forced Pivot

A t the start of 2020, Delta was flying high. It was America's most on-time airline and the top revenue-generating airline in the world. It was beloved by employees, receiving accolades from *Fortune* as one of the Best Companies to Work For and one of the World's Most Admired Companies. (Delta employees have long been known for their loyalty. In the 1980s, when the airline was struggling, its employees pooled contributions to purchase a Boeing 767, *The Spirit of Delta*, for the company.) Based in part on this success, CTA invited CEO Ed Bastian to kick off CES 2020 as the keynote speaker.

Then COVID hit. For a decade, Delta had worked to build up its routes to China, but canceled all US China-bound flights starting January 31. Not long after, Delta paused all international flights at the official request of the president of the United States. The airline faced a liquidity crisis. By March, it was issuing as much as $50 million in refunds per day. Delta received so many customer calls that the company converted its museum in Atlanta into a call center.

With Ed at the helm, Delta's response will go down in history as one of the most resourceful, agile pivots of the pandemic. He managed it in part by focusing on people. Operating at less than 5 percent of its normal passenger load and with more than 500 planes grounded, Delta was able to avoid all but about 2,000 furloughs by limiting schedules and instituting a voluntary leave-of-absence program, which allowed employees to keep their health insurance. Ed approved a plan to use Delta planes to fly medical workers around the country and transport critical medical equipment.

In 2021, Delta Cargo shipped the first COVID-19 vaccines from Brussels to Detroit. As the vaccine became more broadly available, the company transformed its Atlanta museum into a vaccination center, administering doses to some 5,000 people daily.

As the world grappled with the realities of a new "pandemic-era" normal, Delta rebuilt itself—a process captured in an epic documentary, *The Steepest Climb.*[1] In 2023, buoyed by huge numbers of travelers releasing long pent-up desire to see family, connect with colleagues, or simply take a belated vacation, the airline brought idled planes back into service and stepped on the gas pedal. That year Delta saw a record $54.7 billion in revenue and added over forty new Airbus jets to its fleet. In February 2024, it announced that its profit-sharing payouts were its highest ever, with the total greater than the pool of all US peer airlines combined. If there's ever been a story of the great American pivot, it's this one.

What Is a Forced Pivot?

Forced pivots happen when external forces, be it economic downturns, technological advancements, or unforeseen "black swan" events, require businesses to change their strategies or products, or even their entire business models. During these critical moments, the true mettle of leaders is tested, and their ability to adapt and pivot becomes paramount.

In this environment, the best leaders can reassess their priorities and reposition their organizations to thrive in new landscapes. This requires a willingness to let go of the familiar and embrace uncertainty. Change is uncomfortable, and most people don't like to be uncomfortable! But leaders and businesses that seize the moment and take calculated risks can emerge stronger and more competitive on the other side.

Besides a willingness to embrace discomfort and change, the organizations and leaders who succeed in a forced pivot scenario demonstrate a remarkable ability to stay even-keeled. In these situations, you can't default to panic. You need grit. Every leader should have solutions to "what if" scenarios long before they happen, but be prepared to develop new ones in response to the black swan events (or "unknown unknowns," as former US secretary of defense Donald Rumsfeld famously described them) that exceed the bounds of imagined risks.

Seizing the Moment

In early 2020, DroneUp was a small startup based in Virginia Beach, Virginia. Founded in 2016 by military veteran Tom Walker, the company focused initially on connecting drone operators—the people who navigate unmanned drones remotely—to clients who needed their services. Through a central database, DroneUp could find and match licensed, vetted, and skilled operators in locations around the United States.

The company was wildly successful in building a community of amateur pilots. By 2018, more than 20,000 pilots in the US and another 45,000 around the world in sixty-one countries operated using the company's app or its training or community network.[2] But revenue was initially expected to grow slowly, in part because DroneUp focused on small-scale government partnerships to support emergency response.

All that changed in 2020. In the first year of the pandemic, DroneUp pivoted to meet an unprecedented surge in demand for remote capabilities. Businesses that had previously sent people out to do inspections, crawl up cell towers, or scramble onto roofs found it more challenging to dispatch workers long distances or have crews work together in-person. The new reality prompted businesses to look at how they could use drones, supported by human operators, to carry out some of these tasks. That year, DroneUp grew more than 1,000 percent.

The pandemic also forced Walker and DroneUp to rethink their business strategy. In 2019, conversations about drone delivery weren't on the DroneUp agenda. In fact, in Walker's telling, prior to the COVID-19 pandemic DroneUp hadn't invested much in the hardware or infrastructure for last-mile delivery, or the extensive lobbying that goes into getting permission to operate in the highly regulated aviation field. Instead, he traded on an important skill for technology industry leaders: the ability to "make critical decisions to shift in the moment."[3]

Walker recognized that in a highly competitive market, you have to be nimble, agile, and willing to adapt to new circumstances. That helped him identify and seize an opportunity, even if it wasn't one his company had planned for. Enter Walmart. During the pandemic, Walmart recognized an opening to sell COVID-19 tests to consumers who wanted them but weren't always willing or able to get in their cars and drive to a Walmart store. Drones helped Walmart to get over that hurdle in reaching customers, offering last-mile delivery that's safe and fast—with deliveries coming in as little as thirty minutes—and comes with an added bonus of reduced greenhouse gas emissions relative to traditional vehicle delivery. From three locations in Arkansas, DroneUp has now expanded its Walmart partnership to multiple states, reaching 4 million households as of 2023.[4] Months later in early 2024, the company received landmark approval from the US Federal Aviation Administration for operations "beyond visual line of sight" (BVLOS) by the remote pilot in command, opening new horizons for drone delivery.

No one could have predicted the magnitude of the COVID-19 pandemic, which unleashed a wave of forced pivots across the consumer technology sector and a range of other industries. In this environment, some companies panicked. Media headlines touted "the end of commuting,"[5] the death of retail and "the American middle class,"[6] and even the collapse of globalization. Of course, from our vantage point now, it's clear that none of these apocalyptic visions have come to pass. But along the way, technology and technology-adjacent companies focused on, as the *Harvard Business Review* put it, "pivoting to business models conducive to short-term survival along with long-term resilience and growth."[7]

But many of the best pivoters had prepared their online infrastructures and emergency strategies. I think that CTA was on the "better prepared" side of this equation as we carried out our own pivot. We knew that if American white-collar workers stayed home, they needed the devices and tools to keep working and business flowing. More, if kids were stuck at home and couldn't even go to parks and playgrounds, both parents and children (and their mental health and household peace) benefited from access to entertainment. Also, with remote learning, all children needed reliable access to the internet and products that allowed them to access online resources. Put simply, Americans needed access to consumer technology both as a tool and as a diversion.

As a trade association, our challenge was to make sure those working in consumer technology factories, distribution, and retail stores were legally categorized as "essential workers." We shifted from focusing on our innovation agenda and turned our attention to engaging policymakers—often via newly important tools like Zoom or Microsoft Teams. We explained why tech workers were so critical to keeping us afloat in a uniquely challenging time. Thus, in April 2020, our team quietly celebrated a victory when the federal government included technology workers as essential workers exempt from closing mandates. We also began a series of weekly sessions designed to connect with member companies and provide information on hot topics, surveyed members on supply chain and other operational challenges, and even worked with the White House to create a COVID-19 information website for businesses.

Just like CTA, many companies in the technology industry pivoted to new strategies they had never contemplated pre-COVID.

Curbside Pickup and Changing Modes of Commerce

Curbside pickup surged during the pandemic, as consumers opted for a shopping option with more limited in-person interaction. Tech retailers took notice. Best Buy, the nation's largest dedicated consumer technology retail chain, pivoted immediately to a curbside pickup model. Beginning on March 22, 2020, the company announced that it was moving to "contactless curbside service" only at its more than eight hundred retail stores. Best Buy wouldn't fully reopen stores to customers until mid-June that year. Despite these closures, Best Buy managed to meet customers where they were. In-store (or maybe we should call it "adjacent-to-store") purchases fell only 6.3 percent in Q1 that year—a smaller drop than analysts expected—and surged back to rise by 5.8 percent year-on-year in Q2.

How did Best Buy pivot so quickly? The company was able to rapidly roll out curbside pickup in March 2020—the first time it had ever offered the service—in part because it was already a leader in store fulfillment, with many of the technology and logistics capabilities already in place that individual stores needed to support curbside ordering. Best Buy built on years of experiments in giving consumers choices between in-store buying and online purchasing with home delivery or store pickup options. Those experiments paid dividends during COVID when, as CEO Corie Barry explained, "customers were leveraging digital shopping tools at an unprecedented rate and new fulfillment options like curbside pickup were becoming table stakes."[8]

In late 2020, I had the chance to interview Corie for a virtual leadership series in partnership with the Northern Virginia Technology Council. During the session, she outlined three priorities: "The first was [to] keep our employees and customers safe. The second was [to] protect the employee experience for as long as possible for as many as possible. And the third was to come out the other end of this, not just a vital company, but a vibrant one."[9] Those three goals, Corie told me, "allowed the team to constantly prioritize decision-making and help us iterate the operating model incredibly quickly."

When Best Buy switched to a curbside pickup model, they paid all their employees for the next four weeks, including those who were out sick or not needed in the stores. That bridged staff to the first federal stimulus package. When they had to furlough employees, they continued to cover their medical benefits.

Even once safety concerns receded, it turned out that people still wanted the convenience and personal touch that comes with in-store shopping. For Best Buy, that meant leaning into another advantage—their deeply knowledgeable sales associates. For consumers suddenly investing in a full suite of products to host meetings at home or allow kids to interact with their teachers and classmates, Best Buy's sales team offered the opportunity not just to browse tech product options, but to seek guidance from tech product experts.

Best Buy made perhaps the quickest and best-executed pivot in the history of retail. (I'll share more about that success in Chapter 6.) As CEO, Corie received well-deserved and widespread recognition and accolades for her quick action. But she wasn't the only one.

Target, Walmart, and many other American retailers also pivoted to curbside pickup where practicable. At the same time, Amazon and others put more trucks and delivery options on the road, bringing goods directly to our doorsteps. In late afternoons of spring 2020, sessions of catch with my youngest son, Max, on our suburban Detroit street were interrupted seemingly every few minutes by deliveries from Amazon, FedEx, UPS, or the US Postal Service.

Companies also pivoted to meet their customers in other ways. Amid concerns about handling paper bills and coins, companies accelerated the rollout of contactless payment systems and mobile payments like Apple Pay.

Pivoting to Meet Your Customer

Similarly, restaurants survived by offering curbside, carry-out, and home delivery options. Their pivot was supported by food delivery services like Grubhub and Uber Eats, which flourished during the pandemic. Uber in particular is an incredible case study in pandemic pivots, leaning—like Best Buy—on the advantage of years of planning and unique foresight by its leadership.

When Uber's founders were first pitching investors back in 2008, they included the idea of delivery as a moneymaker . . . but only at the very end of the pitch deck. It took the better part of a decade to launch Uber Eats. As CEO Dara Khosrowshahi put it, "When I first joined Uber, I think Uber was much more associated with ride-hailing and Eats was this interesting part-time endeavor."[10] As late as 2019, Uber Eats was losing money and competing in a crowded market, with Grubhub, Caviar, DoorDash, and Postmates all offering similar delivery-to-your-doorstep services. Amazon's brief foray into restaurant delivery was shuttered that year, a sign of the challenges inherent in the food delivery business. But Jason Droege, then head of Uber Eats, knew that the service could be a differentiator.

When the pandemic hit, Droege looked especially prescient. Almost immediately, Uber's ride bookings dropped off a cliff—falling some 80 percent in April 2020. Riders were nervous about being in cars with drivers they didn't know, in environments they couldn't control. Many people weren't leaving their house at all. But when people are stuck at home, it turns out, they still want to order food.

That new environment changed the game. But Uber Eats still needed a nimble, adaptable approach to connect with customers. In 2020, Uber revamped its food delivery app and website, making it easier to find and order food. The company unveiled new features, including a fully contactless "leave at door" option. It also leaned into a renewed desire for hyper-local community building in many American cities and towns by eliminating its delivery fee to support struggling local restaurants. The result? Uber Eats drove nearly all of Uber's growth between 2019 and 2021, with bookings nearly quadrupling from $14.5 billion to $51.6 billion.[11]

This dynamic also transformed the restaurant industry in lasting ways. Today, most fast-casual eateries have a "mobile order" counter, and others—especially in more crowded urban and suburban areas—have dedicated parking spaces just for mobile pickups. And it's not just restaurants! Many grocery stores and pharmacies have dedicated online order pickup parking areas.

COVID and Startups

It wasn't just well-established tech behemoths who found in the COVID-19 pandemic an opportunity to pivot and thrive. In fact, some young tech companies found the pivot to COVID-focused technology relatively easy. In 2020, BioIntelliSense had just begun sales of BioSticker, a wearable Band-Aid-like device used by physicians to monitor vital signs outside of hospital settings. As CEO and founder Dr. Jim Mault explained when the product launched in January 2020, "This isn't a one-time snapshot . . . and that's powerful. We're going to be able to anticipate or prevent a lot of problems that, in the past, took us by surprise."[12]

As it turned out, COVID-19 was that surprise. Mault and his team had previously thought of their device as a tool for chemotherapy or dialysis patients, or as a way for hospitals to monitor pre- or post-operative surgical patients. As hospitalizations rose in early 2020, Mault quickly realized his product could be a key tool to combat the pandemic. Within months, Oakland University in Michigan announced it would use the product, renamed the BioButton, to support early detection of outbreaks and help with contact tracing. The US military used the BioIntelliSense patches on troops deployed in South Korea near the North Korea border. As tourism restarted, the Cayman Islands turned to the BioButton to prevent outbreaks among travelers visiting the popular resort destination.

For other startups, the pandemic posed an existential challenge, forcing business strategies to change nearly overnight. Jason Schloetzer, a professor of business administration at the Georgetown University McDonough School of Business, described the environment: "Everybody is trying to think about . . . 'How do we need to adapt or evolve?' because the way that we used to do things may not be applicable to the next six months or 18 months."[13]

Most of us remember March 11, 2020, as the day the World Health Organization officially declared the COVID-19 outbreak a global pandemic. But for Jason Feldman, it was also less than twenty-four hours before his men's health startup Vault was set to announce a major rebrand and the successful close of a funding round. Standing on the floor of the New York Stock Exchange, Feldman watched as investors panicked amid the largest single-day dip in the stock market in decades. In an interview with Crunchbase News, he recounted the anxiety of the moment: "I thought 'What are we going to do?' Because we had literally just launched the brand nine months before and built all this technology and here we are. Now I'm afraid that peoples' jobs are at risk, and I don't know how we're going to live."[14]

His fear wasn't misplaced: Vault's business model combined at-home and telehealth visits, and within a week the company was forced to suspend its in-home operations in some states. But rather than pausing the planned national rollout, Feldman recognized an opportunity to pivot to testing for COVID-19. To execute that pivot, he maximized a key strength: the company's existing partnership with Rutgers University, which was developing a saliva-based COVID test. While the FDA had put a halt on at-home testing, Vault developed a new model that connected patients virtually to a practitioner who could "watch somebody spit in a tube at home." The company also partnered with UPS to ensure expedited delivery to Vault facilities for testing.

When Feldman stepped onto the NYSE floor that March, the company had fewer than fifty employees. Three years later, it had grown to more than five hundred.

Some pivots marked the birth of new startups, as founders recognized in the pandemic an opportunity for technology to help improve—or even save—lives. Dr. Rachael Grimaldi founded healthcare communications app CardMedic as a way to expand patients' access to healthcare information after reading about a young surgical patient who struggled to understand her doctor through his mask. The app is now used in one hundred twenty countries by more than 55,000 users. Biobot Analytics, a startup founded at the Massachusetts Institute of Technology (MIT), launched a new technology to monitor disease spread by looking at wastewater in sewers. A more advanced version of the platform was recognized as one of *Time's* Best Innovations of 2022 and can now help public health officials detect norovirus and curb drug overdoses.[15] With more than $29 billion invested in US health-tech startups in 2021 (more than double the investment in 2020), the healthcare innovations unleashed by the pandemic are only getting started.[16]

Ultimately, the COVID-19 pandemic was an accelerator, forcing companies to pivot more quickly and more often to survive. Those that did are already reshaping our world. In many cases, these forced changes ended up bringing more success than those companies had ever seen.

From Handwritten Paychecks to Virtual Lip-Syncing

The COVID-19 pandemic had fully taken hold when Jennifer Taylor took over as the new president and CEO of the Northern Virginia Technology Council (NVTC)—the nonprofit trade association representing the vast Northern Virginia technology community.

Northern Virginia is the data center capital of the world—more data flows through the region than anywhere else in the world—and it also has more cybersecurity companies and government contractors than any other region. NVTC's members include major tech behemoths like Amazon, Google, Meta, and Microsoft, alongside major universities, banks, hospitals, telecom companies, and nimble startups. There was a lot at stake.

In September 2020, NVTC had only hosted *in-person* networking events for over three decades. Taylor was a first-time CEO, and the challenges were mounting quickly. Previously, she had been vice president of US jobs at the Consumer Technology Association, addressing the nation's critical skills gap. I recommended her for the NVTC CEO position because I had confidence in her. I knew she would find a way.

When a board member gave her the advice to take advantage of the pandemic in order to rebuild NVTC, she took it.

First, she modernized the way NVTC was operating. In many ways, it had been operating the same way for years—which was working until the pandemic. But now, there was an urgent need to capitalize on the growing digital landscape.

Taylor implemented automation tools to manage membership, accounting systems, and marketing activities, and focused on rapid-fire networking as she got to know the nearly five hundred member companies. "I was able to meet up to ten times the number of people in a virtual setting than I could have before the pandemic," she said.

Her main challenge was how to continue to generate revenue when everything had shifted online and away from in-person events. For one of NVTC's fall events, its annual CFO Awards reception, they used an online networking German technology to host a live virtual event. When it was showtime at seven p.m., the technology failed. No one could log in. Because of the six-hour time difference between Virginia and Germany, NVTC couldn't access customer support, and the event didn't happen that night.

But the team learned from that experience and moved on, thinking of new ways to reach their audience. Bobbie Kilberg, Taylor's predecessor, tapped into her network and invited well-known politicians to be interviewed in a new series called "Masters of Leadership." And for NVTC's annual holiday Tech100 event, where the council gives a hundred awards every year to tech innovators, they hosted a virtual lip-sync contest. They asked members to submit videos of their leadership or employees lip-syncing different songs. The videos were played between award categories, which kept people watching, laughing, and enjoying the event.

Since 2020, NVTC has increased its revenue by 20 percent and membership by 71 percent. "In the end," Taylor said, "COVID-19 was a forcing function that took the NVTC brand and member experience to a whole new level."

■ ■ ■

GPS: Tragedy to Innovation

Tragedies are often the catalyst for forced pivots, and not just in the case of pandemics. That's the case with GPS (Global Positioning System), which enables location tracking, navigation, and mapping in hundreds of devices, from your car to your smartphone.

GPS started as military technology, when the US Navy began satellite navigation experiments in the mid-1960s to track US submarines carrying nuclear missiles. The Soviet Union had launched the first Sputnik in 1957, and American scientists were monitoring Sputnik's radio transmissions. They realized that, because of the Doppler effect, the frequency of the signal being transmitted by Sputnik changed; it was higher when the satellite moved toward them, and lower when it was moving farther away. Because the scientists knew their own exact location, they could use these frequencies to pinpoint where the satellite was along its orbit.

Experiments continued through the 1970s, and as early as 1975, Dr. Brad Parkinson, the chief architect of GPS, described to Congress a system that could serve both military and civilian purposes. While researchers sent detailed signal specs to anyone who requested them, including a group of students at the University of Leeds who built the first civilian receiver, non-military access wasn't guaranteed. It would take a combination of tragedy and entrepreneurial ingenuity to elevate GPS to a technology we all use daily.

On August 30, 1983, Korean Air Lines Flight 007 left John F. Kennedy International Airport in New York City en route to Seoul, South Korea, with 269 crew and passengers aboard. At a refueling stop in Anchorage, Alaska, the pilots learned that their radio navigation beacons weren't working. They switched to the backup, the gyroscope-based inertial navigation system (INS), but didn't realize that it wasn't working properly either.

Flight 007's autopilot took the plane hundreds of miles off course toward the Kamchatka Peninsula in the Russian Far East, home of a Russian nuclear base. When Soviet radars detected an unexpected incursion into their airspace, they scrambled MiG-23 interceptors and shot down the flight, which spiraled into the Sea of Japan. There were no survivors.

Two weeks later, President Ronald Reagan announced plans to speed up the timeline for guaranteeing GPS technology for civilian use. In a statement that day, Deputy Press Secretary Larry Speakes highlighted GPS access as a contribution by the United States to a world "united in its determination that this awful tragedy must not be repeated."[17] That decision, coupled with more than a decade of work by researchers to expand GPS access, opened the door for technology that would change the world.

At CTA's predecessor organization, I recall we filed at the Federal Communications Commission (FCC) in support of opening GPS to civilian usage. Once the commercial system went live in 1988, it rapidly launched a new industry and a new benefit to consumers. During the 1990s, CTA members including Panasonic and Sony pioneered commercially available GPS receivers. At CES 1998, Garmin introduced StreetPilot, described as "one of the first practical and affordable GPS-based road navigation devices," and paved the way for huge growth in the consumer GPS market.

This was a huge step forward for road safety. No more printing out driving directions from MapQuest and trying to read them while driving. GPS eliminated the need for paper maps the same way the internet eliminated the need for the Yellow Pages.

By the 2000s, GPS was no longer just a stand-alone technology. Following new FCC requirements, GPS-enabled smartphones opened the door for all-in-one devices. These products could deliver turn-by-turn navigation or identify the location of a lost or stolen device. In more recent applications, GPS technology provides the foundation for ever-more-complex mobile uses and a whole new industry of "location-based services."

The evolution of GPS reflects a broader industry trend: innovators integrate foundational technology into successive generations of products, spurring development of new products and services. We've seen the same pattern play out for Wi-Fi, Bluetooth, and Near Field Communication (NFC), which enables the latest tap-to-pay technologies. Hundreds of companies simply would not exist without free, global access to GPS signals!

With GPS, ridesharing companies like Lyft and Uber match drivers and passengers, lead drivers to a precise pickup location, and chart out a safe and efficient driving route. GPS-integrated smartwatches allow runners and cyclists to easily track pace and distance, a huge boon for many of us in the pandemic era. Closer to home, GPS-enabled pet collars help families keep tabs on their furry friends.

Today, GPS technology is also revolutionizing "nontraditional" technology industries like agriculture. John Deere has leveraged over a century of experience in building tractors and other agricultural and construction equipment to transform itself into a technology powerhouse, combining GPS with other location technologies to steer self-driving tractors on routes with an accuracy calculated down to centimeters. As Deere CEO John May explained on the keynote stage at CES 2023, GPS hardware, coupled with embedded software, machine learning, and cloud computing capabilities, give their machines "superhuman capabilities." In addition to the time and efficiency benefits for farmers, technologies like these support sustainable agriculture by reducing the use of pesticides, water, seed, and fertilizer. As May explains, that's "good for . . . customers' business, for the planet and all of us." He's right!

Pivoting in Wartime

Of course, the COVID-19 pandemic is far from the only event forcing businesses to adapt to survive. It's not even the most recent. In early

2022, Russia launched a tragic and illegal assault on the independent nation of Ukraine, escalating a conflict that began in 2014. Some members of Ukraine's thriving software and technology innovation community swapped laptops and laboratories for rifles and ammunition as they left their roles to support Ukraine's defense effort. Others found that their tech skills could be applied to the war effort or to supporting Ukrainians whose lives and livelihoods had been upended.

In the first days and weeks after the invasion, Ukraine's technology leaders pivoted to adapt to a new reality of bombings and rolling blackouts. For companies like Esper Bionics, that meant focusing initially on a "people first" approach to ensure that the company's largely Kyiv-based staff were safe. With that accomplished, CEO and founder Dima Gazda turned to carrying out the "Plan B" for wartime business operations developed just days before. Gazda quickly discovered that operating in a wartime environment was "like building a company from zero." While the Esper Bionics products—prosthetic limbs made more agile by constant data collection—were more relevant than ever, they needed new processes and structures to support a scattered team.

The Esper team temporarily relocated to Berlin, returning several months into the war. Other companies made the opposite leap—leaning heavily on backup generators and Starlink connections to support employees still working together in Ukraine. (That made Ukraine's tech community early if unexpected pioneers in leading the growing push for a return to in-office work post-COVID.) Others rushed to provide scattered employees with power banks.

Sofiia Shvets, co-founder of AI startup Let's Enhance, recalled, in comments to *Wired,* hosting regular video calls with team members sitting in total darkness and surrounded by candles amid a blackout.[18] Companies also found new ways to connect and keep staff in touch. Kyiv-based software developer MacPaw developed the new Slack plug-in

TogetherApp to support quick check-ins and location drops between co-workers. Through it all, Ukraine's vibrant technology community—which included some 5,000 companies and employed 300,000 people in 2021—kept shipping new products and software updates.[19] Sometimes, pivoting is required just to stay in one place.

I heard some of those stories from the dozen Ukrainian startups who overcame significant adversity to join us at CES 2023 and CES 2024.

Releaf Paper co-founder and CEO Alexander Sobolenko told us that in the days leading up to CES, he had worked through blackouts and fuel shortages. "It was not the best time for working," he recalled, but after the first few weeks of the war "people adapted [because] they needed to do *something*." In early 2022, his company—which turns the fallen leaves collected from city streets into sustainable paper packaging—had been focused on go-to-market and sales plans. All those plans were upended by the Russian invasion.

The Releaf team pivoted to continue development in western Europe, leaning into plans to manufacture their paper from a facility in France and holding conversations remotely with new prospective partners. "We were looking for any opportunities. We knew we had a good idea, the technology works, we [had] pilot customers," Alexander explained. "We were considering a lot of different directions." While international travel restrictions for Ukrainian men made it challenging to meet with potential customers and partners, he focused on virtual meetings and held multiple negotiations daily through the first months of the war. All that while seeking shelter in emergency bunkers several times a day during periods of intensive bombing.

The resilience and flexibility of Ukrainian startups paid off. Releaf Paper was recognized as a finalist for luxury goods brand LVMH's Innovation Award and received a $2.7 million grant from the European Commission to build a factory in France. Esper Bionics pivoted to bring their products to market more quickly than planned, and were rewarded with the coveted Red Dot Design Award for their bionic hand prosthesis.

Of course, they didn't do it alone. Both were supported by the Ukrainian Startup Fund (USF), a Ukraine government-backed organization officially launched in 2019 to boost the country's startup ecosystem. Just like the startups themselves, USF found that operating in a wartime environment meant pivoting to adopt a new strategy and vision. "By the second day of [the] war, we understood that . . . the whole world had changed," USF's head of ecosystem Karina Kudriavtseva told me. "We needed to adapt to the new challenges we faced not only as a fund but as a governmental institution." That meant seeking support from international and private donors on the way to becoming the largest single investor in Ukrainian startups. It also meant racing to establish a new dual-use grant support program focused on industries—defense, infrastructure, cyber-security, healthcare, and education—that could support the Ukrainian war effort. Several years into the war, USF also found they needed to pivot in the way they were talking about Ukrainian startups. According to Ihor Markevych, former USF head of strategy and development and startup ecosystem builder, "we're [no longer] presenting on how resilient and brave the Ukrainian technical system is. Now . . . we're just saying, consider them equal to any other company in the world. Let them compete."

It wasn't just Ukrainian companies that adapted to the conflict. In the United States, tech companies stepped up to support Ukraine. Google removed Russian state media from its Google News service. Instagram and Twitter made posts from Kremlin-backed outlets harder to find, while YouTube and Facebook blocked outlets like RT and Sputnik News. Apple and Microsoft withdrew their products and services from Russia. Amazon provided $10 million in donations and matched employee contributions to organizations helping Ukrainians like UNICEF, UNHCR, the World Food Program, and the Red Cross. Airbnb offered free, temporary housing for 100,000 refugees fleeing Ukraine. Tech to the Rescue launched a #TechforUkraine initiative that helped tech companies build systems for resource distribution, payments and donations, secure messaging, and other services for Ukrainians.

We also did our part. In an interview with the BBC during CES 2023, I shared my decision not to allow Russian companies to participate in that year's show. The story went global. It was a gut decision, and not one vetted by our board or senior leadership. But I felt it was an easy call and an opportunity to do the right thing.

The Privacy Pivot

Shifting consumer demand can also usher in industry-wide pivots. Unlike a pandemic or a war, which tend to come as sudden shocks to the system and everyone in it, these pivots are often slower and more deliberate. That doesn't make them any less critical for businesses hoping to survive and thrive.

One of those shifts was the growing awareness of—and demand for—data privacy. In some ways, the conversation has been going on longer than you might think. Back in 1967, the US Supreme Court expanded privacy protections in *Katz v. United States* to cover anything that a person "seeks to preserve as private," including information gathered and communicated electronically. But for many Americans, the focus on data privacy is far more recent.

For CTA and several of our members, it started with step counting.

The process of defining "a step"—as in the steps counted by our wearable electronic devices—launched a new way of thinking about personalization of healthcare, the information consumers need to trust and invest in digital health devices, and how that information should be protected.

A decade ago, interest in fitness trackers exploded. I first noticed the trend when Fitbit launched the Fitbit Classic—the company's first model—at CES 2009 to great acclaim. Suddenly, it seemed like everyone was wearing them. Workplaces (including mine) started sponsoring fitness challenges tied to steps walked.

For CTA, the step tracker opened the door to new accuracy standards that support trust in health-tech products. Since then, we've produced more than two dozen digital health standards covering everything from sleep tracking to brain wave activity to mental health. But wearables also launched another discussion, centered around privacy. Privacy concerns have been a regular feature of new technology introduction since the advent of the portable camera. But only in the past decade have concerns become so widespread.

By their nature, wearable devices continuously collect data about their wearer. Depending on the device, that could include heart rate, fitness, sleep quality and quantity, and location. Along with all that data collection came a new question: Who owned the data? Could device makers share data in a way that might compromise consumers' personal information without their permission? Part of the answer depends on the location—different countries have different requirements for the use of personal data.

Industry leaders came to see development of the wearables ecosystem as fundamentally tied to consumer trust. They knew that if consumers felt that their privacy was at risk, they would be less likely to try new devices. That relatively commonsense concept is borne out by consumer research. In a 2020 McKinsey survey, 87 percent of respondents said they "would not do business with a company if they had concerns about its security practices."[20]

Recognizing the challenge, CTA gathered leading wearable device makers, which then included Apple, Fitbit, Google, Samsung, and Sony, and hammered out a set of privacy guidelines for wearable devices. They were clear, fair, and became widely adopted. More, they were what consumers want and would expect: A company's policies to be transparent and expressed in simple language. A commitment that no private information will be sold or shared without express permission. An opportunity for consumers to opt out of data sharing to ensure their privacy will not be compromised.

These privacy commitments showed consumers that the companies making their devices took their concerns seriously. Just as rock climbers look for ropes that will hold them securely and cyclists pick helmets they trust to protect them in a crash, technology users choose products—and the brands that stand behind them—that they can trust with their personal information. As wearable devices and other technology—including smartphones and many of the apps on them—generate an increasing amount of highly personalized data, the demand for assurances that it will be handled judiciously will only grow.

The Environmental Pivot

Another major societal shift is the rise of sustainability as a business priority. My sense from speaking with American business leaders is that most genuinely want to make our world better. Many are alarmed by climate change and are concerned that politicians seem to be incapable of doing much about it. According to research from Accenture, 90 percent of CEOs feel that limited support from the government is negatively impacting their ability to tackle today's interlinked global challenges.[21]

And it's not just big companies. Many startups have been founded specifically with sustainability challenges in mind. In summer 2023, I had the chance to judge a startup competition at Cannes NEXT, an innovation summit at the Cannes Film Festival. In that competition alone,

I saw several innovations that promise to reshape the way we create and use products, including a new plastic bottle technology that biodegrades after just a year.

But of course, CEOs aren't launching new ventures and spearheading new initiatives *just* because it's good for the world. They've recognized that people want to feel good about the products they buy. That means a growing awareness of not just how a product works, but how it impacts the environment. According to a recent survey by McKinsey, 66 percent of all Americans and 75 percent of millennials say they consider sustainability when buying products.[22] The Economist Intelligence Unit, the research and analysis division of the Economist Group, reports a 71 percent rise in online searches for sustainable goods globally between 2018 and 2023.[23] That trend accelerated during the pandemic, with more than half (54 percent) of respondents to a Mastercard survey saying they believe it's more important to reduce their own carbon footprint in the wake of the COVID-19 pandemic.[24]

Social media has played a major role in influencing consumer views on sustainability and the environment. Often that's for the better: in a March 2023 study, Unilever and the UK-based Behavioral Insights Team (BIT) found that "75% of people . . . are more likely to take up behaviors to help save the planet after watching social media content about sustainability."[25] Sometimes, it's for the worse. If you live in one of the (at the time of this writing) eight US states that have enacted plastic straw bans after a brief hysteria around sea turtles, you may share my frustration about how well-intended sustainability efforts can go off the rails.

In any case, sustainability is an especially important issue for technology companies. Our industry feeds into the sustainability challenge, as the technology in our homes, offices, and communities multiplies—using energy and creating e-waste. At the same time, no industry is better equipped to innovate in ways that address these challenges and many more and improve the lives of millions along the way. Industry is rising to the sustainability challenge, making tremendous strides to reduce our collective environmental footprint. That means advancing energy efficiency, e-cycling (electronic recycling), and the circular economy, as well as investing in the research, partnerships, and programs to reach even more ambitious sustainability goals.

What does that look like in practice? As part of plans to put sustainability "at the core of the user experience," Samsung's SmartThings platform offers an AI Energy Mode that can offer up to 35 percent energy savings for appliances. HP released a new line of notebooks with more than 82 percent of its mechanical parts made from recycled materials. In 2023, Delta Air Lines announced a sustainable travel innovation lab and plans to achieve net-zero emissions by 2050.

Voluntary standards agreements are magnifying efforts, bringing industry leaders together to meet ambitious sustainability targets. For example, under an agreement to improve the energy efficiency of set-top boxes used to access video programming—led by CTA, internet and television association NCTA, and CableLabs—the energy use of set-top boxes fell 57 percent between 2012 and 2022.[26] That's good for the environment, but it's also good for consumers, who are collectively saving $2.5 billion a year in energy costs. Building on that success, CTA partnered with the television industry and allied organizations to launch a voluntary agreement that will significantly improve the energy efficiency of TVs, preventing more than 10 million metric tons of CO_2 emissions each year.

Those efforts are paying dividends. Since 2000, we've seen a 50 percent reduction in materials used across all consumer technology products, an 8.9 percent reduction in US greenhouse gas emissions, and over $1 billion spent on recycling efforts—more than any other consumer-facing industry.

The growing focus on sustainability has also prompted a broader pivot in the technology industry to focus on technology's capacity to create a better world. Over the past several years, I've seen an explosion of new startups and innovative thinking from existing industry players, all dedicated to delivering on technology's promise.

Few people capture this spirit better than Dr. Carmichael Roberts, a serial entrepreneur, chair of CTA's 2023 executive board, and founder and managing partner of venture capital firm Material Impact. Carmichael has dedicated his career to investing in technologies that have a real-world "material impact," whether it's solutions for renewable drinking water, wearable sensors to monitor patient health, or the fight against diseases like multiple sclerosis. Through his work with Breakthrough Energy, founded by Bill Gates, he has also supported companies tackling the threat of climate change. As he explains it, "technology can be the great equalizer that can democratize the solutions . . . and technology can do that in a quick, efficient manner."

While technology innovations that can improve lives are happening everywhere, walking the halls of CES each year offers a glimpse into how our industry is responding to the demand for tech-based solutions to big problems. Agricultural tech is helping farmers grow healthier, more abundant crops. Tech tracking food reduces waste and makes agricultural supply chains more sustainable. Digital therapy products can now predict ADHD and seizures, treat epilepsy and spinal pain, and help manage a suite of mental health challenges. Sustainable water technologies can recycle water in your home and in businesses to reduce water waste. Smart home devices can predict falls and prevent injuries. Self-driving wheelchairs are making the world more accessible to people with mobility challenges. In the not-too-distant future self-driving cars promise to do the same—not to mention reduce traffic fatalities.

As we look ahead to the promise of future technology, I think it's also instructive to look backward. In the 1980s, concerns grew about the rapidly expanding hole over the Antarctic, believed to be caused by ozone depleting chemicals used as refrigerants in electronics manufacturing and other processes. Recognizing the challenge, technology industry leaders spent significant time trying to develop a solution. I felt strongly that a tax on electronics companies wouldn't substantially fix the problem. Instead, I helped launch a group called the Industry Cooperative on Ozone Depleting Chemicals, focused on shifting industry processes to reduce or eliminate the use of chlorofluorocarbons (CFCs), which electronics companies typically used to clean device parts. After substantial research and testing, we discovered that high-pressure water could serve as a perfect—and more sustainable—substitute. It was important work, and I was gratified that Stephen Andersen of the US Environmental Protection Agency (EPA) later credited me as a "mastermind" of the successful joint effort. The lesson? Even challenges that seem intractable now may be solvable if we bring the smartest minds from industry together.

The world will be better as we innovate and harness technology to improve the human condition. We must enable and embrace change. If we do it right, people all over the globe will reap the benefits. But while the technology industry is leading the way, technology alone can't solve our problems. It requires people who can harness this technology to make an impact.

Refusing to Pivot: A Cautionary Tale

Just because market conditions may require a pivot for organizations to stay afloat doesn't always mean it will happen. That's the case for radio broadcasters, who have sought technology mandates to prop up their industry rather than pivoting to stay relevant and competitive.

For decades, radio broadcasters were the only game in town for audio news and entertainment. But as is always the case in technology (or any business), competitors emerged. Satellite, the internet, and multiple pre-recorded formats and streaming options were launched, each eroding broadcasting market share for advertising and competing for consumers' time and attention.

Instead of pivoting to new strategies to retain market share, American radio broadcasters chose a wait-and-see approach. For example, the American broadcast industry was a full decade behind their European counterparts in adopting the radio data system (RDS), an FM broadcasting standard that lets your radio display information, like song title and artist.

Rather than making their services competitive, they asked the government to pass a mandate that would require radio to be included in cell phones and other devices. In essence, the broadcasters were urging the government to add to the cost and complexity of smartphones by requiring radio receiving chips and antennas in every phone.

Thankfully, that effort failed. Congress recognized that mandating technology made little sense in a market economy, where consumers voted with their wallets.

After the broadcasters lost that battle, they pivoted to another push for a government mandate—in the form of a law requiring carmakers to include AM radio in every car. In 2023 and 2024, broadcasters poured over $7 million into this campaign. But a federal government mandate requiring installation in *all* new cars made little sense—especially in an era where consumers have an overwhelming number of choices for audio content. FM radio, internet streaming services, podcasts, and other content were, and still are, on the rise, while AM radio market share is in decline. In a late 2023 test of the nationwide Emergency Alert System (EAS), less than 1 percent of Americans heard the alert via AM radio, while 95 percent received it via their smartphones.[27]

My colleagues and I at CTA also knew that success by the broadcasters could delay the transition to electric vehicles. In electric vehicles, electromagnetic currents produced by vehicle batteries interfere with AM radio reception. Solving that challenge is possible but costly, requiring additional shielding components. Nostalgia is great, and those who want cars with AM radio should certainly be able to buy them, but it has no place in policymaking if it stands in the way of the technological innovation that is crucial for progress. Unfortunately, politicians of both parties bowed to the pressure and gave the broadcasters what they wanted—a sympathetic hearing. Whether that hearing will lead to actual mandates rests in the hands of our leaders in Congress, an astonishing number of whom continue to call for regressive legislation that would require twentieth-century technology in twenty-first-century vehicles.

As a rule of thumb, I believe that companies and governments get it right when they pivot toward innovation rather than mandating old technologies. Most of the time, our legislators get it right, but I fear that we're moving away from some of the bedrock principles that have made American innovation the envy of the world. More of that in Chapter 8. But first, let's look at some companies and leaders that found opportunity and inspiration in failure.

CHAPTER 5

The Failure Pivot

ailure pivots can be some of the most inspiring. We all love to hear stories about the entrepreneurs and innovators who face rejection after rejection, or make a terrible decision, or see things go up in flames . . . before dusting themselves off and trying again. Sometimes that self-confidence is rewarded with success. Other times the outlook isn't quite so rosy. But without people who live by the motto "if at first you don't succeed, try, try again," the worlds of technology—and art, culture, and society—would be far worse off.

In April 1956, a young rock musician strode onstage at the Las Vegas New Frontier Hotel. While it was his first gig in the city, he had every reason to believe it would be a success. After all, a single from his debut album was sitting at #1 on the charts, and he'd just signed a multiyear movie contract with Paramount Pictures. But that night, Elvis Presley found that the routine that left teenage fans swooning and screaming for more elsewhere fell flat.

The crowd in the New Frontier's Venus Room just didn't *get it*—and neither did the middle-aged music critics. A writer for *Newsweek* compared Elvis to "a jug of corn liquor at a champagne party" and described an audience sitting "through Presley as if he were a clinical experiment."[1] The *Las Vegas Sun* panned "the brash, loud braying of his rhythm and blues catalog," calling it "overbearing to a captive audience."[2] Opening night went so badly, in fact, that the hotel moved Elvis's name to the bottom of the marquee for the duration of his show's two-week run.

While the business world is rarely as glamorous as show business, I tell this story because it illustrates a key principle that spans industries: even the biggest success stories can start as flops. In fact, I think failure is often a critical ingredient of future success, especially here in the United States. Sometimes, you have a great idea but the timing isn't right. Or you're not explaining your vision in a way that prospective funders or customers understand. Or maybe your initial product just isn't something people actually want or need, and failure will help you better understand the market. More than perhaps any other culture, Americans have come to embrace failure and see it as a learning opportunity. Success can breed complacency, but losses, mistakes, and missteps teach humility and the need to do things differently—as long as we first look backward and learn from our mistakes.

I've actually seen more winning tech companies, ideas, and entrepreneurs that came from failures than companies that gained big traction with the first attempt. As Vinod Khosla, the Sun Microsystems co-founder, said at SXSW in 2013, "I probably have more experience screwing up than anybody in this room." His company was acquired by Oracle for $7.4 billion. Bill Gates's first company, Traf-O-Data, was based on a product that "read the raw data from roadway traffic counters to create reports for traffic engineers." When the State of Washington decided to offer traffic processing to all the cities for free, any potential demand for the product vanished overnight.

PayPal founder Max Levchin started four failed companies before he had his big hit, including an ad banner network and a company that sold white-label classifieds for newspaper sites. He spoke about it at a conference called FailCon: "The very first company I started failed with a great bang. The second one failed a little bit less, but still failed. The third one, you know, proper failed, but it was kind of okay. I recovered quickly. Number four almost didn't fail. It still didn't really feel great, but it did okay. Number five was PayPal."[3]

Las Vegas Pivots

Las Vegas wasn't always an iconic event destination. In fact, while CES and Las Vegas are now closely intertwined, the show didn't start in Las Vegas at all. Our journey there started with, you guessed it, a failure.

Until the mid-1970s, CES took place in Chicago . . . in January. Our 1977 show was something of a bust, with weather so cold—a record-breaking -45°F windchill—that guests could not leave their hotel rooms. After that weather debacle, CES founder Jack Wayman moved the 1977 CES to Las Vegas, making it the city's first major business event. We never looked back, and CES has grown with Las Vegas for over four decades.

Today, Las Vegas has three of the ten largest American convention centers and 155,000 hotel rooms. With over three million visitors in 2023, it ranked that year as the top travel destination for Americans by Google searches.[4]

Not all of the city's pivots have worked. Attempts to market Las Vegas in the 1990s as a family destination were a mixed bag, after many parents discovered to their chagrin that laws excluding children from casinos *are* actually enforced. But one Las Vegas marketing strategy became part of American culture. Thanks to the brilliance of Rossi Ralenkotter, former president and CEO of the Las Vegas Convention and Visitors Authority

(LVCVA), the city launched an indelible slogan that still draws visitors today: *"What happens in Vegas stays in Vegas."*

At my first Las Vegas CES show in 1981, I recall that the lone convention center was so small, CES had positioned its largest exhibitor on a basketball court in the multiuse facility. Still, the technology innovations on display more than made up for the uninspiring surroundings. The Walkman was hot; the CD was making its public debut, launching the digital versus analog debate in the music industry; and car and home speakers were coming of age. Major tech companies debuted some of the first camcorders, alongside the first electronic gaming systems. CES was (and remains for me) the most exciting destination on the planet.

In 1982, CES creator Jack Wayman persuaded me to leave the big law firm where I was working as his outside lawyer and join the association as a full-time employee. One of our first big projects was an effort to secure more exhibit space in Las Vegas. While the Las Vegas hotels were gradually adding exhibit space and the Las Vegas Convention Center would eventually expand, Jack didn't want to wait. He wanted more space for the upcoming January show.

We approached four Las Vegas event industry leaders with a big idea: building a structure next to the existing Las Vegas Convention Center. Only one organizer was interested—Sheldon Adelson, creator and owner of COMDEX, then a fast-growing show for IT professionals. By the summer, we'd signed a three-way contract with Las Vegas to use their land to build the 120,000-square-foot structure. We rushed into production so it could be used for the late November COMDEX. For a building thirty times the size of a large American home, it is shocking, in retrospect, how little it cost: just $1.5 million, of which we paid half.

That investment in a Las Vegas event space catalyzed others around the city. Shortly afterward, Barron Hilton expanded exhibit space at the iconic Hilton Hotel. The convention center then tore down the basketball court that had played host to the 1981 CES and added newer buildings. Sheldon Adelson sold COMDEX and built the Sands Convention Center and the Venetian. Steve Wynn built the Wynn hotel properties, and Kirk Kerkorian developed the MGM Grand. The Las Vegas strip was booming. More recently, in 2021, the Boring Company opened the LVCC Loop, a series of tunnels connecting Convention Center buildings to quickly move visitors around the complex.

Las Vegas continues to reinvent itself. The city has welcomed professional hockey and football teams, hosted the 2024 Super Bowl, and joined part of the Formula 1 circuit. No other American city has transformed so rapidly.

Women in Tech

Let's start with a frank admission: the tech industry has not always supported and advanced women in leadership. As an industry, for a long time, we've failed.

Women make up just one-third of the overall tech workforce and hold just a quarter of tech leadership roles. But women-owned companies on average generate higher returns,[5] women-run companies generate a 35 percent higher ROI (return on investment) than companies managed by men,[6] and women-owned startups and startup teams with women founders deliver higher returns on investment, generating 10 percent more in cumulative five-year gains. That's despite receiving, on average, less initial funding.[7]

The failure to promote women in business and women in tech has been harmful to our economy and harmful to our country's potential for innovation. Thankfully, companies have recognized the failure, and women are gaining ground. In a 2021 survey of CTA members, for example, nearly 90 percent reported companywide efforts to increase representation among women.[8] Data from 2022 showed that large technology companies are steadily increasing the number of women in their workforces, with the largest gains happening in leadership roles.[9]

Highlighting women in leadership is also something we think about as the owners and producers of a highly visible platform like CES. To strengthen the current generation of women in tech and create role models for the next generation, it's not enough to simply bring more women to the table. We want to highlight them on some of the biggest stages in the tech world. Since 2020, nearly half of the speakers on CES stages have been women. As a policy, we also decline offers for CTA spokespeople to speak on "mannels" (all-male panels) that have at various points generated well-deserved criticism. I am not sure I got it or ever will get it entirely right, but I'm proud of CTA's commitment to ensuring diverse representation at our events.

What Does Flushing Your Toilet Have to Do with Failure?

In 2015, Dutch media mogul Arthur Valkieser looked at his flushing toilet and thought, "It's crazy that in the twenty-first century, people keep using precious water to flush their toilets."

Water is becoming scarcer. The average household consumes five hundred liters of water per day. And yet droughts are common. Clean water is harder and harder to come by. So Valkieser teamed up with serial entrepreneur Sabine Stuiver to invent Hydraloop, which launched globally at CES 2020. Hydraloop's product filters and recycles domestic water from showers, baths, washers and dryers, heat pumps, and air-conditioning units so homeowners can reuse water and reduce their overall usage.

It had an immediate impact. Winning out over more than four thousand competitors in different categories at CES, the company was awarded Best of Innovation in the categories of sustainability, eco design, and smart energy.

The path wasn't easy. It took five years to go from idea to launch. And Valkieser is no stranger to failure. In 1991, the company he owned at the time nearly went bankrupt. A friend of his took him to dinner and confronted him. "Either quit," his friend told him, "or be willing to adjust your goal so that you believe in it, and your team will believe in it, too." Valkieser took the lesson to heart. When he was developing Hydraloop, many early prototypes didn't work. The journey was one built on trial and error. He and Stuiver ate many dinners in his garage as they iterated the product. By 2020, they finally had a working prototype, but several investors who were in talks to invest pulled out because of fears around COVID-19 tanking the market.

In an interview with the podcast "10 Lessons Learned," Valkieser noted, "You will fail. You will fail—bottom line." But he says he doesn't see obstacles as problems, but as favors. It's an attitude that has helped his product gain a foothold across Europe and Africa, and recently in markets across the US. *Popular Science* called it one of the best home innovations of 2022. It's a product that could fundamentally shift water usage around the world.

This Entrepreneur Went from a Spot on "F*ckedCompany.com" to a Billionaire

Nick Woodman always wanted to be an entrepreneur. During college, he vowed to create a successful business before the age of thirty. He made a deal with himself that if he still hadn't done it by then, he would get a "real job."

He founded his first startup, a website called EmpowerAll.com, just after graduating from college. It was a flop. The idea was to sell electronic goods for a markup of a dollar or two, but he encountered too many obstacles, and the site didn't even go live.

It wasn't his last failure. He then started a gaming platform called Funbug, which gave users a chance to play games while winning cash prizes. He raised millions of dollars in funding, and Funbug started getting a lot of media attention. It seemed like a sure hit—until the dot-com bubble burst. In 2001, like so many other online companies that had begun with so much promise, Funbug crashed and burned. Woodman lost not only his own money but his investors' money. Even more humiliating, Funbug landed on a site called f*ckedcompany.com—a list of the dot-com era's biggest failures. He was twenty-six years old. Four years left to make it big or go find a desk job.

Reeling from the loss, Woodman did what a lot of people do—he escaped. He set off on a five-month surfing trip around Australia and Indonesia. He and a group of friends lived in a van while they moved from beach to beach, hoping to catch the perfect wave.

Some of them did—but no one else would know. They tried to take photographs and videos, but they couldn't get good enough pictures from shore. That's when Nick had his next idea. When he got home, he created the prototype of a waterproof wearable camera that surfers could take with them. The stakes were high, because to do it, he had to borrow $200,000 from his father. To make ends meet, Woodman sold shell necklaces he'd bought in Bali.

The cameras were a success. Surfers wanted them, and Woodman created the next iteration of the product, which could take ten-second videos. He called it GoPro. By 2014, the company went public.

GoPro, however, grew too big too fast. At its height, it was pulling in more than $1 billion in annual revenue. Some eighteen months after launching, the company had more than doubled its staff, and we hosted

Woodman as a featured speaker at the annual CES Leaders in Technology dinner. Then, the 2015 iteration of the product turned out to be bug-ridden and full of problems. By the end of that year, GoPro had had its first unprofitable quarter. A new product in the works, perhaps appropriately called Karma, faced repeated delays in its release date. Then GoPro was hit by a class action lawsuit, accusing the company of failing to disclose flaws in its products. Struggling to bounce back, GoPro laid off a quarter of its workforce.

Woodman had to pivot, again. He dialed back expenses and stopped focusing on hyper-complex products. GoPro pivoted back to the simple products that had gotten them such success to begin with. He told *Inc.* he had learned a huge lesson: "When things are going really well, you can be lured into thinking that everything's easier than it is. Just because you're a World Series–winning pitcher doesn't mean you can go play quarterback."[10]

As of this writing, the company has made significant improvements to regain market trust and market share. Investors are predicting a big turnaround, and I'm one of many rooting for them. At CES 2023, the company released a much-lauded HERO11, which won one of our coveted CES Innovation Awards, and the even more recent HERO12 has received accolades as the best overall action camera in the game. With more products set to release in 2024, GoPro showed how much a great pivot can reinvigorate a company.

When Failure Means You're Ahead of the Market

In 2003, three students from Finland's Aalto University won a local game development competition and took their success as a sign: the time was ripe to start a mobile gaming business. At first, the three did nearly all the development work for the new company, which they called Rovio, creating games for mobile platforms such as Java-based mobile phones like Motorola and Nokia. Then, investor cash gave them resources to expand the company to twenty-five people. After a few years, the young company found that while they could survive by working on contracts for larger companies in the gaming ecosystem, they faced an existential problem: they'd released more than fifty games, but none of their independent games had made it big.

By 2009, Rovio was almost bankrupt. Co-founders and cousins Mikael and Niklas Hed had to lay off more than a third of the company's staff. Despite these challenges, the Heds saw a market shift that could prove transformative, if they could harness it. In mid-2008, Apple had launched its App Store, which allowed iPhone users to easily download apps. More important for developers, the App Store provided a centralized platform where developers could easily distribute their games to a global audience, and an easy-to-use interface where users could discover new games. "The iPhone opened up the whole world," Niklas told *Wired*. "You had one contact, plus worldwide distribution." They decided to take one last shot at creating a hit game.[11]

To make it happen, they built on lessons from their failures. While previous games had been marketed to a niche audience, the new game needed mass market appeal. (As Mikael Hed put it, "we tried to profile the iPhone user and it turned out that it was everybody.") That meant a game that was easy to load, easy to play, and easy for players to connect with. With the company on the line, a graphic designer brought a single concept image of disgruntled birds trudging along the ground to a meeting—and the idea of Angry Birds was born.

Of course, that didn't guarantee it would be a success. The team was confident they had the makings of a hit game, especially after an early tester (Niklas's mother) got so wrapped up in the game she burned the Christmas turkey. They also knew that Rovio stood to benefit from the App Store's early days as an open playing field, where anyone with game development skills could see their game rise in popularity. But failure had also taught them the virtue of patience.

While the game shot up the charts in their native Finland, it didn't initially make waves in bigger gaming markets. The company focused on smaller European markets, attracting enough downloads to help Angry Birds get a big break: a featured spot as game of the week on the UK App Store. Within three days, it surged from the six hundredth position on the most-downloaded list to the first. Within weeks, it claimed the same spot on the US App Store list.

Today, the Angry Birds franchise remains one of the most-downloaded game series in App Store history. Starting from near-failure, Rovio has also capitalized on the smash success of Angry Birds to execute a pivot I'll explore at greater length in the next chapter: the success pivot. The founders quickly recognized that their game wasn't just successful because of its high-quality game play. People also *liked* the characters. A year after launch, Rovio began to market plush character toys, and by the early 2010s was earning some 40 percent of its revenue through toys and other licensing deals.[12] By 2019, a decade after its launch, the company had sold more than 1.8 billion consumer products, produced an animated series for Netflix and YouTube with over 10 billion views, and released two animated movies grossing nearly $500 million. As CEO Kati Levoranta tells it, the company used the success of Angry Birds to pivot, transforming "from a gaming company into a games-first entertainment company."[13]

Lawsuits, Taxes, and Bankruptcy

In 1998, an eager young entrepreneur named Travis dropped out of college to help his friends found a startup—a peer-to-peer file sharing service called Scour that helped people search for files they wanted to download. But just two years later, the Motion Picture Association of America

(MPAA), the Recording Industry Association of America (RIAA), and the National Music Publishers Association (NMPA) teamed up to file a $250 million lawsuit against Scour for copyright infringement allegations. Scour filed for bankruptcy in September 2000. It went up for auction and was ultimately sold to a communications company in Oregon.

Travis pivoted quickly. A month later, he launched a networking software company called RedSwoosh, which developed client-side technology to support, manage, and distribute media files. He later described it as his revenge company. "The idea was to take those 33 litigants that sued me and turn them into customers," he told an audience at FailCon 2011. "So now those dudes who are suing me are paying me."

In 2001, that company, RedSwoosh, ran out of money. The company owed $110,000 to the IRS, and Travis and his co-founder were nearly prosecuted for tax evasion. While there are differing accounts of who was responsible, ultimately, a new round of funding provided enough cash to repay the IRS. His co-founder left, and Travis moved back in with his parents to save money, going without a salary while he tried to save the company. RedSwoosh struggled on with just Travis and one engineer—who left to work for Google in 2005, losing RedSwoosh a potential deal with AOL.

Travis didn't give up. Eventually RedSwoosh was acquired in 2007 by a competitor, Akamai, for $23 million.

Who was this persistent entrepreneur? Travis Kalanick, who went on to co-found Uber in 2009. Travis managed to pivot in his approach to business while holding on to his self-belief—even when it seemed everyone doubted him. In fact, I was one of those early doubters myself. I had dinner with Travis at the 2012 Democratic National Convention. Back then, I didn't entirely understand the Uber concept and certainly had no idea how important it would become!

■ ■ ■

One Hundred Rejections

In 2013, nineteen-year-old Australian teen Melanie Perkins was earning extra money while at university by teaching students how to use design programs. All her students felt the same way: the programs were just too hard to use, and expensive to boot. Perkins knew there had to be a better way.

Perkins's mom was a teacher who was also in charge of her school's yearbook, and designing it took her mother hundreds of hours a year. So Perkins and her boyfriend, Cliff Obrecht, created an online school yearbook design business, Fusion Books. Students could use the online program to design their own profile pages and articles. They sold yearbooks to schools across Australia; the software was free, and schools only paid for printed yearbook copies. In their first year of business, only sixteen schools signed up. By year three, a hundred schools were using the software. In 2008, the founders received the Western Australia Inventor of the Year award.

Perkins and Obrecht knew they had a great idea, so they set their sights on Silicon Valley next, with a company that made design accessible to non-designers. They called it Canva, and they connected with investor Bill Tai, an early investor in Zoom, who agreed to invest $25,000 to start. But that was the only bit of good fortune they had for a while. In their first fund-raising round, they received rejection after rejection by investors—more than a hundred, in fact. Investors were wary that Canva was based in Australia, not in California; that its founders didn't have MBAs; and that the price of Canva was too high.

But Perkins and Obrecht didn't give up. Eventually, Canva ended up raising $1.6 million from angel investors like Bill Tai and Lars Rasmussen, the co-founder of Google Maps and Google Wave, as well as venture capital firms including Blackbird, Matrix, and InterWest Partners. They were also able to get a grant from the Australian government for $1.4 million, bringing their total seed raise to $3 million.

Today, the program has 60 million users around the world. Perkins is the CEO of one of the few profitable "unicorn" startups. Canva has raised more than $560 million in investments and has a $40 billion valuation.

Why Failure Matters

I recently had the opportunity to sit down for a conversation with Panasonic North America chairwoman and CEO Megan Myungwon Lee. To put it bluntly: she's very impressive. Over a thirty-five-year career with Panasonic, she rose from an entry-level role as a legal secretary and through the ranks of HR, before taking on responsibilities for strategic planning for Panasonic's North America business line. In that time, she helped reshape Panasonic North America as it shifted from consumer electronics to a more business-to-business focused model. So when I asked her what she was most proud of, I expected a little bragging.

Instead, Megan told me that as head of strategy, she'd made a lot of mistakes—and that *was* what made her proud. "It's okay to live through the mistakes and learn from the mistakes. Success, everyone knows," she explained. "But when you go through painful mistakes, that's when you learn. That's when you test yourself. And that's when you grow."

I couldn't agree more.

CHAPTER 6

The Success Pivot

Some of the biggest pivots are deciding what to *stop* doing, even if you're doing that thing well and doing it successfully. The tech industry leaders who enjoy lasting, long-term success don't rest on their laurels. They're constantly innovating, iterating, and pushing the boundaries of what's possible. The trick to longevity in business is pivoting at the right time. Businesses must change their products, services, actions, and attitudes as opportunities arise and market conditions shift. The value of a pivot built on prior success—rather than one prompted by failure, or the fear of it—is the luxury of time, resources, and a deep knowledge base to devote to investing in new areas of growth and opportunity.

There's an important lesson from Panasonic there, too. I've watched Panasonic grow for decades, from the early years of CES when Panasonic was known as a giant in the consumer electronics field, producing TVs, phones, VCRs, and VHS tapes. For those who aren't keyed into the technology field, those products may still be what the Panasonic brand name evokes—but that understanding is now fifteen years out of date. Panasonic's consumer electronics segment now represents just a small fraction of its North American business, dwarfed by growth in the company's business-to-business solutions in areas like batteries and energy storage used in electric vehicles and other cutting-edge technologies.

How did that pivot happen? According to Megan Myungwon Lee, "We didn't think we were introducing this grand strategy. But looking back, that's what we did." Senior leaders began to realize that the market for TVs, one of Panasonic's flagship products in the American market, was increasingly tight as models from lower-cost manufacturers became available. At the same time, the company was getting more calls from automakers and retailers, who were interested in using Panasonic's core technology.

"Don't get me wrong, it's been a painful transition," Megan told me. But to execute the pivot, she and Panasonic's leadership team were able to lean on a long-standing company philosophy: if we're serving our customers, the business should prosper. Amid declining TV sales Panasonic made a pivot away from TV sets, leaning on a century of R&D to eventually make an ambitious bet on electric vehicle batteries. That bet has paid off in spades, helping Panasonic's leaders to reinvent a century-old company to compete for the next century.

"Success pivoters" are excited about change. They love a challenge. And, most of all, they're visionaries—often even more so than those who execute any other type of pivot. They're able to see emerging trends and where things are headed, and to get out in front.

Another great example is Best Buy. While I already discussed Best Buy's COVID response in a previous chapter, the company's pivot has ultimately been larger than the pandemic. As CEO, Corie Barry has not just grappled with questions about the value of brick-and-mortar retail in an increasingly digital world, she's answered them decisively. At CES 2024, she sat down with then–Fortune Media CEO Alan Murray during our Leaders in Technology (LIT) dinner. Alan said to her, "A decade ago, I heard smart people say, 'Best Buy will be gone in five years.' So how is it that Best Buy not only still exists, but is succeeding?"

One answer is that Best Buy found its niche: it *humanizes* technology. When a person comes into their stores, an employee can see their purchase history and find solutions to their exact questions, down to accessing the manual for the microwave they bought five years ago. A Geek Squad crew can come to your home to help you set up your television. More recently, Best Buy has leaned into the healthcare space, from installing connected devices that help with aging-at-home, to partnering with hospitals around the country to install medical technology in patients' homes post-surgery.

"Whole sections of our store leave, and new ones come in," Corie told Alan. "Ten years ago, if you'd told us we'd be selling doorknobs and bikes, we would have been like, 'What are you talking about?'" But embracing new technologies like smart doorbell cameras and e-bikes has been the foundation of Best Buy's continued relevance. That also trickles down to their approach to the workforce. As Corie put it, Best Buy has succeeded because they've focused on "rewarding adaptability versus perfection." With the exception of a few industries—surgeons and pilots come to mind—that's an approach that any leader could benefit from adopting.

A Revolution in Surgical Care

I had a front-row seat to another success pivot, this one in the field of health technology. In the early 2000s, Neal Kassell, co-chair of neurosurgery at the University of Virginia (UVA), was getting increasingly frustrated. While he had successfully treated thousands of patients, he'd worked with dozens more who had brain tumors in surgically inaccessible locations or had maxed out on surgery and radiation and chemotherapy. With the technology available at the time, there was little else he could do to help them.

One day, a colleague—a cardiac anesthesiologist—mentioned research he was doing on the heart muscle using ultrasound and microbubbles, which are contrast agents for targeted drug delivery. A light bulb went off in Neal's head. What if he used ultrasound to treat those otherwise untreatable tumors? The idea, essentially, was to take multiple beams of sound and have them converge to destroy tumors in hard-to-access areas of the brain. Research from decades prior had shown it was possible, though technology limitations at the time made it challenging to pursue.

Neal immediately launched efforts to raise the money and institutional support for a Focused Ultrasound Center at UVA. He had good reason to be optimistic. Just a few decades before, he'd successfully launched the country's first Gamma Knife Center at UVA, making it a center of excellence for another radiation-based treatment. But while donors shared Neal's excitement, he discovered that UVA administrators didn't. In a more risk-averse academic environment, UVA leadership refused to commit to what they saw as a new and unproven technology.

Neal spoke to our mutual friend Bill Crutchfield, an entrepreneur and creator of the amazing electronics retailer Crutchfield, and a member of the UVA board. Bill suggested Neal take the money committed to the project and create a nonprofit instead, which would fund focused ultrasound programs at other institutions. Not long after, Bill called me and insisted I attend a luncheon in DC where Neal was slated to speak. Bill told me I'd hear about a new technology that could change the world, and I believed him. Luckily, he wasn't overpromising. Over lunch, Neal showed us a "before" video of a patient with an essential tremor so severe he couldn't hold a cup of coffee. After the treatment, the patient was fully cured. I became an enthusiastic supporter at that point.

Focused ultrasound is nothing short of a miracle. It is often a better alternative to chemotherapy, radiation, or invasive surgery. It has achieved thirty-five regulatory approvals as a treatment for different conditions around the world, including nine in the United States.

While the technology itself is incredible, its success wasn't preordained. The Focused Ultrasound Foundation was founded in 2006, and for nearly a decade Neal balanced his surgical work at UVA with his philanthropic work at the foundation. Then, in 2016, he realized that something had to give. The decision to leave UVA and focus full-time on running the foundation was really hard, he told me, "because I had the best job in the world. It's hard to describe how rewarding… [it was] to challenge the most feared and devastating diseases." But, he explained, "It really became a moral imperative." As a neurosurgeon, he was helping hundreds of patients a year. With focused ultrasound, he knew he had the potential to help millions.

That decision paid off in spades. In 2022, 100,000 people were treated at 1,000 treatment sites. Soon, one million people annually will benefit from a treatment that can shrink tumors both in the brain and outside of it, and offers the promise of new progress in treating degenerative conditions like Alzheimer's and Parkinson's. Focused ultrasound is medicine's best-kept secret. Thanks to Neal Kassell's career pivot—and willingness to completely change the trajectory of a successful medical career—focused ultrasound technology is taking off. And don't just trust me. I'm joined as a member of the Focused Ultrasound Foundation board of directors by luminaries including the author John Grisham, the financial wizard and healthcare philanthropist Michael Milken, and Amazon board member Tom Ryder—himself a beneficiary of focused ultrasound therapy.

Success Means Flexibility

Sometimes success pivots are radical, creating entirely new markets and revolutionizing the way our world works. Perhaps the best-known example is Amazon Web Services (AWS). At the 2015 AWS re:Invent conference, Amazon CEO Andy Jassy told the story of a senior retreat at then-CEO Jeff Bezos's house back in 2003. The executives in the room that day went through an exercise to identify Amazon's core capabilities. By that point, the company was already highly successful as an online retailer, but they wanted to dig deeper.

The executives quickly recognized that over the course of several years, Amazon had created a shared layer of basic infrastructure services that formed the building blocks for each Amazon function and feature. That helped speed up project development internally, but it also created a valuable product. Amazon's leadership team also realized that the company had built expertise and know-how in running reliable, scalable, cost-effective data centers. In short, they already had all the tools they needed to create AWS.

At the offsite, Amazon's senior-most leaders took the next step: deciding it could be a business. That step was a major pivot for a retailer focused on marketing itself to consumers who bought "new, used, refurbished, and collectible items."[1] But for Amazon's leaders, who saw the company as a "technology company that had simply applied its technology to the retail space first," the new business venture represented boundless opportunity. Jassy and others had a vision for AWS as a service that could provide startups and small businesses with a platform to easily build and scale applications. They had dreamed up the concept of cloud computing as a business.

As with many radical pivots, some people didn't immediately get it. In 2006, when Amazon first launched its Simple Storage Service, market watchers were skeptical. "I have yet to see how these investments are producing any profit," sniffed one Piper Jaffray (now Piper Sandler) analyst, suggesting the new product was "probably more of a distraction than anything else."[2] Amazon executives steeled themselves to fall back on a long-standing company principle: "As we do new things, we accept that we may be misunderstood for long periods of time." (Another valuable asset of the success pivot: well-earned confidence in your capabilities.)

Luckily for Amazon, developers immediately saw the value. Some 12,000 signed up on the very first day of the product launch. Since then, both AWS and the cloud computing market have grown exponentially. In the first ten years after its launch, AWS reached $10 billion in annual sales, powering nearly a third of the cloud computing market. If you've checked Facebook or LinkedIn, watched a show on Netflix, traded stocks on Robinhood, placed a bet on Sportsbet or DraftKings, or ordered lunch on DoorDash, you've benefited from a pivot that reinvented the way we use the internet.

Elon Musk is another radical pivoter. His first company was a searchable business directory (basically an online Yellow Pages with maps). Eventually, he scaled a purely electric car company—Tesla—to a valuation worth more than every other major car company in the world. He has created companies boring huge underground transportation tunnels, commercializing space exploration, advancing robotics, and pioneering brain-computer interfaces. While not all his companies have been mega successes—the recent challenges of X (formerly Twitter) are a recent example—and he's certainly a polarizing figure, his ability to envision and pursue big ideas and get funding behind new industries is unmatched in recent history.

I find award-winning author Walter Isaacson's biography of Musk to be especially insightful. As Isaacson tells it, Musk takes big risks and focuses on failing fast and pivoting. He recognizes that technology can and must play a role in improving the world, and constantly challenges his people to do the impossible. Plus, he's not afraid to roll up his sleeves and immerse himself in every aspect of the technology. Even if you're not a Musk fan, there's no question that our world has benefited greatly from his ability to pivot and advance new and emerging fields of technology.

■ ■ ■

Past Lessons Feed Future Success

In the early 2000s, John MacFarlane, Tom Cullen, Trung Mai, and Craig Shelburne were riding high on the success of their startup Software.com, a major player in early internet messaging. After selling the company to another young software firm, the founders knew that they wanted to work together on another venture. Having been "at the core of the Internet as it was blowing up," as Cullen put it, they had learned some key lessons: digitization and digital products were the next big trend; prices were plummeting for the technology components that made up smart home products; and the internet was developing as a "programmable" platform to deliver tailored and individual content.[3]

They took that knowledge and applied it to solving a shared passion: music. Any music buffs my age will remember the tangle of stereo and speaker wires and expense (for those who could afford it) of installing products for high-quality or surround sound. MacFarlane, Cullen, Mai, and Shelburne set out to build products that would allow music lovers to play their favorite songs anywhere in their homes. They called the new company Sonos.

While it might not seem so now, in 2002 the concept of music streaming was an ambitious idea. In fact, when they began to brainstorm, almost none of the technology needed to make their vision a reality actually existed. Americans were still listening to the AOL dial-up sound and fewer than 16 million American households had high-speed broadband. The founders needed a team that could take a great idea and build the systems and components needed to create functional prototypes. Luckily, they were able to build on another hallmark of the success pivot: a strong reputation and a big network of talent.

They hired engineers who were willing to make their own lives more difficult, in the form of trickier technical challenges, in order to produce a better user experience. Ultimately, the team pioneered several new approaches and patented dozens of new technologies that allowed for seamless, synchronized music across multiple areas. Sonos made its debut at CES 2005, where the company's multizone Digital Music System won one of our Best of Audio Innovation Awards. The first products shipped later that January.

Sonos wasn't just selling high-end audio products. It was selling consumers an entirely new way of listening to music in their homes. As one executive recounted, "When I started working with Sonos . . . we'd go to speak with retailers and installers. You had to ask, 'Have you heard of Spotify?' If they said yes, then you could explain what Sonos was and how it worked. If they didn't, then you'd have to explain music streaming, which blew their minds."[4]

The ethos of constant innovation has stuck with Sonos. It was also the foundation for another, more recent, pivot from success. Going into 2020, Sonos had successfully navigated a forced pivot to voice activation and was benefiting from a growth market for smart home devices, including speakers. But leaders at the company recognized a new opportunity in curated music streaming. In 2019, surveys showed people were spending a whopping eighteen hours a week listening to music, with nearly 90 percent using an on-demand streaming service.[5] While Sonos speakers could already connect to more than a hundred music streaming platforms, executives felt there was an opening for more curated, high-quality audio content.

In April 2020, Sonos launched Sonos Radio, a slate of original content focused on genre-based stations and artist-created channels. It was a bold move. The company was competing with a wealth of original content across dozens of platforms. But that pivot paid off. Thanks to the company's long-standing investment in partnerships with musicians and radio stations, brand recognition, and its sterling reputation, Sonos saw overall listening hours increase by 33 percent in 2020 from the previous year. Sonos Radio played a significant role in that growth, becoming the fourth most-used service on the platform and the most popular radio service.

After so many years focusing exclusively on hardware, Sonos CEO Patrick Spence capitalized on the lessons of a long career at both Black-Berry and Sonos: while bold pivots have some execution risks, the mindset for pivoting is opportunism and pragmatism. In other words, when success gives you the opportunity to take a chance and make a profit, seize it!

The 45-Degree Pivot

Often pivots, especially success pivots, aren't 180-degree turns in strategy or approach, setting people or businesses on a diametrically opposite course. Instead, think of pivots as a range of tactical changes in direction. They can be more like a 90-degree turn, or even just a 45-degree quarter turn! That describes scenarios like Sonos's introduction of Sonos Radio, which enhanced the overall listening experience for Sonos users. Rather than a complete pivot, it was an expansion of Sonos's existing product offerings that enhanced the value of its products and further engaged its users.

In the technology field, many traditionally hardware-centric companies have—like Sonos—successfully executed 45-degree pivots by adding software, streaming, or subscription services (or sometimes all three) to their portfolios, complementing and enhancing the allure of their hardware products. Think Peloton, which is pivoting away from hardware and accelerating its transformation into a software-first company focused on content. Even those without Peloton-branded equipment can subscribe to access fitness classes ranging from cycling and running to yoga and strength training. Apple has ventured into subscription services with offerings like Apple Music, Apple Arcade, and Apple TV+. Wearables maker Garmin offers Garmin Connect, a software platform that allows users to track and analyze their activities and participate in fitness challenges.

The expansion into software and services helps companies create "sticky" demand and weather downturns in the hardware market. Software subscriptions can enhance the value of hardware products and help establish positive relationships with customers. Companies that pivot in this direction are also tapping into a large and growing market. CTA's 2023 software and services analysis showed more than $150 billion in spending as software and services expanded to capture nearly one-third of the technology market.

Roll with It

Few people know that Eggo waffles first started as . . . mayonnaise. When brothers Frank, Anthony, and Sam Dorsa created their own mayonnaise concoction in the 1930s, they called it "Eggo" because they used the sales pitch of "100% fresh ranch eggs" as their main ingredient. Their product was a hit—and they started thinking of other egg-based products they could sell. It wasn't a stretch to move from mayonnaise to waffle batter—which is also made of eggs. Their waffle mix, which needed only milk to make waffles, was also a big seller.

In the 1950s, grocery stores started featuring more and more types of frozen food. The Dorsa brothers were doing just fine with mayonnaise and waffle mix, but they saw an opportunity. They created a machine that allowed them to make and flip thousands of waffles in an hour, which were then frozen for grocery stores. They called the waffles Froffles (frozen waffles).

The name was fine, but "Eggo" had become such a strong household brand by that time that customers simply called the waffles "Eggo waffles." The Dorsa brothers rolled with it. They stopped using the name Froffles after just a few years. Sometimes, your customers know your brand better than you do.

Seizing the Opportunity

Michael Chasen, former CEO and co-founder of Blackboard, started his new ed-tech company, Class Technologies, after seeing his kids struggle with virtual education platforms during COVID.

In a 2021 Masters of Leadership interview with NVTC, he said, "My daughter was in second grade at the time, my son was in eighth grade, and my older daughter was in tenth grade. And they were having a hard time really engaging with the students in online schooling. So I spoke with a number of teachers and asked them why they were having a hard time engaging with students, and they said, 'These virtual meeting tools are great for lecturing online, and they're great for having group discussions, but they don't actually bring everything in the physical classroom online. We do a lot more in the physical classroom—everything from taking attendance, to handing out assignments, to giving tests or quizzes, to talking one-on-one with the students.'"[6]

So he came up with the idea for Class—a Zoom classroom that mirrors the physical class experience. Class is changing the way the world learns by adding teaching and learning tools to Zoom for K–12, higher education, and the workplace. It's also making learning more equitable.

Chasen said in a 2022 *Forbes* interview, "You can run Zoom and Class from your iPhone or your iPad, cheaper than a computer, and you can be miles outside the city and another country. If you can access live instruction, for maybe the first time, you can help raise entire societies out of poverty."[7]

By 2022, Class had raised over $160 million in funding from prominent Zoom board members and investors, including SoftBank, Salesforce, GSV, and even NFL quarterback Tom Brady. But Chasen never forgot the lessons of his entrepreneurial beginnings. When he started Blackboard, his former boss at KPMG allowed him to take some chairs from their office.

"I sat in that chair for 20 years," he said, "because it always reminded me of our scrappy beginnings." Class is an almost entirely virtual company; while they're headquartered in DC, they tap into talent all over the world. This also means they can cut down on the unnecessary costs of a large physical office.

Chasen always tries to stay one step ahead. When he started Blackboard, he was told by school after school that they wouldn't have any use for an online classroom software solution. Some even said they thought it would be illegal to have grades available to view online. But by 2005, it had gone public with a valuation of $350 million (today, its valuation is in the billions). In 2023, Class announced it was bringing ChatGPT to the classroom, allowing it to capitalize on the massive opportunities of AI. Its AI classroom tool can generate study guides, answer student questions based on what was taught in class, and elaborate on specific sections of lectures.

Seeing the Opportunity

In 2012, entrepreneur Adam Gross played a recreational tennis match with former professional tennis player Dr. Melissa Hunfalvay. When Adam congratulated Melissa on her win, they started talking. Melissa mentioned that she is a scientist and researcher, and was working on developing products based on eye-tracking technology. Adam's interest was piqued. He had just had a successful exit from his previous company in the healthcare space, and he immediately saw the potential of her work.

So Melissa and Adam teamed up to develop RightEye—an eye-tracking medical device that, within minutes, can measure objective eye movements, visual tracking, and more. These quantifiable evaluations can do everything from helping doctors diagnose vision issues or concussions, to helping athletes and elite military improve their visual skills. Certain eye movement patterns can also be strong indicators of clinical conditions like Parkinson's and Autism-spectrum disorders.

RightEye developed a successful market within the medical, military, and athletic communities, but Adam knew there was still an untapped opportunity beyond the software and the device. After all, eye-tracking serves as a sensitive measure of a person's state, encompassing attention, health, and performance. And together, he and Melissa had amassed decades of data that includes raw eye-tracking data, gaze patterns and videos, demographic and epidemiological data, and clinical notes from doctors. It is, in fact, the largest and most diverse longitudinal, scientifically validated repository of PII-redacted eye movement data in the world. More than eight million users have used the RightEye device to date. "Our data is growing about 145% per year," Adam said, "which enables us to build more and more accurate machine learning and AI models. This growing dataset helps connect the dots between a person's eye movement patterns, demographics, medical and vision conditions, and more."

RightEye began acquiring other data sets, partnering with universities and organizations like MIT and the US Veterans Administration to build new models for biomarkers for Parkinson's, Lyme disease, Alzheimer's, and more. In total, RightEye has more than a hundred user states that range from distraction and fatigue to vision and neurodegenerative diseases.

In 2022, they were approached by some tier one tech firms who asked if their data and models could be deployed in environments beyond the medical device. It was at that point that Adam and Melissa realized that the same data they had collected and procured over the past ten years could deliver even more value to the world.

So in 2023, they launched HarmonEyes to put that data to work. VR/AR headsets, driver- and pilot-monitoring systems, 3D monitors, and phones and tablets increasingly have the requisite technology built in and can benefit from HarmonEyes's solutions, anytime and anywhere. Gaming companies can use its plug-ins to solve real problems and enhance user experiences. Surgical training applications can alert doctors when they are fatigued and confirm they are looking at the right place at the right time. Special Operations teams in the military can develop expert profiles to select the people best suited to perform certain tasks. And it could be life-saving. "For example, we know what kind of vision skills are required to be an elite sniper," Adam said, "and where someone is the fastest (or slowest) visually. This type of critical, granular information can be used to put them in the best physical spot during an operation where they'll be at their best."

Or, consider Parkinson's disease: One of the biggest challenges for clinical drug trials is that there are a lot of comorbidities with Parkinson's, making it difficult to differentiate what conditions participants actually have. But there is a specific ocular marker that people with Parkinson's have, which is different from the ocular marker for, say, essential tremor (ET). Differentiating between these two conditions could be the difference between a successful and failed clinical trial for a disease-modifying therapy. So there are vast opportunities for eye-tracking data to enable the success of various types of drug development.

"I've learned that the flexibility and willingness to pivot is as important as your first go-to-market plan," said Adam. "Identifying new opportunities based on market feedback is critical for long-term value creation. It takes guts to take the risk to pivot to new opportunities. But remaining open to new and better product-market fit can result in success. Many companies that have become big successes have pivoted multiple times. It's something that is common and doesn't get talked about enough."

When Industries Pivot

Sometimes the changing, evolving needs of our societies prompt entire industries—even successful ones—to pivot. Getting an industry to align on one strategy is like herding frogs into a wheelbarrow. By definition, industries are made of companies with similar businesses. And businesses are, still, run by people. Egos, grudges, personalities, jealousies, and deal-making history often interfere with efforts to move an industry to pivot so it can seize opportunities for growth. That's why it's especially impressive to see industry pivots executed well. The cable industry's strategic transition in the 1980s is a great example.

In 1975, HBO became the first television network in history to deliver a continuous signal via satellite for its broadcast of the "Thrilla in Manila," a live boxing match between Muhammad Ali and Joe Frazier. The program was so popular that cable companies began to produce more and more content throughout the '80s, ushering in a "programming deluge" driven by the rise of MTV.[8]

But cable industry leaders knew they couldn't just create content. With the growth of satellite and telephone companies and even wireless phone service, they foresaw huge entertainment competition on the horizon. And they knew that in order to reach viewers, they had to reach consumers where they were—at home. With that goal in mind, industry leaders strategized and came up with an ambitious plan to back up their entertainment revenue stream: broadband. The new technology supported high-speed internet access and high-definition digital content. In addition to the traditional entertainment services they had offered, cable operators would provide the technology making that entertainment accessible.

To execute this pivot, broadband operators couldn't work alone. They needed to collaborate. That meant working together to identify issues, troubleshoot shared technical problems, and invest in developing technologies that would support and shape the future of entertainment. In 1988, cable operators came together and created CableLabs, a nonprofit research and development consortium based in Louisville, Colorado.

At the cost of just a few cents a month for subscribers, CableLabs quickly established a collaborative process for developing public and shared standards for cable technologies. In the 1980s and '90s, that meant technologies that could support bigger and better cable pipelines into our homes. Then it meant technologies to handle massive digital content, including full motion internet video. While their work often flies under the radar—how often do you think about who is working on the standards that help connect the internet-enabled devices in your home?—CableLabs today successfully manages key public infrastructure for the whole cable industry. That includes embedding digital certificates to ensure that data and content is protected and secure, a growing concern with cyberattacks on the rise.

The cable industry is a rare example of leaders in major industries deliberately shifting course. Of course, 1980s cable industry leaders also had an advantage: because cable companies literally strung cables—or, more recently, buried them—through a city, cities and towns often granted only one cable company a franchise. That meant cable companies weren't in direct competition with one another. It's easier to come to agreement as an industry when the players at the table can focus on cooperation rather than competition.

Cooperation

Still, until fairly recently, most successful companies and business leaders saw partnering as a "nice if it works out" opportunity, but not a big deal. In my conversations with CEOs early on in my time as the head of the Consumer Technology Association, there frankly were just not a lot of people focused on it.

Then the internet came along and partnerships became much more important. I now hear more and more executives embrace a corporate philosophy built on a *need* to partner—especially with small companies.

No single company has all the answers anymore, and big brands recognize that startups are often better positioned to bring new and innovative ideas to life. According to a 2022 HubSpot report, 65 percent of organizations already view partnerships as essential to their future growth, and half of organizations surveyed attribute a quarter or more of their revenue to partnerships.[9]

The reality is that technology has advanced quickly, gained complexity, and innovations and patents have multiplied in shorter time frames. As a result, leaders are recognizing that partnerships, strategic alliances, and even simple licensing deals can expand their market, increase their revenue and brand recognition, and produce products that are simply better. Take the automotive industry. Car companies are partnering with audio hardware companies like Sony, Bose, and Harman to provide consumers with high-quality audio as a way to meet consumer demands. In 2020, Jeep and McIntosh announced a "great American comeback story" between a classic American car maker and a company whose systems are beloved by serious audiophiles.

Today, innovation is about collaboration. Collaborating with other businesses may be the quickest way to get to market, beat competitors, and grow the top and bottom line.

Creating products and services consumers want increasingly requires using another company's intellectual property. Products are more and more complex and use an array of semiconductor chips, resistors, capacitors, mechanical controls, sensors, software, and design elements. Patent licensing allows a business to use another's inventions. Cross-licensing is common in the technology industry. This is when two businesses agree to license each other's intellectual property.

For any new business collaboration, strategy, or relationship, one key consideration must always be the conditions for and cost of a breakup or split in the relationship. Having reviewed and signed thousands of business contracts, I have learned to focus on that factor and require it to be outlined in the contract.

I recall a dinner I enjoyed with Scott McNealy, who created and then headed Sun Microsystems. He said that anyone, including a government agency, that bought software or an IT system should know not only the purchase cost and annual fees for what they buy but should understand the cost of leaving the system—and the time and resources it takes to set up and adapt to a new system. This is good advice for anyone in business considering investing in a platform, system, or software.

Partnerships are also growing across industry verticals, as larger companies promote smaller ones using their hardware and software. In recent years, we've seen dozens of those partnerships showcased at CES. Nemo's Garden—a startup focused on underwater crop cultivation—has touted its use of Siemens's digital twin technology to test and fine-tune underwater greenhouses. Siemens software also powers Space Perspective, a consumer-focused space travel company. Microsoft is acknowledged as a partner (and software provider) for companies as diverse as Wejo, a data insights company for connected vehicles; Touchcast, an enterprise metaverse company; and Rockwell, a manufacturer of industrial automation components. Lidar technology company Ouster used booth space to promote the technology driving automated forklifts from Third Wave Automation and autonomous robots from Ottonomy.

In previous eras, each of these companies might have developed its own proprietary software systems. Or, if they were licensing software built by other companies, it was far less likely to be publicly acknowledged, much less celebrated. Today, successful companies have recognized that fostering cooperative relationships among industry players is key. It allows them to pivot as they navigate through disruptive changes and capitalize on emerging opportunities. It allows them to cross-promote to increasingly selective consumers. And it helps them stay competitive in the market and manage risk.

Collaborations can also help companies work across geographies. Hundreds of billions of dollars are invested in technology companies each year, often with the expectation of growth and returns that can only come from tapping into international markets. But it's rare for companies—especially small and midsize companies—to have the cultural and legal knowledge, not to mention contacts with media, government officials, and relevant players, to enter a new country market by itself. Even companies that choose to create a subsidiary in other countries must still find distribution and marketing partners and those with local knowledge.

That knowledge is critical. One company I know created a European unit and hired scores of employees. Business leaders quickly discovered their products were ill-suited to the market and wanted to pivot and shut down the European facility, only to learn that Europe's employment laws required huge payments and several months' notice to employees prior to closing down a facility. Not knowing the local laws before entering the market was a major mistake!

Cooperation . . . with Competitors?

Cooperation is certainly easiest when you're not chasing the same market, but it's also possible—and often profitable—even between rivals. As a young boy, I remember watching in awe the images from Apollo 11, the first manned mission to land on the moon. The moon landing is now remembered as the triumphant culmination of a decades-long space race between the United States and our Cold War rival, the Soviet Union. And while there's no doubt it was a triumph of American ingenuity, that's not the whole story. In fact, lunar exploration almost began as a cooperative venture with the Soviets. In early meetings with Soviet premier Nikita Khrushchev, then-president John F. Kennedy proposed a joint mission to the moon, a diplomatic gesture that ultimately didn't survive the tensions between the US and the Soviet Union.

Fast-forward some fifty years to another collaboration that almost was: a cooperative venture between Jeff Bezos's Blue Origin and Elon Musk's SpaceX. In the early 2000s, the founders met to discuss their "mutual obsession" with the future of space exploration. While both are famously competitive, they recognized that sometimes companies—even competitors—can be more successful working together than going it alone.

That idea is called "coopetition," and it's defining how the technology industry seizes opportunities and pivots. Though coopetition isn't new, it has taken decades to build momentum. The term was first coined in the 1996 book *Co-opetition* by Adam M. Brandenburger and Barry Nalebuff, who advocated for companies to seek out and cautiously work with their competitors, where possible. Back then, there weren't many examples of tech competitors pivoting to work together. After all, there's always a risk that any cooperation will give a rival some competitive advantage.

Perhaps the best-known early case is Microsoft and Intel. In the early 1980s, the companies were jockeying for slices of the personal computer market. With Microsoft known primarily as a software and services company and Intel as a hardware provider, executives found a complementary strategy that would allow them to dominate the market—together. Every personal computer would be powered by Intel chips and would come with the Windows operating system pre-installed. The companies also worked together on new technologies and standards, including the USB.

This "win-tel" strategy was embraced by major computer companies like Dell and Compaq (later HP) and gave the PC market strength and huge dominance over more niche non-PC competitors, which at that point included Apple. Their savvy, brilliant cross-promotion and marketing investment created successful PC marketplace domination. It also delivered a sea change in the technology industry, making computers an accessible at-home technology for first thousands, then millions of Americans.

Trade associations are, by their nature, a platform for collaboration among competitors. For example, the Motion Picture Association of America ratings code gives parents confidence in determining children's appropriate viewing. Drink milk, buy Florida oranges, or enjoy avocados are all healthy food campaigns by trade groups representing their agricultural sectors. The National Association of Home Builders and the National Association of Realtors publish economic statistics and advocate for housing construction and sales. And the National Association of Manufacturers advocates for manufacturers and promotes jobs in manufacturing to America's youth.

I probably know more than the average person about coopetition after decades at CTA. Many of our more than thirteen hundred members compete for market share in the same industries or have overlapping interests. Despite those concerns—no company wants to give away information about its focus areas that might benefit a competitor—they often find common cause in working together toward goals that include influencing government action, conducting market research, setting standards, or promoting growth of an industry as a whole.

Trade associations don't always work well. Consider the 2019 revelations that National Rifle Association (NRA) board members were being rewarded with lucrative NRA contracts.[10] Another painful example is the US Chamber of Commerce. In 2019, after media reports of excessive staff spending including a $600,000 private plane trip by the CEO to China, I wrote to Chamber board members sharing my concern that our nation's top business association was tarnishing the image of other business associations.[11]

I also expressed my concern about the Chamber's willingness to put its name on paid media campaigns designed by special interest groups.

I felt that in many cases, they were supporting proposals that could harm American businesses, including fighting against lower healthcare costs and financial protections for workers, or allying with an anti-tech campaign funded by the content industry that could shut down internet sites. At least one Chamber insider told me the letter prompted major changes, including a quicker leadership transition to now-CEO Suzanne Clarke, who has positively pivoted the Chamber in visible and substantive ways that support better governance, transparency, and effectiveness.

The Good Side of Coopetition

Social media sites offer a positive example. While many specialized social media sites compete with Facebook for users' time and eyeballs, Facebook allows more than 160,000 websites to use its credentials as a way to authenticate log-ins. That helps smaller apps and websites, which may have a less-well-developed security infrastructure than more established social networks, while giving Facebook an opportunity to cross-promote every time users log in. It offers additional benefits to users like me, who struggle to remember the dozens of passwords needed to access various accounts and websites.

Coopetition can benefit direct rivals, if it helps free up other resources that keep companies competitive in the broader market or meet an untapped need. In 2020, cooperation between pharmaceutical manufacturers Pfizer and BioNTech allowed the companies to share development and manufacturing capabilities and know-how. We have benefited from the result: highly effective COVID-19 vaccines created and brought to market at record speed.

Recently, tech giants like Google and Samsung (mobile phones) and Microsoft and Samsung (smartphones, tablets, and other mobile devices) have entered into cross-licensing agreements for the high-performance computing technology that goes into microprocessors and more. These agreements allow both companies to focus on innovation and product development.

It's also happening in the mobility space, as nearly every auto company pivots to embrace electric vehicles. In the mid-2010s, Ford and GM announced a partnership to jointly develop automatic transmissions for front-wheel-drive and rear-wheel-drive vehicles. Ford led the market in ten-speed transmissions, while GM was known for their nine-speed components. The deal saved both companies money, allowing both to make huge investments in upgrading their Michigan production factories. It helped Ford and GM adjust to changing market conditions—in this case new regulations around fuel efficiency for US-bound vehicles. Most important, it freed up engineering talent to help both companies execute a pivot to electric. Less than a decade later, GM CEO Mary Barra proclaimed in her CES 2022 keynote address that the auto industry was "at the tipping point of electrification" and announced GM's vision for an all-electric future.

We see a similar trend in electric vehicle charging. General Motors and Ford are partnering with Tesla to use Tesla's North American charging network and technologies for their growing electric vehicle fleets. Volvo, Rivian, Mercedes, and others have announced plans to adopt Tesla's charging standard to access the company's more than 12,000 superchargers.

As tech companies diversify and move into new markets, opportunities for coopetition grow but become more complex. Take Amazon Prime, which among many other services has built out a formidable offering of both original and owned content. That puts it in competition with other streaming services like Netflix, Hulu, HBO Max, and Peacock. Amazingly, all of those platforms run on Amazon Web Services, allowing them to benefit from huge economies of scale. That means that one part of Amazon is working with and for some of Amazon's top competitors in the content space.

Cooperation, collaboration, and coopetition are going to define the next decade of what we buy, drive, consume, wear, and work with, not just because these principles allow tech to develop faster, but also because they allow the *right* kind of tech to develop.

Public-Private Partnerships

Sometimes, lawmakers cannot quickly or easily agree on how to address new developments in technology. That's a function of the slow-moving nature of our federal government system, and entrepreneurs in emerging technology fields like self-driving are struggling with the lack of federal guidance. But having been involved in several public-private efforts, I learned they work best if there is strong agreement on a big goal.

One example is the Energy Star seal of approval, authorized in 1992, which recognizes the most energy-efficient products in several product categories. Since then, consumers have bought over 2 billion Energy Star products, most of them consumer technology products. The program has helped American families and businesses save more than $500 billion in energy costs and helped prevent 4 billion metric tons of greenhouse gas emissions from entering the atmosphere.[12]

Another example is HDTV. By the late 1980s, we knew better television technology was on its way, but TVs require an agreed-upon standard for broadcasting and receiving. Under the volunteer tutelage of revered former FCC chairman Dick Wiley, the FCC created public-private committees to set testing criteria and recommend a system for US adoption. Eventually, Congress set a date to end analog broadcasting, and the US led the world with a robust digital standard. We saw a similar process for the launch of the commercial internet and airplane mode, as I shared in Chapter 2.

More recently, White House–led efforts to enhance cybersecurity are a fantastic example of the power of collaboration between industry experts and government leaders. Both recognized a shared goal of helping consumers build trust in the security of their devices, and an imperative to work against the growing threat of cyber intrusions. With the backing of government leaders, CTA worked with the National Institute of Standards and Technology (NIST) and other stakeholders for more than five years to develop a set of consumer-connected device security recommendations as the framework for a voluntary national cybersecurity labeling program. That program, dubbed the US Cyber Trust Mark, will help consumers identify secure products by authorizing use of a standardized mark and QR code on products that meet certain technical specifications—similar to the way the Energy Star program certifies energy-efficient products.

The US Cyber Trust Mark was formally announced in 2023, with the first qualifying products hitting store shelves in 2024. CTA won the Chairman's Award from the World Innovation, Technology and Services Alliance (WITSA) for its work, but ultimately the winners are the millions of American consumers who will benefit from more secure devices. The lesson here is that leaders lead best by getting buy-in. They mandate only as a last resort.

Now that I've covered the four types of pivots—and the qualities that make great pivoters—we're going to take these ideas to the next level. In Chapter 7, I'm going to share the pivots happening *now* in the technology industry, and how companies and our societies are pivoting to meet them. Of course, technology can't do it alone. Innovation doesn't happen (or at least, happens far more slowly and inconsistently) without good policies and an ecosystem that rewards pivoters and people who are willing to take a risk and try something new. In Chapter 8, I'll take a look at how to create that innovation-friendly environment, highlighting a few "overpivots" in reaction to technological developments. I also offer some suggestions for how US policymakers should pivot if they're serious about maintaining America's status as a global leader in innovation.

CHAPTER 7

The Emerging Technologies
Reshaping Our World

I n 2011, Marc Andreessen wrote a now-famous blog post focused on the idea that software is eating the (financial) world. In it, he explained that "more and more major businesses and industries are being run on software and delivered as online services—from movies to agriculture to national defense. . . . Over the next 10 years, I expect many more industries to be disrupted by software."[1] Just over a decade later, it's clear those predictions have come to pass. Consumers live in an increasingly digital and on-demand world offering streaming services, food delivery, customized shopping experiences, and more. Meanwhile, almost all businesses—even so-called mom-and-pop shops—have now established an online footprint of some sort.

But what's next for the tech innovations shaping our world? The upheaval of the COVID-19 pandemic created an inflection point—or, you could say, a pivot point—for a variety of technologies, which moved from "nice to haves" for our homes and businesses into necessities that help us work, live, and connect on a daily basis. These technologies are laying the foundation for a reimagined modern economy and providing solutions for some of the world's biggest challenges.

But in essentially every technology field, the only constant is change. Leaders who predicted in the 2010s that AI would see only incremental advances in the decades ahead weren't counting on the breakthrough represented by generative AI. To understand what's possible and what's next in the world of technology, I first want to highlight some of the technologies that saw pivot points during the COVID pandemic. The entrenchment of virtual and hybrid workforces and increased online consumer activity has transformed the modern economy. At the same time, businesses are confronting an ever more complex set of challenges and tradeoffs, which include:

- A more vulnerable cyberspace as greater online activity raises the potential for increasingly costly attacks.
- A growing workforce gap as heightened demand strains labor resources.
- The need to offer flexible working environments for staff while also ensuring business productivity.

Innovation in cybersecurity, cloud computing, AI, quantum computing, and robotics can and will play a big role in helping us mitigate these challenges—and set us up for the incredible pivots to come.

Cloud Computing

Early examples of cloud computing date back to the 1960s, but large-scale cloud computing—essentially, outsourcing your computer needs—is far more recent. Still, we've already seen a massive impact on the way businesses operate. With cloud computing, businesses can access powerful computing resources without having to invest in their own hardware. This means they can put their resources into creating new products and serving more customers, as well as serving up more customized and tailored support for that growing customer base.

During the pandemic, cloud computing showed its agility and reliability for greater remote and hybrid models in what may have been the ultimate stress test for the technology. Now, it's indispensable. Worldwide public cloud spending in 2023 was $591 billion, an increase of 20.7 percent from 2022.[2] Fifty percent of the world's total data will be stored in the cloud by 2025.[3] It's also efficient: it's 34 percent less expensive to adopt a multicloud environment than using a single platform.[4]

In mid-2020, just a few months into the pandemic, Microsoft CEO Satya Nadella talked about how his company had seized on these advances to pivot. He explained that the company had seen two years of digital transformation in two months, as its customers started adopting cloud solutions. PayPal CEO Dan Schulman summarized this trend with a bit more animation: "We went from being the Flintstones to the Jetsons in nine months."

As a general rule, cloud computing can create efficiencies for companies that make their operations more sustainable, reducing a company's carbon footprint by shrinking or even eliminating power-hungry onsite infrastructure. In fact, the switch from on-premises computing to cloud computing may prevent more than one billion metric tons of carbon dioxide from 2021 through 2024.[5]

A number of businesses—like Citibank, Hertz, Verizon, Allstate, and GAP—have pivoted to move all or most of their applications to the cloud, which reduces both cost and environmental impact as well as the risk of data loss, minimizes security risks, and allows companies to be more mobile. In fact, disaster recovery is one of the most important benefits of cloud computing. If there's a power outage or a natural disaster like a hurricane or an earthquake, businesses can still access their data and continue to operate without interruption.

The power of the cloud allows companies of all sizes to have greater scalability in their operations with minimal disruptions, which allows them to more effectively balance the demands of workers in hybrid working conditions with minimal disruption to overall business connectivity. Considering a transition to the cloud? Maybe it's worth framing this change—whether internally or externally—as part of your organization's next success pivot.

Cybersecurity

The future of cloud computing is also by necessity closely linked to the expansion and development of the Internet of Things (IoT). The IoT essentially runs anything we know as "smart"—from smart watches and security systems to driverless cars and smart cities. This ecosystem of connected devices already creates massive amounts of data that needs to be stored and processed, and as an even greater number of our daily use devices capture and create data, that amount will only grow. With more than 14 billion IoT-connected devices already in operation around the world, our collective online presence has increased exponentially.[6] Along with that growth comes new risks, and the need for more advanced cybersecurity.

To quantify bytes of digital output the world generates daily, data scientists use the term "quintillion." One quintillion is equivalent to one billion billions. Multiply that by 2.5, and you're looking at how many bytes of data we're spinning up every twenty-four hours. All that valuable information is an irresistible target for today's threat actors in cyberspace.

In response to the shifting security landscape, companies and individuals are demanding a tapestry of protection, from personal identity protection to more complex business cybersecurity solutions, to lower the risk of data breaches. In 2023, nearly half of organizations experienced a ransomware attack of some kind,[7] and the global cost of cybercrimes in 2023 reached $8 billion.[8] According to a 2022 report from IBM, the costs associated with cybercrime—$10.5 trillion annually by 2025—are estimated to exceed worldwide cybersecurity spending by forty times.[9]

This threat landscape is only set to evolve further. During multiple conference sessions at CES 2023 and CES 2024, cybersecurity experts said they are closely watching AI. The concern is that the technology will be as useful to criminals and others involved in nefarious or black market activity as it is to those working for the public good. Adversarial AI will likely contribute to increased frequency and complexity of attacks like large-scale phishing attacks that can also be personalized to better target individual users. At the same time, defensive AI will play a key role in responding to and eliminating these threats with advances in areas such as threat detection automation, like those outlined during CES 2023 by CrowdStrike CEO and co-founder George Kurtz in a conversation with Jen Easterly, director of the Cybersecurity and Infrastructure Security Agency (CISA). So cybersecurity experts will have to tread carefully.

The post-quantum decade is also shaping up to be a major turning point for cybersecurity. Firms and enterprises are devoting significant resources to innovating existing tools or developing new tools to ensure cyber resiliency for digital systems with the pending arrival of regular quantum computing.

In response to these changing threats, we're seeing concerted efforts across both government and industry to bolster the cyber ecosystem. Breakthroughs in hardware and software will offer stronger protection, but the technology itself isn't the only solution. To protect cybersecurity—for critical infrastructure as well as our own personal data—we'll need to see enhanced collaboration and cooperation between the hardware, software, and services providers, as well as the government agencies who monitor and combat cyber threats.

That's why I'm so proud of the role CTA played in developing the US

Cyber Trust Mark I mentioned earlier, a voluntary national cybersecurity labeling program that helps consumers identify secure products.

For many leaders, recognizing and responding to cyber threats also requires a pivot in mindset. Good cybersecurity is expensive. But it's also an investment—in your company's resiliency and reputation. As I shared earlier in this book, good reputations are built over years—but can be destroyed or undermined in seconds.

Artificial Intelligence and Quantum Computing

While AI will certainly affect the cybersecurity space, AI technology itself is "horizontal." That means it cuts across *every* area and business in the technology industry. Developments in AI will generate downstream impact on the performance and operation of nearly every technology product and technology business, reshaping industries along the way.

At CES 2023, I sat down with Nasdaq CEO and board chair Adena Friedman to talk about technology advancements and our modern economy. As head of one of the world's largest stock exchanges, Adena speaks with CEOs and other business heavyweights on a daily basis, so I was eager to hear her perspective on the trends animating business. I asked her to identify the technologies that are poised to transform industry. "Definitely AI," she told me, with quantum computing delivering vastly higher processing power and offering tantalizing possibilities for even more data-driven decision-making. "And then you also have the cloud, [which has] really unlocked the ability for data to be leveraged in new ways. So you've got the cloud being able to bring scalability to data, AI coming in, and being able to make sense and intelligent solutions on the back of that vast amount of data."

Venture capitalists are betting big on AI. By September 2023, they had invested $14.1 billion into generative AI.[10] By 2026, the market for AI hardware, services, and software will be an estimated $300 billion.[11]

It's easy to see why AI is generating such buzz, and such big money. Simply put, it's one of the coolest tech innovations in history. At CES 2024, we saw AI chips in TVs and keyboards delivering "smart" capabilities; machine learning and low-code/no-code AI platforms powering e-commerce, software development, and gaming engines; digital twins for limitless research; and smart assistants that help people shop, drive, and even sleep better.

Or take the AI Aquarium—the world's first interactive aquarium that can display marine life information in real time according to the visitor's line of sight. Wherever your eyes are looking, its screen will tell you what you're looking at, and give you information about that species. The field trips our grandchildren go on will look a whole lot different with technology like this than ours ever did.

Speaking of digital twins, one of my favorite recent AI innovations at CES was re;memory, an AI-powered device that creates a "digital twin" of a deceased loved one that allows family members to be able to talk with— not just to—those they have lost. It restores the voice and appearance of a person by collecting and analyzing photos and videos of them. It could completely transform the way we grieve. Right now, it's not very accessible to the masses; it costs upward of $10,000 to create a digital copy of the deceased, with each conversation an additional cost. But like all great innovations, it's only the beginning.

AI's capacity to power digital twins, or digitally simulate a physical environment, could unlock limitless research and development at a fraction of the cost.

Siemens showcased this potential at CES 2024 with its NX Immersive Designer in partnership with Sony, and the Industrial Metaverse in partnership with NVIDIA. This spatial content creation system, which relies on an XR (extended reality) head-mounted display with high-quality visuals and controllers, provides intuitive interaction with 3D objects to power development efforts for a variety of enterprise and industrial applications. For example, Red Bull's Formula 1 team is already deploying this technology in the design of their championship-winning race cars.

AI is delivering especially critical advances in healthcare. Withings's BeamO goes beyond the traditional ability to measure temperature to measure and transmit data to healthcare professionals about heart and lung sounds. A Machine Vision Bedsore Management Mat uses artificial intelligence to track patients' lying positions and adjust their bodies correctly to prevent bedsores. PERISCOPE's AI-driven software can help doctors predict post-surgery bacterial infections and reduce the risk of complications. Early detection of health concerns can even extend to your dog or cat. The pet healthcare software TTcare uses AI software to analyze a photo of your pet and alert you to potential eye, skin, or other issues.

Further, the transformer technology (or the T in ChatGPT) can be used to predict protein sequences at the atomic level, which could unlock millions of new proteins and rapidly accelerate drug discovery.

The lifesaving potential of artificial intelligence even extends into the arena of safety. At CES 2024, Bosch unveiled a Gun Detection System, which pairs video and audio AI to help identify and issue alerts about guns in school or other public buildings. For these innovation efforts, this system received one of our CES Best of Innovation Awards for Artificial Intelligence.

AI will also improve productivity, lower inflation, and improve global economic and physical health. It will analyze and learn from vast data sets, and it will extend our lifetimes and our ability to engage with the world around us. With advances in generative AI, we may learn how animals and even insects communicate—making it possible to "talk" to other species!

What does this mean for business? If you're not already thinking about how to integrate AI into your business, it's likely you're already behind. That doesn't mean every product needs to put AI front and center. But you should consider how AI tools can enhance productivity, strengthen customer relationships, and help your employees do what they do better. This is the age of the AI pivot, and working without it risks being left out of advances that are reshaping what's possible.

Robotics

AI increases the performance and efficiency of a variety of other technologies and fields, from cybersecurity to digital health to smart homes to a vast ecosystem of technologies, which includes robotics.

As already existing workforce shortages meet increased demand for service providers, robotics will play a key role. That doesn't just mean replacing humans, but working alongside or in conjunction with people to enhance human productivity. Like the larger AI ecosystem, robotics act as a horizontal technology, and the already rapidly growing market is poised to explode: quadrupling from 2023 to 2030 to reach $290 billion.[12]

Every year, I eagerly await the product debuts in robotics at CES, because the progress on display year to year is astounding. At CES 2024, we saw complex robots designed for everything from Mars exploration to mixing your favorite drink at the bar. Looking back a year, one of the highlights of CES 2023 was Ameca, the world's most advanced human-shaped robots that can talk, draw pictures, and express a range of emotions, from gasping in surprise to pursing its lips in disappointment.

And then there are robots for every kind of work and play you can imagine. Yo-Kai Express's boba cooking robot is expanding the universe of autonomous restaurants. The iVolve Pro tennis robot can shoot a ball dynamically and move across the court, simulating the experience of actually playing against another person. And Parky, an autonomous EV recharging robot, brings a charging station to any parking spot—eliminating the need for built-in charging stations at places like apartment complexes or stores.

ADT Commercial, a premier provider of commercial security, fire, and life safety services in the US, has been working in partnership with Norway-based robotics company Halodi Robotics to develop a humanoid robot that can conduct autonomous safety and security patrols in commercial facilities. What the robot can do is pretty remarkable: open doors and operate elevators; inspect and remove hazards or obstructions; interact with employees; and perform tasks using fully articulated hands.

The question everyone asks is, "Will robots replace people?" From my experience, the answer is complicated—and also yes, in some cases. As of early 2024, the world has roughly 150 robots per 10,000 workers, more than double the number measured only six years ago, and that number will surely grow even larger by the time you're reading this. China has surpassed the US in density with 392 robots per 10,000 workers compared to 285 in the US.[13] Globally, automated systems and robotics will comprise 25 percent of the capital expenditures of industrial companies over the next five years.[14]

That's a pivot we should embrace. Robotics are an inevitable part of our human future—and that's a good thing! There are tasks that we *want* robots to do for us, like going into hazardous areas, or fighting fires, or crawling into tight spaces. Robotics also opens the door for a slew of new jobs—many of which don't even exist today. These jobs go beyond the obvious designers, programmers, engineers, technicians, and servicers. We'll need linguists and speech pathologists to help make robotic speech sound more realistic, veterinarians to replicate robotic pets, agriculturalists to design robots that work on farms, and teachers to program robots that interact with or educate children.

If the early 2000s represent the start of the digital transformation era, where companies and users began to experiment with technologies like cloud, cybersecurity, AI, and robotics, the advances of the past five years confirm that we've pivoted into a new period. As businesses address new challenges and shifting consumer expectations, these technologies are no longer options, experimental, or seen as upgrades. They're necessities for both enterprises and consumers as they navigate the modern economy—reshaping what's possible.

That leads us to the next section: the pivots that are helping us re-imagine how we can create a more sustainable, accessible, and healthy world for the generations to come.

Pivots for Tomorrow's Challenges

Technology doesn't just play a role in addressing the economic challenges described earlier. It's also helping us to meet and grapple with the world's ever-growing list of existential environmental, social, and health challenges:

- A changing climate that has economic, health, and even socio-political implications.
- A rise in the need for chronic health condition management as mortality from noncommunicable diseases like cardiovascular disease, cancer, and diabetes increases and life spans extend.
- A need to ensure that more individuals can access the advances of technology regardless of ability.

While global governments and innovation leaders are already grappling with these challenges—and we're seeing the advent of technologies specifically designed to solve them—look for pivots that will deliver solutions at scale and in new and creative ways over the next five years. Some of those will offer individual or household solutions. Others will need coordination and implementation at a local or national level to truly make an impact. Either way, the success of the pivots in these technology areas will be the difference between a world where these crises spin out of control and one where they remain challenging but manageable.

Sustainability

Technology will play a critical role in keeping Earth habitable for those of us who live here now, and for future generations. At CES every year, I see hundreds of exhibitors showing technology that is making our world cleaner, greener, and healthier for the next generation. At the World Economic Forum's annual meeting in Davos, Switzerland, sustainability is regularly a top focus of global leaders.

In response to increasing consumer demand, companies are increasingly incorporating sustainable features into their technologies, considering more environmentally friendly materials in their supply chains, and exploring ways to reduce their carbon footprints. In fact, CTA research from mid-2023 showed that 31 percent of American consumers have made a technology purchase based on sustainability in the past year. Look across the ocean to Europe, and that number grows to nearly 50 percent.

Sustainability pivots are already underway across the tech sector, but we'll see rapid expansion over the next decade, as these technologies scale and see greater integration. In 2022, technologies to remove or reduce carbon emissions were valued at a collective $905 billion. By 2027, they are estimated to reach a value of $1.4 trillion. According to PitchBook, "green industry"—the decarbonizing of chemicals and raw materials—will be the most valuable climate tech segment, with an estimated value of $657 billion in 2027.[15] And according to the World Bank, green buildings represent one of the biggest investment opportunities of the next decade— $24.7 trillion across emerging market cities by 2030.[16]

There's a strong business rationale behind these kinds of investments— not just an environmental one. Financial losses resulting from severe weather exceeded $300 billion globally in 2021, and those costs are rising.[17]

Luckily, new technologies are changing how we use precious natural resources and incorporate alternative materials in product design. This starts with the very batteries that power many tech products. Panasonic announced at CES 2021 a plan to move toward cobalt-free batteries, which could reduce the environmental impact of batteries as well as move production away from conflict zones where cobalt is often sourced. Industry has taken the idea of more sustainable battery development and run with it. At CES 2024, we saw German automotive supplier Schaeffler unveil a new solid-state EV (electric vehicle) battery, alongside EV battery innovations from SK Group and dozens of other mobility companies at the show.

Meanwhile, Schneider Electric is making power sockets and switches from recycled fishing nets. CES 2024 also showcased incredible solutions like Powerfoyle by Exeger, which are fully customizable solar cells that can be built into a wide range of products from headphones to GPS-enabled dog harnesses to power them sustainably.

In transportation, we're seeing equally exciting advances, including the electrification of the automotive industry, with EV innovations at CES coming from all around the world, including Germany, Italy, Turkey, and Vietnam. This includes Xpeng AeroHT—one of two "flying cars" at the 2024 show—and an emissions-free vehicle that can switch from a more traditional road configuration to flight mode by unfolding its propellers. Inokim, an Israel startup, produces light and foldable electric scooters. Goodyear has developed a tire from 90 percent sustainable materials.

Startups are also in the game. GreenSwapp founder Ajay Varadharajan wrote an algorithm that pulls information about various edible products from published research papers, enabling him to assign a carbon footprint to every food's barcode. Nanoleaf debuted the first nonflammable graphene battery at CES 2022, which would have a 25 percent reduced carbon footprint compared to their lithium-ion counterparts. Italian company Wiseair developed a sensor that measures air pollution down to the block-by-block level within cities.

Like AI, sustainability is a horizontal trend that can cut across every tech sector and can help not just companies, but entire industries pivot to a greener tomorrow.

The evolution of agrifood tech is a strong example of this horizontal trend and this industry is going to play a key role in making our world a more sustainable place to live. The combined enterprise value of foodtech companies is $1.4 trillion, per Dealroom.co.[18]

Food technology truly spans farm to table. On the farm, companies are creating autonomous tractors, systems that increase yields and reduce pesticide use, and satellite-based farm management software for sustainable food-chain production. One technology that could improve the quality of our food is John Deere's See and Spray. It enables targeted application of herbicides on weeds within corn, soybean, and cotton fields—leaving the actual food that gets to our tables untouched.

CES 2024 also showcased novel sustainable agriculture tech (agtech) innovation with Midbar's AirFarm, a portable and inflatable smart farm that can grow food sustainably in desert or drought-impacted areas. This could have a strong mitigating effect on resource tensions driven by environmental insecurity from climate change.

On the table side, companies are innovating customers' food experience through sustainable innovations like Sevvy's Smart Cooker, which can enhance the taste of food with less baking fats and sugars, all while cooking the food via electrical pulse technology that uses 90 percent less electricity than traditional cookers.

AI is also reducing food waste in both professional and, increasingly, home kitchens. Tech from companies like Orbisk and Nuvilab uses computer vision and data-based algorithms to track everything from food nutrients to days until spoilage, giving users more insight into the life cycle of their food. WasteShark, an autonomous aqua-drone, can clean pollution from waterways. Gropod, a startup in Indiana, built an appliance with a seed pod subscription that is like a sustainable "Keurig for food."

One of my favorite technologies, because of its expansive potential, is Nemo's Garden, which I mentioned briefly in Chapter 6. Founded in 2012 by Sergio Gamberini—the president of Italian scuba diving equipment manufacturer Ocean Reef Group—and his son, Luca Gamberini, Nemo's Garden is like an underwater greenhouse, cultivating herbs, fruit, and vegetables underwater. This leads to multiple benefits, from temperature stability to protection from pests. Nemo's Garden has since partnered with Siemens to train a machine-learning algorithm to monitor plant growth and the environmental conditions within the domes.

Digital Health

While preserving our planet is certainly important, it's no surprise to see parallel technology innovations focused on preserving ourselves—especially with rapidly aging populations in so many top technology producing countries.

The value of the global digital health market was estimated at more than $240 billion in 2023.[19] Like sustainability, industry pivots are positioning the technology of health for explosive growth, with estimates suggesting it will reach nearly $800 billion by 2030—powered by increasing smartphone penetration, improved internet connectivity, and advancing healthcare IT infrastructure. The digitization of healthcare continues to lay the groundwork for new products, new therapies, and more seamless interactions between patients and their doctors, leading to better health outcomes. Many Americans—in fact, nearly half of us, according to the CDC—manage chronic conditions, and digital health devices allow for greater ease and often lower-cost solutions to better manage these conditions.[20]

Abbott entered the continuous glucose monitoring (CGM) market officially at CES 2024 with the unveiling of their new Lingo CGM device, which works as a "biowearable" and trains users to lead a lower glucose life.

Evolutions in solutions that can manage chronic conditions like diabetes, cardiovascular disease, and more are critical considering that by 2050 these diseases will account for 86 percent of the 90 million deaths each year, according to the World Health Organization.[21]

The COVID-19 pandemic also spurred advancement in health tech and digital health. One of the major areas is telehealth. According to Kaiser Permanente, 60 percent of typical ER visits can be solved via telehealth appointments with caregivers. Telehealth is freeing up in-person visits and doctors' time and resources for urgent and complicated health cases. The effects of this may be hard to see immediately, but it's having a huge impact.

At CES 2024, Withings unveiled the BeamO AI tool, which placed sensors on a board that could detect four different sets of vitals data that could communicate in real time to your health provider during a telehealth appointment. NuraLogix displayed similar breakthroughs at the show as technology works to empower patients to better manage their conditions from home.

Wearable and portable tech are two of the biggest up-and-coming trends in health tech—from a patch by Epicore Biosystems that can monitor hydration, to Movano Health's Evie Ring, now cleared by the FDA, and the first consumer wearable that is also a medical device. The ring can give women information on everything from resting heart rate and period and ovulation tracking, to sleep stages and skin temperature variability. Virawarn has designed a small breath analyzer that can detect COVID-19, influenza, and RSV in less than sixty seconds, and Valencell created a cuffless, fingertip blood pressure monitor.

This wearable trend even extends into the use of VR headsets for healthcare and therapy for aging populations. At CES 2024, Mynd Immersive launched the Elderverse project, which provides older adults with exercises and experiences to promote cognitive and physical health. This campaign, supported by a collaboration with AT&T, HTC Vive, and our own CTA Foundation, underscores an ongoing pivot in the health tech sector toward better addressing an aging global population in addition to rising chronic conditions.

Accessibility

The health tech sector's focus on "age tech"—technology that allows people to remain connected and engaged with their friends, families, and communities—is another important shift in the overall production, design, and delivery of technology products. Increasingly, technology companies aren't just looking to serve up "cool" technology that's exciting to the early adopters—now Millennials and Gen Z. They're focused on creating products and services that make the marvels of tech advancement accessible to as many people as possible.

Accessibility tech is growing at a pace I've almost never seen before in the tech industry. At CES 2024, our annual accessibility roundtable had a lengthy waiting list. Scores of people with vision, hearing, mobility, and other disabilities attended CES, both as advocates and industry members. At our 2023 show, I visited some exhibitors with All Access Life's (AAL) Bradley Heaven, an innovator who communicates by using eye tracking and a keyboard to spell words on a screen. He and AAL partner Dan O'Connor shared that even those companies at CES that weren't educated on accessibility, or that didn't realize the impact their product could have on someone with a disability, were always willing to listen and eager to adapt their product.

Accessibility tech in the coming years is going to push the boundaries of what we imagine the category to be. One of the products that received the most buzz at CES 2023, for example, was CRDL, an interactive care-instrument from Cardiol Therapeutics that translates touch into sound. The instrument enables new forms of contact between people who have difficulties with communication and social interaction—such as people suffering from dementia, autism, and mental disabilities—and their surroundings.

Another innovation, debuted at CES 2024, was the XRAI Glass AR smart glasses. Designed for the hearing impaired, these glasses allow wearers to see conversations as subtitles generated in real time across the frames. As someone speaks, the words are translated to digital text that scrolls across the screen, allowing people with hearing impairments to follow along and participate in verbal conversations.

CES 2024 built on the role that eyewear can play in improving accessibility with the Italian company EssilorLuxottica, owner of Ray-Ban and Oakley, bringing their Nuance Audio glasses. These glasses pair prescription lenses with advanced open-ear audio technologies that can help those with mild hearing loss better hear the person speaking to them. The open-audio nature of the technology allows the glasses to offer discretion for those who want it and a chic frame, which goes along with how EssilorLuxottica likes to fittingly describe the purpose of these technologies: "From stigma, to style." The advances in hearable technologies, from Nuance Audio and other companies like Nuheara in the hearing space, reflect a greater push to make technologies that address hearing loss more accessible.

I was thrilled that after a decade of advocacy by CTA and our partners, 2023 marked the first full year in which consumers could purchase FDA-approved over-the-counter hearing aids. These products opened new doors for millions of Americans with mild to moderate hearing loss who can't afford the four-figure cost of prescription hearing aids and audiologists—a great example of the power of technology innovation paired with good policy. The new OTC hearing aid category also generated new innovations that popped up at CES 2024, and promises to expand opportunity for the nearly 400 million people around the world with mild to moderate hearing loss.

In many ways, accessibility isn't just a category, but a design trend that can and should cut across every single industry.

For example, CES 2024 keynoter and multiple Innovation Award–winner L'Oréal's smart makeup applicator helps disabled users more easily apply mascara or lipstick. A small onboard computer distinguishes unintended hand movements from intentional ones, helping to counter tremors and similar challenges. The Relumino feature from Samsung, a TV mode for visually impaired viewers, uses AI to dynamically outline and enhance television images to improve the viewing experience for the visually impaired. Garmin unveiled their Venu 3 at CES 2024, which adds a feature for wheelchair users to track pushes, follow wheelchair-specific workouts, and more, which brings long-standing fitness tracker technology that many may take for granted to a whole new community.

Here, we can see how accessible design at past CES shows can help the beauty, entertainment, and fitness industries reach a greater number of people. I'm excited to see how these approaches will influence the technology development and products at future CES shows.

The technology we're seeing now reflects a new thoughtfulness and focus on not just what people with disabilities *need*, but what enables them to live a more fulfilled life that is not marked by their disabilities. In many ways, it's a recognition that disabilities likely will affect many of us temporarily or permanently over our lifetimes, which means this continued pivot toward accessible design can ensure that we all continue to benefit from the advancements of technology, today and tomorrow.

These pivots are reshaping the technologies that are available on the market now, and what's to come in the years ahead. Along the way, they're helping to create a world that's healthier, safer, and more sustainable. Ultimately, that's not just for us. It's for our children, grandchildren, and generations to come who will inherit the world we create.

CHAPTER 8

How the US Must Pivot

The United States is one of the world's greatest startups. When it was founded, its leaders had all the qualities of great entrepreneurs: long-term vision, discipline, adaptability, and persistence. But the world is changing, and the United States could use a good success pivot. We need to find a way to get beyond partisan politics and undertake a fundamental reckoning with our approach to innovation policy, free speech, competition, trade, and more. After all, global competition is heating up. To illustrate just why I'm so concerned, I'd like to retell a story I originally recounted in my first book, *The Comeback*.

In 2008, I sat at the head table of an elaborate banquet in the beautiful oceanside city of Qingdao, China. CTA was partnering with our Chinese association counterpart and the city of Qingdao to produce SinoCES, a business exhibition modeled after our hugely successful CES show held each January in Las Vegas. The banquet was a SinoCES tradition, drawing several hundred Chinese VIPs, government officials, and business leaders to celebrate the event's annual opening day. Chinese officials strolled from table to table, making toasts, shouting "*ganbei*" (the equivalent of the Western "cheers!"), and downing shots of baijiu.

At this banquet, I was seated next to the Chinese Communist Party head for Shandong province, who presided over more than 100 million Chinese citizens. For some reason, our interpreters were not with us, but we managed to cobble together some basic conversation. Some twenty years later, one brief exchange stuck with me. Halfway through the meal, the official turned to me and slowly raised his fist in the air, his thumb extended to the ceiling in a proud thumbs-up. "China," he declared, a big smile on his face, "is going up."

I couldn't help but nod my head in agreement. Cranes punctuated the skyline of Qingdao and every other major Chinese city. When I visited the country, I was chauffeured around on new roads and traveled on high-speed train tracks. Cars and trucks were swiftly replacing bicycles. In every city I visited in China, I saw shiny new factories, new apartment buildings, and new retail stores, thanks to the government's huge investments in modernized infrastructure.

Then the exchange turned sour. The Chinese official turned his thumb downward, lowering his arm to the floor as he said, "America going down." His message could not have been clearer. In his mind, while China was ascending, the US was in decline.

The incident stuck with me because, despite the rude delivery, there was some truth to the message. China found a way to pivot its economy and its society. While that economic growth has come at the expense of human rights and freedoms—a price Americans would rightly reject—there's no denying China's success in transforming its economy to lift hundreds of millions of people out of poverty and nurture technology companies that can go toe to toe with industry leaders on the world stage.

Our CES events in China motivated me to ring the alarm bell as visibly as I could about a powerful China long before US media and policy-makers seemed to be paying attention. As part of my job to attract global companies and attendees to CES, I first visited China in the early 1990s. Although tall buildings were few and bicycles dominated the streets, the scores of visible construction cranes in every city I visited foretold rapid growth and a stronger economy.

I also learned that China doesn't play by the same rules the US does. As just one example, take the SinoCES show I just mentioned. It originally began when a Chinese association took our CES brand and launched a new event. We tried to convince the Chinese show's leadership to change the name, but they refused, and we quickly learned that we had little recourse. It was a clear lesson that American companies have scant intellectual property protection in China.

So instead of fighting the association, we joined them—offering to help the show succeed and formally licensing the CES brand name. It wasn't a bad idea. The event had the support of the Chinese government and Chinese industry, as well as a strong exhibitor, audience base, and media following. But we soon found that our partners had lower quality standards than we insisted on for our other events. Our government-imposed partner also refused to move the show to the more global city of Shanghai, where we felt it would have a better reception, and required huge payments that sucked all profitability out of the event. In the industry's eyes, the event was wildly successful; the show footprint grew quickly. But the Chinese clearly saw us as captive foreigners who they could saddle with big charges.

While we did ultimately re-launch CES Asia in Shanghai, ultimately costs and increasing crackdowns by President Xi Jinping put an end to the event. China put up a digital perimeter blocking access in China to all non-Chinese news sources, making it challenging to attract global journalists. Even more concerning, China imposed a new law subjecting foreigners to arrest for anything viewed as critical of the Chinese Communist Party (CCP), creating risks not just for the media, but for our own staff. In 2020, we announced CES Asia was on hold. It has yet to be resurrected.

The lessons of China are many. First, the US needs to get smart and build an innovation strategy that will keep us competitive. Collaboration between our countries is certainly possible, but tougher to achieve with different cultures, values, languages, and views of human rights. Doing business in China is tough, and while the US and Chinese economies are still strongly intertwined, many companies in the technology field are figuring out how to reduce their investments and reliance on China. While strong individual relationships can be formed and foster great collaboration, you can't fight a government hostile to American success and unwilling to protect American intellectual property.

I am an eternal optimist, and I've long seen the United States as, to borrow a phrase from President Ronald Regan, the "shining city on a hill." Much like President Reagan, I believe the United States is a beacon for freedom and opportunity. Our country has long created opportunities for nearly everyone to succeed and live a meaningful life and offers rewards for those with good ideas and the will to make them a reality.

But we can't rest on our laurels. The US and our leaders need to find a way to pivot, too. If we don't, we will continue on a trajectory of US decline that is closer to the Chinese official's vision than most of us would like to admit.

If anything, I've only grown more concerned in the years since I wrote *The Comeback* in 2008. Part of that concern is personal: since that book was published, I've watched my two younger sons go through childhood and my older children become adults, with one now immersed in the joyful and exhausting process of raising children of his own. I desperately want my kids, their cohorts, and future American generations to enjoy a life at least as good as that lived by my generation. As a proud American, I think we have all the ingredients at our fingertips to offer young people even better, more fulfilling, and healthier lives.

Sadly, we seem too locked in partisan divides these days to realize our potential. Our national confidence is shaken. Our national direction lacks focus. Bitter political feuds have seeped out from the halls of Congress to local town halls. Our elected leaders are polarized and polarizing. They seem to lack any strategy for getting us out of this mess or even a desire to develop one. Some are focused on operating the levers of government in bad faith, seeking to punish political opponents or consolidate their own political power. Others recklessly throw money at their favored constituents, significantly raising the national debt without even acknowledging the problem we are creating for our children.

In my 2008 book, I raised this problem and even flagged the risk of rising interest rates causing a debt crisis. Incredibly, in 2023 alone the United States spent more money to service the interest on our debt than it did to fund our national defense. Given the ballooning federal debt, we've now reached a point where vast cuts to programs benefiting millions of Americans are the only real solution. Even as I write, one major credit rating agency has downgraded the US credit rating due to concerns about "erosion in governance" in addition to our growing deficits.

I've also been concerned to see our country become more hostile to the freedom and openness that are America's special sauce. In fact, Americans now seem increasingly skeptical of the core ideas of America itself! A 2023 survey by the *Wall Street Journal* and NORC showed, as the *Wall Street Journal* put it, Americans "pulling back from the values that once defined [us]," including patriotism, hard work, and investment in community.[1] Nearly a third of Americans now say that other countries are better than the United States, up nearly 10 percent from just five years ago. The only "value" the *Journal* tested that has actually grown in importance in the past quarter-century is money! This retreat from our core values manifests in many ways, from politicians refusing to respect election results to both parties showing an increasing hostility to free speech and expression.

These issues would all be concerning on their own. That the United States is locked in a geopolitical battle with China makes them even more pressing, especially because China on some metrics appears to be winning. A 2023 report by the Australian Strategic Policy Institute found that "Western democracies are losing the global technological competition, including the race for scientific and research breakthroughs, and the ability to retain global talent," with China leading in thirty-seven out of forty-four advanced technology research areas.[2] China is outpacing the United States in the production of STEM PhDs, with the gap growing each year.[3]

Childhood looks very different for China's children than it does for American children. China limits the number of hours children can play video games to an hour or less per day. From elementary school through high school, Chinese students are not allowed to use calculators. Learning is based on rote memorization, compared to the US approach of inquiry-based learning. While I don't necessarily agree with China's approach, Chinese students have historically outperformed American students in testing in recent years—especially in STEM subjects. In 2023, the Defense Department called for a major initiative to support education in STEM, citing the fact that there are eight times as many college graduates in these disciplines in China as in the United States.[4]

In 2022, China outnumbered the US for the first time in *US News & World Report*'s ranking of the world's "best" universities.[5] Five of the world's top ten programs in AI were in China, and China also led in nano-science, nanotechnology, engineering, and physical chemistry.

The difference can even be seen in social media. In China, TikTok content focuses on math, science, and model behavior. In the United States, it promotes laziness and sloth, and magnifies divisive and anti-American narratives.

I am not someone who believes that any future course is preordained or inevitable. We can change the arc of our history. We can pivot to define our future. As Robert Kennedy once put it, "the future is not a gift. It is an achievement."

I know how important this power and perspective is, because in 1943, my wife's grandfather Marek returned to the Warsaw ghetto apartment where he lived with his wife, father-in-law, and five-year-old son. He found the apartment empty. Marek immediately assumed that his son and father-in-law had been taken for rail transport out of Warsaw. He grabbed loose diamonds he had hidden and ran to the area of the ghetto where Jews were gathered before transport.

Marek found his father-in-law and son about to be put on rail cars. He begged a guard to spare their lives, offering the diamonds in return. The guard said he could choose: his son, or his father-in-law. Marek chose his son. His father-in-law was killed, either on the horrific train ride or in one of Europe's brutal concentration camps.

I have visited Auschwitz, where 1.3 million people died in less than two years. It's made me reflect on the role of governments, which play a huge role in propagating both good and evil in the world. We should demand that our government be open, follow processes, and not intimidate, harass, and target whatever group the current officeholders do not like. We should encourage diversity in every government. And we should examine our role as citizens, especially as Americans, in ensuring that genocide, torture, and evil are met with our resistance.

I can't help thinking that if Marek's son—my father-in-law—had not survived the horror and bombing of wartime in the Warsaw ghetto, my wife would never have been born. Nor would our sons, Mark and Max, be alive. I'm hopeful that learning the lessons of the past will lead to a brighter future for Mark, Max, and millions of children like them.

The Overpivots

The United States is the world's technology leader. It's not because we're uniquely nice or smart, or eat pancakes for breakfast, but because over 250 years of our national history, we've mostly made the right decisions. We also have the capacity to pivot and course correct when we get it wrong. The United States has made its share of mistakes—during WWII, we offered asylum to far fewer Jewish people than we should have, to give just one example—but our citizens have the power to criticize our government and advocate for change. That's not the case for some of our global adversaries, and it gives us a unique power and perspective.

Unfortunately, our government can also overpivot and overcorrect. In fact, I think that's becoming more common as our government grows more polarized. In my role at CTA, I've seen many of those overpivots firsthand.

In seeking a scapegoat for America's problems, elected leaders of all stripes have seized on American business. Instead of focusing on kitchen-table issues that matter most to the average American—inflation, jobs, the economy, healthcare, national security, and the environment, just to name a few—politicians have chosen to demonize many of America's biggest and best companies, including many of the American technology companies that are driving economic growth and bolstering our investment portfolios and retirement plans.

They've also set up a false dichotomy, pitting "big businesses" against "small businesses." The reality is that our economy needs both. I would know: at the Consumer Technology Association, more than 80 percent of our member companies are startups or small businesses. We also represent global technology's leading names. While companies of different sizes have different needs, they all need one another. Startups deliver the innovation and new thinking that forces established industry players to adapt and complete. Big businesses have the resources and know-how needed to nurture innovation and help it thrive.

That's why I've been so concerned to see efforts across our government to punish big businesses for their success. Case in point: the US Federal Trade Commission (FTC). I began my legal career in Washington as a law student working with a firm of former Democratic FTC commissioners and lawyers. The firm had big investor clients, and every time a major public company announced plans to buy a smaller company, I was dispatched to rush to a local library for research to determine if the merger would pass antitrust muster. I loved analyzing markets and the prior rulings of the judge assigned to each case to see how they would likely rule. Speed was everything and all-nighters were common.

The FTC was highly respected and almost always took a bipartisan approach to antitrust issues. FTC leadership and staff were the best and brightest. For the ensuing four decades, through successive administrations, the FTC—the agency focused on promoting the welfare of American consumers—has served our nation and attracted the best and brightest career staff. Sadly, FTC Chair Lina Khan has undermined and hollowed out the agency. Between 2021 and 2022, FTC senior attorneys left the agency at a pace not seen since 2000, and data from the Federal Employee Viewpoint Survey[6] showed a drop in staff morale and commitment from 80 percent in 2020 to under 50 percent for the three subsequent years. During Khan's tenure, the FTC has fallen from one of the government agencies rated highest by its staff to one of the lowest. These issues and recurring patterns of mismanagement that created a "culture of fear" at the FTC are well documented in a damning 2024 report by the US House Judiciary Committee.

Under the traditional consumer welfare standard, business conduct and mergers are evaluated to determine whether they harm consumers. Generally speaking, if consumers are not harmed, the antitrust agencies don't step in. For anyone who's worked in the tech sector over the past several decades, that concept has served as the gold standard. Competition—the free exercise of innovation—is what we should all be after. Instead, the FTC under Chair Khan has launched a series of lawsuits that seem to rest on a new and alarming idea: that big companies should not acquire smaller ones. In pursuing this anti-tech agenda, Khan has made the agency deeply ineffective: the FTC lost every single merger challenge it brought between mid-2021 and the end of 2023. By the time you read this, the US legal system may have dealt Khan's FTC even more losses. In advancing the theory that acquisitions by larger companies create "kill zones" for investment, the FTC isn't just wasting taxpayer resources. It's working against the interests of the startups who actually create the competition the FTC is supposed to protect.

The idea that protecting existing competitors actually *harms* competition isn't just common sense—we have proof! The "big is bad" theory advanced by the FTC is similar to regulatory structures in Europe, which have relentlessly smothered business and crushed innovation. The results in the technology industry are striking and sad. As of 2023, *Forbes* reports that none of the world's largest tech companies are based in Europe.[7]

In bringing antitrust lawsuits against American tech leaders including Google, Amazon, and Meta, Chair Khan—at times overruling the guidance of longtime FTC staff—has advanced a novel and concerning approach: even if the lawsuits themselves don't or can't succeed on the merits, they'll make big companies think twice about acquiring smaller ones. It's telling that Khan has never worked in the private sector. Despite a losing court record in vertical merger cases, she seems to be proud of lawsuits that prevent acquisitions simply because companies don't want to take on the cost and uncertainty of a legal battle.

This approach is disastrous for the vibrant American startup ecosystem. Thousands of startups have lost out on funding or even gone under as venture capital firms pull back on spending in response to FTC hostility. If acquisitions by a large company are off the table, that removes a crucial outlet for many fledgling startups. If you're not already persuaded, the example of my good friend and CTA board member Dr. Ximena Hartsock may help to explain why we should all be alarmed.

Ximena is a product of the American Dream. Growing up indigenous and poor in Chile, she came to America and earned a doctorate in education and served as assistant superintendent of DC schools. She's also a serial entrepreneur, having built and launched two companies. The first was Phone2Action, which offered software that made it easy for people to contact their elected representatives. After a few years of growth, the company was successful, but Ximena—one of the hardest workers I know—was exhausted. So when an opportunity arose, she sold Phone2Action to another company. Then that company was acquired by an even larger company.

Now, Ximena is seeing her software offered as part of a suite of tools that she could never have developed on her own—and she's thrilled! She's also made a positive impact on our society, advancing our democracy by getting people more involved in the issues that impact them. While she needed a breather, Ximena quickly seized the chance to pivot to a new opportunity. Recognizing the skills gap, which I'll discuss later in the chapter, she launched a second successful venture helping companies create successful apprenticeship programs. Change a few details, and that story could be shared by thousands of entrepreneurs and founders. The most successful and visionary founders aren't always the right people to scale businesses. Allowing big companies to acquire small ones is critical not just to provide an outlet for investors, but to allow serial entrepreneurs a chance to do what they do best: launch new ventures.

Good governance means recognizing that businesses both small and large have an important role to play in our economy and our society. We've pivoted away from that perspective, but it's not too late to go back. Despite the challenges, I remain an optimist. While CTA generally opposes government involvement in the market—and we don't advocate for funding to our industry—we long ago bowed to the reality of Washington by boosting our lobbying presence. And in recent years, we've seen some positive momentum behind the cause of American innovation.

Free Speech Makes Us Great

Growing up as a Jewish boy in the 1970s, I still remember the all-out fight over efforts by Nazi sympathizers to demonstrate in Skokie, Illinois. While the issue divided many households, I was taught to value and elevate freedom of speech—no matter how much we disagree with what is being said. (Ultimately, the Illinois chapter of the ACLU—led by another Jewish man—prevailed in efforts to allow the demonstration to go forward.)

While the courts have helped define limited exceptions, we always come back to the fundamental principle that we are built as a nation on a shared desire to freely express and receive differing views. Since our nation's founding, innovative technologies like radio, telephone, television, computers, and the internet have enhanced our ability to create, share, and receive new ideas. They have also fueled our country's global economic success, and in many of these areas the US has led the world. I cannot help but compare us to China and North Korea, whose citizens are literally blocked from receiving external information or views.

Today, I worry that our nation is devaluing First Amendment principles. We are shutting down the diversity of opinions on college campuses and even in the media. Both major political parties are pushing proposals clearly in conflict with the letter and spirit of the First Amendment. Florida's Republican governor signed a law that tells social media platforms what content and speakers they must allow, and even sanctioned Disney—a private company—for expressing its views. A Democratic senator tried to use her position in Congress to intimidate, threatening to punish a company for what she described as "snotty tweets." And both parties play games with online free expression, trying to browbeat internet platforms into leaving up speech that helps their side and removing speech favored by their opponents. For both parties, upholding the principle of free speech seems less important than scoring political points.

I am especially concerned by efforts to remove or alter Section 230 of the Communications Decency Act, established by Congress in 1996. To borrow a line from journalist and author Jeff Kosseff, Section 230 includes the "26 words that built the internet"—allowing all of us to create the trillions of words that fill our blogs, social media sites, and video sites. Thirty years ago, to speak to an audience of millions you needed an invitation to appear on a TV network or radio station, or the connections to have your words appear in a newspaper. Today, all you need is a smartphone and a data connection. Anyone can create content, and millions do. More than 50 million YouTube channels give musicians, film producers, and artists a venue to display their creativity. That's not to mention TikTok, Instagram, Twitter, Facebook, Substack, and many more.

In efforts to remove the protections of Section 230, which put liability for speech on creators, not platforms, detractors threaten to destroy the open internet. Platforms face an impossible task. They are asked to determine the truthfulness of political speech and what is offensive in real time—in dozens of countries and different languages. The reality is that content moderation at scale is incredibly daunting, and platforms will inevitably make mistakes. Facebook users post 350 million photos per day. X (formerly Twitter) users post 200 billion tweets per year. Moderation decisions anger both sides of the political spectrum.

While 2023 Supreme Court rulings in *Twitter v. Taamneh* and *Gonzalez v. Google* left Section 230 intact, brewing legislative proposals could threaten Section 230's existence. Without Section 230, online platforms carrying user content would see a blizzard of lawsuits. As just one example, restaurant review sites could find themselves dragged into court every time someone reported a bad meal or a cold coffee. In such an expensive and litigious environment, many founders would stop building, VCs would stop investing, and the internet would become unrecognizable. This is not the direction we want to go in as a country. If we do, we will undoubtedly accelerate our decline as the world's tech leader.

Spending Isn't the Solution

For decades, I have been urging elected officials to address out-of-control government spending and reduce our national debt. A quick look at our debt shows that advocacy has largely fallen on deaf ears. When I traveled to China for SinoCES in 2009, our debt was $10 trillion. In the intervening years, the US federal debt has exploded. And it's only getting worse. The national debt has increased every year for the past decade, exceeding the $30 trillion mark for the first time in history in early 2022. That new highwater mark is, in large part, the result of enormous federal spending during the COVID pandemic, as the government spent lavishly on payments that discouraged workers from taking jobs and kept bad businesses afloat, in addition to programs that kept viable businesses and industries afloat through the economic shock.

Marc Goldwein, senior vice president and senior policy director for the Committee for a Responsible Federal Budget, highlights the challenge: "Debt held by the public . . . is about as large as the economy. In a decade, it'll be larger than any time since World War II. Meanwhile, we have the highest inflation rate we've had in 40 years, and there doesn't seem to be any sign that the borrowing is going to let up."[8]

Federal interest rates at 5 percent—as they stood in 2024—force the United States to pay over a trillion dollars annually in interest payments on our federal debt. These payments will either drown out other government programs or our annual deficit will grow almost exponentially. That spells serious trouble. But while the huge sums dedicated to paying off debt are choking off our ability to invest in our future, political leaders in both parties seem incapable of taking any meaningful action.

With executive branch decisions increasingly rubber-stamped by members of the president's party, the Supreme Court is one of the last backstops against excessive spending. Increasingly, I feel there ought to be a "cost threshold" that would make executive action, if weakly tethered to a statute, unconstitutional based on sheer magnitude. A Commerce Department action costing a million dollars, even if challenged, is unlikely to prompt a hearing—or even attract much notice. A billion-dollar action may attract attention in the halls of Congress, but the agency is still likely to get legal deference to their interpretation in any legal hearings. What about trillions? Can a president bind us in a nonwartime action for a $30 trillion expense, liability, or forgiveness without clear statutory authority of Congress?

I was thrilled to see the Supreme Court provide a resounding "no" in its decision to void President Joe Biden's nearly trillion-dollar loan forgiveness program. Although I feel for indebted former students (I was one of them for some fifteen years!), I do not believe a president has the authority to create huge debts unless clearly empowered to do so by Congress. Yet President Biden, as of this writing, is ignoring the Supreme Court and seeking to forgive nearly a trillion dollars in debt by executive order—a cost that will ultimately be borne by taxpayers.

The magnitude of our fiscal policies should matter. Supreme Court justices don't like to believe they act on the basis of economic impact when it comes to statutory interpretation, but I think they should. So should the president and Congress. Taking it a step further, perhaps it's time for a constitutional amendment requiring higher scrutiny or clarity for costlier federal interpretations of congressionally appropriated funding. While there is an active and rich debate over the limits on executive authority, there's no precedent for granting any president the expansive authority to spend an unlimited amount of money Congress has not authorized.

Antitrust and Competition in the Tech Sector

Recent government efforts to use antitrust laws to rein in "Big Tech" are, to put it bluntly, catastrophic for American innovation and our startup ecosystem. In 2021, a few members of Congress pushed the American Innovation and Choice Online Act (AICOA), which threatened to degrade the performance of beloved tech products and platforms under the guise of promoting "competition" by ensnaring them in a web of restrictions.

The bizarre thing is that the technology sector has always been highly competitive—consumer demand has dictated who has risen and who has fallen (think Blockbuster). Policymakers in Washington seemed to forget that what they smeared as Big Tech was actually born of ambitious imaginings. Apple, Hewlett-Packard, Dell, and Microsoft all got their start in a garage. Tech leaders, innovators, and entrepreneurs were once small startups who took risks and dreamed big. In other words, our largest technology enterprises represent the best of what our country has to offer—the possibility that if you have big ideas and the drive to make them a reality, you can make it big.

For entrepreneurs, bills to limit mergers and acquisitions aren't just bad policy, they represent an existential challenge. Just look at Ring—an American-born company that succeeded in scaling over decades but has recently struggled to compete on an uneven playing field against Chinese competitors who benefit from government support, low-cost capital, and limited intellectual property enforcement that allows copycat products. In mid-2022, Ring got a boost when they brokered a deal for acquisition by Amazon.

The reality is that iRobot, like most small companies, did not have the resources or funding to rapidly take its products to the next level. That's certainly why chairman and CEO Colin Angle was open to, and perhaps even initiated, acquisition talks. Sadly, those hopes—and an opportunity for American-led innovation in the cutting-edge field of robotics—were dashed by the imposition of undue and disproportionate regulatory hurdles. European regulators made clear they would block the merger, aided and abetted by antitrust warriors at the FTC. In undermining the deal, regulators not only tanked iRobot's stock price and forced mass layoffs of nearly a third of the company's staff, it likely ensured a market with *less* competition and *fewer* consumer options. And ultimately, as Amazon president and CEO Andy Jassy pointed out in a mid-2024 interview with CNBC, "regulators were saying . . . they trust these two large Chinese companies [iRobot's primary competitors] with maps of the inside of U.S. consumers' homes more than they do Amazon."[9]

Acquisition is the dream of many entrepreneurs. Usually, they're great at building and launching big new ideas. They're often (with some notable exceptions) not as great or not as interested in scaling and running businesses long term. Acquisitions give startup founders the time and money to go off in search of the *next* big idea that they can bring to life. While we're most familiar with companies that get big and go public, they're actually pretty rare. To put it in perspective, in 2020, 886 venture-backed companies were acquired, while just 103 went public.

I've always fought fiercely for startups to be given every advantage to succeed, and that means allowing entrepreneurs the freedom to build a company, and then sell it. They're the bedrock of the tech industry and the bedrock of this country. And the last thing they need is to be forced to pivot (or shut down entirely) by our own government.

How the US Must Pivot

If there's one thing the United States is known for, it's that we're not afraid of hard work. We're determined, and disciplined. But in other ways, as a country, we've lost some of the qualities of great pivoters. We've lost our grit. We've become too comfortable being comfortable. And we've also lost some of our long-term vision—the ability to see *and act* for the future.

We need a national strategy that focuses on what America does well: develop innovative new ideas and help them grow into reality. That means promoting entrepreneurship, investing in infrastructure, encouraging highly skilled immigration, ensuring worker choice, focusing on math and science education, promoting competitive broadband, protecting free speech, and entering free trade agreements. Companies big and small need consistency to make business decisions, and our elected leaders on both sides of the aisle should support policies that advance American innovation and ingenuity.

Immigration

In 1969, a young family pivoted and emigrated from Poland to the United States to escape communism and seek a better life. Like many immigrants, they traded the comfort of their country, language, and community for a life of economic precarity and exceptionally hard work in the slums of Detroit. While both Jolanta and Edward held medical degrees and were practicing physicians back in Poland, those degrees meant little to the state medical board in Michigan. They needed to retake medical boards to requalify as doctors. Even before that, they needed to learn English. Eventually, both succeeded in establishing themselves, Jolanta as a dermatologist and Edward as a cardiologist. This couple is the classic immigrant success story. They also happen to be my wife's parents, who risked everything to give her the opportunity for a better future than their own.

Like most children of struggling immigrants, my wife, Mal, did them proud. She studied hard and made good decisions. She excelled at school, graduating at the top of her class from a joint BS/MD program at the University of Michigan. She scored first in the country on ophthalmology exams, and now supervises all the retina questions on the board exams. She cares deeply about preventing blindness and, in fact, as I mentioned earlier in this book, she invented "slurry Kenalog," a low-cost treatment for eye swelling commonly associated with diabetes. It is free for any eye doctor in the world to use.

While I certainly am biased and feel that she's unique and special, Mal is part of a proud and long-standing tradition of immigrant invention and innovation. The United States is an immigrant nation, full of people with a diversity of backgrounds and perspectives. Immigrants are medical professionals, engineers, and lawyers. They work in our factories making products for domestic use and for export. They drive us and maintain our cars and homes. They plant, harvest, process, deliver, cook, and serve our food. They work their tails off, not only to survive but so their kids will have a better life. And we need them! Foreign-born workers make up 17 percent of the US labor force, with even higher percentages in many labor-intensive industries.

Immigrants are mostly makers, not takers. They not only fill the jobs that Americans won't do, but also are disproportionately entrepreneurs and innovators. Immigrants have founded 55 percent of US startups valued at $1 billion or more. If you include the children of immigrants, that number shoots up to 64 percent. They hold leadership or development roles in 80 percent of these "unicorn" companies.[10]

The US is wildly successful not only because of immigrant sweat and blood, but because our immigrants make us the most diverse nation on earth. This diversity fuels American ingenuity, helping our nation lead the world in creativity and innovation. Our music, movies, pharmaceuticals, software, computer and internet-related companies, and biotech and healthcare science companies are global champions and drive our stock market and economy. That creativity is perhaps most obvious in emerging technology fields. Sixty-five percent of the top AI companies in the US were founded or co-founded by immigrants.[11] The founders of OpenAI, best known for its generative AI breakout ChatGPT, include immigrants from South Africa, Canada, and Poland.

Immigration is also our competitive advantage. Very few people are lining up to immigrate to China or Russia and build new lives and new careers. America remains a beacon for the best, most ambitious, and hardest-working people from around the world, at least for now.

Unfortunately, we're at risk of losing out. Immigration has become a third rail in American politics, with lawmakers unwilling to tackle the basic problems plaguing our immigration system. The system is broken for both illegal and legal immigration. Our cap for H-1B visas—the "working visa" for most high-skill foreign nationals in the United States—is far too low: only 85,000 visas are available annually, and applications hit that cap soon after the system opens each year.

The failures of our system are not lost on other countries. In 2023, Canada unveiled a new Tech Talent Strategy, offering work permits designed to attract high-skill immigrants in the United States who hold H-1B visas. That program reached its 10,000-applicant cap within two days. France has developed a visa expressly for tech innovators. Britain has increased its Exceptional Talent visas by 100 percent. The competition for top talent is stiff—and it will only grow more intense in the years to come.

While we must regain control of our borders, we should also push for immigration reforms that allow and encourage international graduates of American universities with STEM and other advanced degrees to remain in the United States. America has the world's finest universities, which attract students from across the globe. When they finish, many of them want to stay here, build their businesses, and employ Americans. Those who share our national values should have a green card attached to each of their diplomas. Forcing brilliant students graduating from top American universities to go home (or to other, more immigration-friendly countries) to start their businesses is a colossal mistake.

Part of nurturing that talent is to provide the tools and resources leaders, and upcoming leaders, need for success. This doesn't just mean building an exceptional education system, or eliminating bureaucratic red tape from innovation and growth. It also means something as basic as reliable internet.

Internet Access

The pandemic made clear that Americans need access to high-speed internet to work, learn, and connect to dozens of critical services as they increasingly go digital. I was personally struck by reports from across the country in 2020 of students forced to camp out in the parking lots of libraries and fast-food chains (sometimes dubbed "McClassrooms") to access the Wi-Fi they needed to participate in virtual classes or complete assignments.

But few examples demonstrate the stakes for broadband access better than healthcare. In 2019, relatively few Americans had access to telehealth appointments with their providers. That year, just 840,000 Medicare patient visits took place on telehealth platforms—a number that sounds big but was just a fraction of all visits. That all changed as the pandemic kept us inside our homes. It meant connecting patients to vital healthcare services through videoconferencing, remote monitoring, virtual consultations, and wireless communications. For many routine visits, it just made sense to "visit" your doctor through a laptop or smartphone. I saw that phenomenon in my own home. In 2019, my wife's practice didn't even offer telehealth consultations. By mid-2020, she was hosting scores of virtual sessions monthly and teaching others in her field how to do the same.

Remote access to healthcare wasn't just a popular alternative because it reduced the risk of exposure to COVID; virtual appointments also tend to be cheaper than in-person appointments on a per-visit basis. While a visit to your doctor's office costs $146 on average, the average telehealth visit costs just $79. While more people have grown comfortable returning to medical providers' waiting rooms, telehealth is here to stay. That's because people like it! In studies, most patients say they are more satisfied with telehealth and virtual care visits than with in-person appointments.

Digital health technology can be a great equalizer, giving people with mobility challenges, or caretaking obligations, or who live in remote areas access to medical care. But it also highlights the inequities in high-speed internet access. As of 2021, some 43 percent of adults in households making less than $30,000 a year—more than 25 million American adults—lacked a high-speed internet connection.[12] Those with limited or no internet access can't communicate online with their physicians, obtain electronic medical records, or access online health resources, all of which can improve health outcomes. In fact, researchers at the University of Chicago found that lack of internet access was one of the most consistent factors associated with a high risk of death due to COVID-19 in the United States.

It's not just healthcare. From improving our education system, to creating jobs, to expanding opportunities for innovators and entrepreneurs, virtually every key challenge we face counts high-speed internet access as a key condition. Broadband internet is the foundation upon which our digital future is built. It is the lifeline that connects individuals, communities, and businesses, transcending geographical boundaries and unlocking boundless possibilities. To truly unleash America's potential, we must prioritize and invest in competition between internet providers and widespread access to broadband internet, ensuring that no American is left behind in the digital divide.

Trade

American leaders from both parties treat trade as a zero-sum battle and trade policy as a vehicle for scoring political points at home and abroad. But our recent isolationist approach to trade is moving the United States in a dangerous direction, making what should be a team effort with our friends a go-it-alone "Hunger Games" strategy.

Politicians and political talking heads these days love the idea of "reshoring": bringing (or bringing back) manufacturing to the United States. The Biden administration went one step further, shepherding the CHIPS and Science Act—a bill designed to expand and rebuild America's semiconductor manufacturing industry—through Congress and signing it into law in 2022. While I'm deeply skeptical of big spending bills, and CTA as a principle never advocates for funding for our industry, it's hard to deny that the CHIPS bill, alongside manufacturing incentives in the recent infrastructure bill and the Inflation Reduction Act, has been effective in pushing companies to make major investments in US advanced manufacturing. Intel Corporation, Micron Technology, and others have pledged more than $100 billion in new investments, bringing thousands of good-paying jobs to Ohio, New York, and other states.

Increasingly, that investment is coming from foreign firms as well. Norwegian battery maker Freyr announced plans to invest $1.7 billion in a gigafactory—a facility that produces batteries for electric vehicles on a large scale—located in Coweta County, Georgia. Just a few months later, Volkswagen made an even bigger announcement, unveiling plans to invest more than $7 billion in North American manufacturing as part of a planned rollout of new EVs. The announcements aren't limited to EVs. Enel, Italy's biggest utility company, will add 10,000 EV chargers to a network spanning the United States.

The problem with these financial incentives (other than the huge and needless additions to our national debt, pushing unpayable debt onto our children and grandchildren)? They send the wrong message to our allies and friends abroad, telling them they must manufacture in the US or be treated the same way we treat our enemies. The reality is that not all technology products can or should be manufactured in the United States. A 2023 study commissioned by CTA and conducted by consulting firm Kearney found that reshoring manufacturing of all technology products now taking place in mainland China and Taiwan for the US market would require a direct investment of well over $500 billion and as much as ten times the current US workforce.

Instead, we should focus on strengthening ties to fellow democracy-loving countries. Our trade policy—for technology, but also for a range of other products and inputs—should focus on reducing trade barriers with our allies, including countries across the European Union, Canada and Mexico, Australia and New Zealand, Japan and South Korea, and many others. While the decision to stay out of the Comprehensive and Progressive Agreement for Trans-Pacific Partnership (CPTPP) was shortsighted, it's not too late for the US to join. We can also double down on building bilateral and multilateral trade ties to allies and partners. Some five years ago, the US initiated multiple trade wars, fueling inflation and shifting production to new locations, many of which do not have free trade agreements with the US. As supply chains shift, in response to both the COVID-19 pandemic and geopolitical tensions between the US and China, we should provide companies from our "Trade BFFs" the same opportunities for market competition as their American counterparts.

The other reality we must confront is that American factories require reliable, affordable sources of energy. That means encouraging a shift away from many fossil fuels and toward wind, solar, and nuclear energy—as well as experimental emerging energy sources—while recognizing that oil and gas will be an essential component of our energy mix to meet today's manufacturing, business, and consumer needs. This is especially important given that emerging technologies like electric vehicles, quantum computing, and generative AI use massive amounts of electricity.

We should also recognize and pivot to correct areas where our trade policy has gone off the rails. Our current approach to tariffs isn't so far from the Smoot-Hawley tariffs that got us into the Great Depression almost a century ago. You don't need an economics degree to recognize that tariffs aren't paid by foreign countries. Despite claims to the contrary by the Trump administration, they are taxes paid by American businesses—and ultimately consumers. That's true for tariffs on friends *and* foes, and it's particularly egregious in the case of our tariffs on China. While they were designed to push China to end its unfair trade practices, our tariffs on a range of goods imported into the US from China instead hurt American businesses and consumers. In the technology industry alone, American companies paid an estimated $47 billion between July 2018 and June 2023.

■ ■ ■

New Political Options

One final important "big picture" pivot could significantly boost US success. We're a country that loves options—we're inundated with our choice of cars, food, shoes, entertainment, vacations, schools, and even religion. Yet, while Americans may have more choices than most, there is one choice we lack compared to other democracy-loving countries. In most elections, we have only two real choices when it comes to casting a vote. More, the primary system in our country pushes each party and its candidates to the fringes, encouraging them to take ever more extreme positions that alienate many Americans. No wonder that a record number of Americans—nearly 50 percent!—identify as Independents in 2023 polling. According to Gallup analysts, this isn't just a fluke. It's the result, as journalist Mike Allen explains, of growing "disillusionment with the political system, US institutions, and the two parties, which are seen as ineffectual, too political, and too extreme."[13]

As most Americans are not extremists and want problems solved, new groups have emerged. No Labels is a group focused on fighting extremism in politics and on negotiating solutions to the biggest national problems. I am proud that CTA has been a No Labels supporter since its early days. No Labels created the bipartisan Congressional Problem Solvers Caucus, a group of centrist Democrats and Republicans committed to working across the aisle, which has racked up several impressive legislative wins, including the bipartisan Infrastructure Investment and Jobs Act signed by President Biden into law in 2021.

These important movements within our political system won't just fight extremism in our country internally, they'll also have a major impact on our global competitiveness.

■ ■ ■

Innovation Countries

The US isn't the only country known for its innovation. Others are excelling at it, and in many cases even surpassing us.

French president Emmanuel Macron has laudably focused France on entrepreneurship and innovation. He has been a visible presence at CES events in Paris and Las Vegas. He has invited innovators and scientists to settle in France and helped open a startup incubator in the heart of Paris. A French company, L'Oréal, gave the first-ever beauty keynote at CES 2024.

I have known President Macron from the time he was a junior minister, and his passion for innovation is truly authentic. I had been traveling to France for decades to meet with company executives and hold press briefings promoting CES Las Vegas. With the support of several French leaders, we launched CES Unveiled in France more than a decade ago. Macron came to the event and spent hours talking to exhibitors, clearly enjoying himself. I urged him to come to CES that January in Las Vegas, and he did. We stayed in touch over the following years as he created a new, forward-thinking political party. The first (and still only) time I embraced a non-US political candidate was his run for president. In 2021, President Macron formalized our relationship by making me a French chevalier and bestowed on me the Legion d'honneur, an incredible honor I will always cherish. It allows me to wear a red lapel insignia, a symbol recognized globally.

The Netherlands has long been another strong ally in innovation. Our CES Amsterdam event has grown through a friendship with Prince Constantijn, the brother of Dutch king Willem-Alexander. Despite being royalty, he is humble, quiet, and self-effacing, but passionate about Dutch innovation and entrepreneurship. Although we held annual modest press events each year in Amsterdam, it was Prince Constantijn's continued support of the event that led to the growing presence of Dutch and other European exhibitors at CES. Prince Constantijn's visibility and enthusiasm for Dutch innovation along with Dutch government support, wonderful partners, and our efforts to attract European media helped transform our event from a few dozen attendees to over a thousand people annually and close to a hundred exhibiting companies, including Dutch startups and others from Czechia, Germany, Hungary, Poland, and Slovakia.

Despite its small size, Belgium is one of Europe's emerging innovation powerhouses, drawing top talent from across the continent, investment in an innovation ecosystem that supports small and growing businesses, and continued focus on innovation investments in R&D and beyond. In 2023, I had the opportunity to meet with Belgian prime minister Alexander De Croo, who previously served as minister of a broad portfolio that covered the country's digital agenda. De Croo shared his vision of a world in the midst of a digital transition, and I was impressed by his commitment to making Belgium a leader not just for Europe, but for the world.

India has made a remarkable transformation into a country of innovation—and an important technology ally. In the fifteen years between 2007 and 2022, the internet penetration rate rose from 4 percent to nearly 50 percent, making India the world's second-largest online market.[14] It is a pioneer in mobile banking. Most Indians access the internet via increasingly inexpensive mobile phones, bringing this transformative technology to people across the country, including India's many rural communities.

While North Korea isolates itself, banning most communications technology and harming its population (with some 42 percent estimated to be malnourished), South Korea relies on democratically elected leaders with competing visions and parties but reliant on free markets.[15] It took a few decades, but great tech companies like LG, Samsung, SK, and Hyundai emerged, creating wealth and allowing the bamboo shoots of thousands of startups to emerge with ideas and innovations likely to change the world.

I visited South Korea in late 2023 and was astounded at the culture of hard work and innovation in meetings with Seoul's mayor Oh Se-hoon and other leaders from government and industry. The innovation ethos animates Seoul and the surrounding areas, home to thousands of start-ups worth an estimated $177 billion, including fifteen unicorns. Indeed, at CES 2024, hundreds of Korean companies exhibited on the show floor, and Korea sent the largest delegation to our startup area, Eureka Park. Over 16,000 executives, journalists, and government leaders came from South Korea to Las Vegas, demonstrating a huge focus on the future of technology for this country of only 51 million people.

Israel

Israel has succeeded economically, choosing democracy and welcoming global immigration. The country has produced incredible innovation and companies, from Mobileye and SodaStream to Wix.com.

I am Jewish, and I have made several trips to Israel. I have seen the shared desire for peace, security for their families, and a better life for their children. A few months before former Israeli prime minister Shimon Peres's 2016 death, a handful of tech executives, my wife, and I met with Peres at the Tel Aviv peace center he created to bring together Jews and Muslims.

He spoke in a whisper. He described how technology is a solution to the world's most pressing problems. That meeting bolstered the purpose of our global event and resulted in a partnership with the UN, focusing on fundamental human securities.

Sadly, I will never forget my meeting with a Palestinian business leader about a joint business opportunity with Israelis. He told me he couldn't do it; terrorist leaders would kill him for any cooperative venture.

Many US leaders have made great strides in brokering peace. President

Jimmy Carter with Egypt; President Donald Trump's son-in-law Jared Kushner obtaining the Abraham Accords between Israel, Bahrain, and the United Arab Emirates in 2020; and President Biden, who came close to a peace agreement with Saudi Arabia. Increasingly, it looked like peace was breaking out in the Middle East.

That peace ended October 7, 2023. On that holy Saturday, from Gaza, from land given in turn for peace, thousands of Hamas terrorists broke through the Israeli border and brutalized, killed, and kidnapped thousands of Israeli citizens. Immediately after the Hamas attacks, Israel made several pivots. It went from executive control by the conservative government to a coalition government controlling its military operations. It went from a technology- and business-oriented economy to calling up most reservists. And it shifted from a defensive "iron shield" strategy to an offensive effort to recover hostages and dismantle Hamas.

It remains to be seen how recent events will affect Israel's innovation economy—and the rest of the world.

China

China has made more pivots than a point guard in a season of basketball games. It has used several strategies to grow rapidly from the world's low-cost manufacturer to one of the world's top economies and a center for high-tech innovation and production. While the US has dawdled, China has surged. It produces millions of engineers annually, limits litigation, and sends students abroad to study at our top universities and learn and "borrow" knowledge from American businesses. China has focused on key future industries including artificial intelligence, self-driving vehicles, robotics, and cybersecurity. It has created national strategies and laws unbound by lawyers lobbying for compensation. Those are the positive pivots.

At the same time, China made moves to tilt the playing field in its favor. The Chinese government created laws excluding, restricting, or burdening non-Chinese companies from owning land, operating without Chinese partners, or repatriating profits from China. It created the Belt and Road Initiative, investing in low-income countries, like Pakistan, Afghanistan, Ethiopia, Rwanda, and more in turn for huge unpayable debts to China. China hits our governments and businesses thousands of times daily with cyberattacks. And it has created different rules for popular social media platforms in and out of China. In China, social media promotes math, science, and engineering and blocks harmful content, while allowing dangerous and deadly content in other parts of the globe.

While we isolate ourselves from friends and allies, the Chinese government is pouring people and money into projects in Africa, Asia, and Latin America. In doing so, they're propagating their cultural and governing values, too. Countries like Russia and Iran, among others, are eager for Chinese investment and support and seem unconcerned about China's penchant for repressing political activism or human rights violations.

But China is weakening in some ways. When President Xi took control of innovative Chinese tech companies, it spurred an exodus by global companies. Our decision to shut down CES Asia in 2020 was tied to increasing government restrictions, in addition to the COVID-19 pandemic. President Xi's announced intention to take over Taiwan positions China as a hostile force rather than a major world player seeking global harmony and growth. The decision to isolate millions of Chinese citizens during the COVID pandemic created an economic slump. It also added one more reason for Western democracies to seek supply chains outside of China.

Meanwhile, China's real estate bubble is bursting and millions of Chinese businesses teeter on bankruptcy as higher interest rates, a weakening economy, a low birth rate, and an aging economy converge to threaten the wealth Chinese citizens gained. And while China can lay claim to investments and success with green energy, it still relies on and keeps building coal plants. Although it is a vocal supporter of the Paris Agreement aimed to reduce carbon emissions, its obligations under that deal are nonexistent. It can pollute as much as it wants until 2029 and then has a voluntary commitment to not exceed 2029 levels. China is still the world's top air polluter.

China has increasingly isolated itself from the world, and the question is whether President Xi or his successor can again pivot China to its rightful place as a global leader—starting with a respect for human rights and a willingness to treat foreign businesses fairly.

While the US can and should have a mutually respectful relationship with China, we must be cautious not to let misunderstandings result in armed conflict. More, we must reduce our vulnerability to sole reliance on China for strategic elements and products.

We are battling China not only to be a world leader on innovation, investment, and economics, but also in our promotion of the values of democracy, human rights, and our way of life.

Innovation Abounds

Of course, this is just a short and regrettably incomplete accounting of the technology hubs flourishing around the globe, and the world-changing innovations happening everywhere. While a full country-by-country assessment could easily be its own book, this chapter would be incomplete without at least a mention of top technology leaders like the United Kingdom, Finland, Sweden, Norway, Germany, Spain, Switzerland, and more in Europe; our neighbors Canada and Mexico; Australia; and Asian technology powerhouses like Japan, Singapore, and many more.

CHAPTER 9

The Personal Pivot

As an aspiring lawyer, I worked under Ed Day, the "inventor" of the zip code and the former postmaster general for President John F. Kennedy. Ed put me to work for a client, an association of electronics companies. Soon I was working hard, first as a law student, then as outside counsel, and ultimately as an embedded inside counsel, protecting and promoting the VCR—an innovation that allowed people to record TV programs and play prerecorded tapes. In short, it freed people from watching only what TV networks wanted them to see.

Almost immediately, broadcasters and movie companies tried to block the sale of VCRs and video rentals through the courts and in Congress. I began working around the clock trying to build alliances to fight these well-heeled lawyers and lobbyists and keep them from using their political and legal might to quash the nascent VCR and movie rental market.

By age twenty-five, I was running a weekly meeting of representatives from consumer groups, retailers, and manufacturers as we plotted our PR, grassroots, and legal strategy. We were outgunned and outmanned by the broadcasters and motion picture industry. As audio recorders grew in popularity, the music industry lobby joined the battle against us and tried to impose cost-prohibitive taxes on audio technology or ban it outright. But we had one thing on our side: these huge industries also underestimated what a small association could do.

It was a huge multiyear battle. Our ragtag team included unpolished gems like David Rubenstein, who went on to create the Carlyle Group, and Ron Brown, who later became head of the Democratic Party and served as US secretary of commerce. I didn't realize at first what a small "David" we were, compared with the Goliath of the huge industries we were up against. Our Washington opponents were dismissive of us and of consumer choice. As a result, they were lazy in their effort to protect their status quo monopolies. They didn't think they needed to pivot—and that was their Achilles' heel.

We knew we had to have an evolving strategy focused on the benefits of innovation, consumer choice, and the new industries and jobs created by the growth in technology. Without a willingness to evolve, we would be dead in the water. We pivoted frequently to new approaches, shaped by weekly debates on strategy. Ultimately, we won almost every battle in Congress; even the US Supreme Court tipped in our favor, ruling in a close 5–4 case that recording TV shows for later consumption was "fair use" and that Sony and other VCR makers could not be held liable for copyright infringement simply for producing the technology.

We didn't win in spite of our underdog status. We won *because* we were the underdogs. We had to be smarter. We had to move quickly and pivot to survive. When the motion picture industry tried to block movie video rentals, I organized video retailers into a potent political group who got their customers to allow video rentals. When the content lobbyists asked Congress to pass a law requiring recording devices to turn off in response to copyrighted music, we showed how the proposed "spectrum notch" would ruin the sound on recorded home videos, especially the Wedding March used in so many wedding processions. The bill died a quick death.

The pivots of this era are among my proudest, because they taught me lessons I took with me through the rest of my career. Never assume defeat. Don't be cocky. Be hungry. Believe in your cause. Move quickly even with imperfect information. Don't be intimidated by anyone. Hold your ground. Fight for your cause. The status quo must be challenged to move forward.

What makes our country great is our bias toward the new, the better, and the bold. But that progress isn't preordained. Even today, we see trial lawyers opposing efforts to reduce carnage on our roads, unions advocating for laws that would force union dues on skeptical workers, and lobbyists using the levers of government to hamstring innovative new competitors. Even as I write, as mentioned in Chapter 4, AM radio advocates are using fanciful safety arguments as a smokescreen to convince Congress to mandate their pre-WWI technology in every new car. They may even win, because politicians tend to favor the free publicity from radio broadcasters' promotion. That's unfortunate, because stale technologies don't last long in a country focused on the new, the next, and the innovative.

If You Want to Be Right, Be Willing to Change Your Mind

Jeff Bezos says being right more often than not requires the willingness to change your mind regularly. That's an idea I've taken to heart. In some ways (typically the less glamorous ones), being a big association CEO is like being a player in the NFL. People in both groups start out confident, but inevitably we all make mistakes. Sometimes, we miscalculate or overlook weaknesses. Other times, things that are totally out of our control go wrong, or spoil otherwise well-thought-out plans or strategies. It's how we pivot from those mistakes and setbacks that defines our future. Those who can't get over their failures move on, whether voluntarily or not, to less visible high-stakes careers. Those who learn from their setbacks find that failure can breed future success.

Perhaps no one understands that concept, or my analogy, better than my friend and former Seattle Seahawk and NFL Hall of Famer Steve Largent. As a receiver at the University of Tulsa, Steve earned All-American honors and emerged as a standout for the program. After three years as a starter at Tulsa, he entered the 1976 NFL Draft and was thrilled to be drafted by the Houston Oilers, if a bit disappointed to be picked so late in the draft. Then, his plans were upended. Despite throwing himself into drills and practices, Steve was released before the first game of the season, informed by his coach that they had all the receivers they needed.

Luckily, Steve caught a break. In 1976, the NFL expanded to include two new franchise teams. Looking to pick up talent, the newly created Seattle Seahawks traded a future draft pick to get Steve into their lineup. By the end of his rookie year, Steve had fifty-four receptions for 705 yards and four touchdowns. (For those who aren't big football fans: that's a lot.) Despite lacking the height and speed of many receivers, Steve went on to play fourteen seasons, setting NFL records for receptions, yards, and touchdowns. How? He focused on the "intangibles" that he could control and that could make a player great. During his time in the NFL, Steve became a fan favorite for his ultra-precise running routes and ability to catch nearly any ball thrown his way.

I know Steve not because of his success in the football stadium, but because of another big life pivot. After retiring from the NFL, Steve started an advertising and marketing firm, and then, hooked on local politics, parlayed his name recognition into a seat representing his home state of Oklahoma in the House of Representatives. After several successful terms, he decided to run for Oklahoma governor. Sadly, after a highly competitive election Steve lost his bid by fewer than seven thousand votes. At that point, Steve could have enjoyed an easy retirement. Instead, he demonstrated the mental flexibility that had served him well on the football field and in the halls of Congress and pivoted into an entirely new industry as the head of CTIA, a trade association representing the US wireless communications industry.

For years, Steve and I enjoyed regular lunches as we compared notes on running technology associations. I often joked that in an association headshot competition, I didn't stand a chance against a tall, good-looking NFL Hall of Famer and former member of Congress. But what I lack in height, agility, and credentials, I make up for in passion and a willingness to embrace opportunities when they come knocking.

Delta Air Lines CEO Ed Bastian is another example of a leader whose willingness to change his mind showed great integrity of character. In September 2023, Delta announced plans to scale back its loyalty program, making major changes to the way fliers earned its elite "Medallion Status" and lounge access that rewarded overall spending rather than number of flights. More, those with premium American Express cards would no longer have unlimited lounge access. As a frequent Delta flier myself, I can attest that the backlash from Delta customers was immediate, and it was intense. To his great credit, Ed recognized that the feelings went beyond simple frustration, and he acted. In an email to SkyMiles members, Ed shared that he had "read hundreds of your emails," and that the "response made clear that the changes did not fully reflect the loyalty you have demonstrated to Delta."[1] He committed to making program adjustments. More, he admitted publicly that Delta "probably went too far" with its changes.[2]

Ed's candor and change in policy was a great lesson to CEOs. Just a few weeks after that, *Chief Executive* magazine announced that Ed had been named 2023 Chief Executive of the Year by his peer CEOs. A well-deserved recognition.

■ ■ ■

Take Risks

Some people avoid risk at any cost. Others embrace risk-taking, and even find it exhilarating. In general, I strive to be somewhere in the middle. When I first became a manager, an HR colleague gave me what I considered a great compliment, observing that I was willing to take risks and pivot but only after thinking through the potential benefits and consequences. Decades later, that still describes my approach.

Still, among my cohorts in the association world, a famously cautious group, I stand out for my willingness to speak my mind on contentious issues. When I was first promoted to head up the Consumer Technology Association, then under the Electronic Industries Association (EIA), I confessed to EIA president and my personal mentor Peter McCloskey that I didn't fully understand what I was allowed to do and say. His response was simple and clear: "Gary, you have a great job. You can do or say anything you want, until you're fired!"

While I've tried my best to keep the confidence of my volunteer executive board, the fear of getting fired has never dictated my decisions. That may be because I experienced it early: getting fired at sixteen from a 4-H camp counselor job for bringing alcohol onto the campgrounds. The experience was painful and searing at the time, but it taught me that while actions have consequences, getting fired didn't define me or my life. And since I've been commuting to Washington, DC, for work from my family home in Michigan for two decades, my mantra was the worst thing that could happen was I would end up spending more time with my family. Not a bad option!

The irony is that because of this awareness of consequences, I took more (calculated) risks. Looking back at pivots in which I have played a role, I realize my mistakes and successes both occurred because I am change-oriented. I want to move forward. I want something to happen to seize an opportunity or make a positive change in the world.

Get Buy-In

I've learned from experience that making big decisions or pivots in business is especially challenging. They are often fraught with uncertainty, conflicting goals, and even multiple ethical issues. Big decisions often affect people's livelihoods and involve big risks.

Business executives and leaders have multiple constituencies they must consider. The law imposes a fiduciary duty to the business owners or shareholders. This means that not only must big decisions or pivots be approved by the top executives and typically a board of directors, but the top executives and those on the board must consider the financial, legal, reputational, and ethical impacts of major shifts in strategy.

I once interviewed an impressive former CEO for a senior position at CTA. While her credentials and presentation were stellar, I knew that she was job hunting after being fired from the CEO role by the company's board of directors. So I asked her why. When she told me she had no idea, I asked if anything notable had happened in the months before her firing.

Her response floored me: she said she exercised her authority to remove her chief financial officer, and some board members got upset. I asked if she had consulted board members in advance, and she replied that she didn't see it as necessary as she had clear authority to fire employees. Based on that explanation, I immediately knew we would not be making her a job offer, though I wished her well in future endeavors. In fact, I empathized with the board members who'd fired her. She surprised her board after a pivotal decision. She did not see the value of consultation and input and lacked judgment. Management pivots should be discussed with top board members before executing.

Of course, it is not just CEOs who should consult others before a big decision. Good business leaders and executives care about how a big decision or pivot affects employees. People working full-time are giving much of their waking time to their company or organization. According to a 2021 McKinsey study, some 70 percent of Americans say they define their sense of purpose through work.[3] The financial security and emotional well-being of a firm's employees are tied not only into the actual work and work conditions, but the company's role in the world. More than nine out of ten employees told *Harvard Business Review* pollsters that they'd willingly trade a percentage of their lifetime earnings for greater meaning at work.[4] Just as with customers, pivoting generally requires engaging employees as part of the process. More, the process of consultation may reveal facts or ramifications not previously considered. As I tell my employees, "all of us are smarter than any of us."

Existing customers matter. A business often has a mission or values statement, which likely includes an obligation to serve customers. Depending on the pivot, engaging customers by asking their views could not only help with the shift and uncover weaknesses in the idea or reveal related opportunities, but it also helps existing customers embrace a major change in strategy. People are more willing to accept change, even changes they disagree with, if the decision-maker consulted them first.

Thoughtful leaders should also care about the future their children will inherit. This means corporate leaders should consider how their pivot affects society and the environment.

Thoughtful leaders should also care about their local community. This means corporate leaders should consider how their pivots impact the society and environment around them, and get buy-in from local leaders. This is not a book on ESG (or environmental, social, and governance, common shorthand for corporate accountability and sustainability efforts), but ESG considerations in one form or another must be part of the mix. As then Fortune Media CEO Alan Murray wrote in his 2021 book, *Tomorrow's Capitalist*, businesses increasingly consider ESG in decision-making because it makes good business sense, even if many are backing away from the term itself.

I'm keenly aware of the challenges as someone who lives just outside Detroit, a city that struggled amid the decline of the auto industry in the mid-twentieth century. It's been heartening to see a growing cohort of companies, including Detroit-based CTA members like Stellantis and Bosch, focus on partnering with local schools to help shape a future workforce with the skills companies need to hire local.

In his 2023 book *Leading Through Disruption*, Andrew Liveris writes: "This century's businesses won't thrive unless society and the Earth also thrive. The global enterprise I call Humanity Inc. needs to evolve aggressively for everybody's survival, which is why adopting and embedding ESG metrics is minimal table stakes of a business's license to operate in the twenty-first century."[5]

In his review (and praise) of the book, Alan Murray summed it up well: "Those are strong words for a man who was running a petrochemical company."[6] We'd do well to heed their advice.

Set Your Ego Aside

In 1964, college track-and-field coach Bill Bowerman set up a handshake partnership with Phil Knight, who had run under him at the University of Oregon, to start an athletic footwear distribution company called Blue Ribbon Sports. Knight's job was to manage the business side, while Bowerman—while still coaching—worked on the design. They started by importing running shoes from Japan to sell in the United States, until eventually Bowerman made his big breakthrough—he used his wife's waffle iron to create the pattern for the bottom of a sneaker that eventually became the famous Nike "moon shoe."

Initially, their partnership was 50–50. But not long into the business, Bowerman requested to change it to 51–49—*giving Knight the higher ownership.* He willingly gave up his equal standing with Knight because he knew that if they each had half the business and didn't agree on something, there would be no way to resolve it. He trusted Knight's business savvy and allowed him to have the final decision-making power. Today, Nike is valued at more than $30 billion.

Humility has always been an important virtue to me, especially in those I hire and those I work with. My family lived modestly; my father was an elementary school teacher and I was the third of four sons. We were always doing something extra to make money, and I did my part.

Because my father's teacher salary had us on a fairly tight budget, we were always coming up with new, inventive ways to make a few dollars. We would buy soda cheaply by the can and sell it at local sporting events. Every winter I would knock on doors to shovel driveways and sidewalks. Every summer I mowed neighbors' lawns. Once I convinced my father to buy an edger, and he required me to give back 25 percent, along with paying the gasoline and blade costs. I still have my record book from this venture.

I started working very young, holding jobs at a lamp factory and in restaurants, starting as a dishwasher and working up to busboy, waiter, and eventually manager. While in school, I managed the Jones Beach Theater Restaurant, where Guy Lombardo and the Royal Canadians performed each night. I woke up at five a.m. most summer days and biked five miles to empty boxes of eggs from a semi-trailer truck. I was paid four cents a box, and usually unloaded about eight hundred boxes in a few hours. Any success I have enjoyed in my work I attribute to the lessons my parents taught me back when we were making foam curlers and recycling newspapers.

I learned from that experience that ego can be a big hindrance in life, and in business, and I've taken that lesson very seriously. In the 1980s, I launched the first Leaders in Technology dinner at CES, which has become an annual tradition that continues today. We host a dinner to bring together our top international guests, volunteers, customers, and board members with legislators and regulators from around the world, featuring government speakers and CEOs who have something interesting to say. Over the years, our audience has heard from leaders of eBay, Ford, Lyft, Impossible Foods, Best Buy, and many more.

The annual dinner is a hot ticket. Each dinner is a schmoozefest, with a who's who of innovation business and policy leaders. Part of the tradition is that following the "Star-Spangled Banner," the Nevada governor or a Nevada senator welcomes the international audience to Las Vegas. At CES 2019, this tradition almost went totally awry.

Our predinner reception was in full swing, with several hundred of our guests arriving and mingling. Our big name interviewer, Fox Business's Liz Claman, asked me to take her into the banquet room to show her the stage setting for her interview of that year's featured business speaker, Waymo CEO John Krafcik.

Walking with Liz through the room as the servers laid salads on the tables, we noticed a visibly angry man huffing by us to get to the exit. It was a senior elected official—whose name I'm withholding at the advice of my editor—due to speak at that evening's event. He told me no one from our team had greeted him when he entered, and he had found Secretary of Transportation Elaine Chao in the backstage green room. She didn't belong there, he said, because she had never held elected office.

The official threatened to leave. While I never want any of our guests to feel unwelcome, that threat was particularly concerning because he had already been announced as a speaker for the evening.

So I acted quickly. I took responsibility for our failure to recognize and greet him at our registration area. I told him how important he was to our event, and how much I respected him as a leader.

He said he didn't care, and that's when I went into ninja mode.

I got on my knees, and, with genuine tears in my eyes, begged him to stay. I told him I would do whatever it took, including a written or on-stage apology, as long as he agreed to stay.

It somehow worked. He saw I was willing to humiliate myself, and he relented. I stayed near him, introduced him to VIPs and made sure his every need was met. He welcomed our guests, and they felt special. It all worked out.

I share this slice of event life vignette because it captures the stress of dealing with powerful people, but also the importance of being willing to put your ego aside for your business and your cause.

Admit When You Get It Wrong—and Make a Change

Here's another one: At CES, we've grappled with the ways that companies use gender and sexuality to sell their products. I have struggled with the question of sex at CES for decades, and it's an area where I made some of my biggest blunders and have had to admit mistakes.

In the 2010s, we were embroiled in debates around so-called booth babes, the spokesmodels for companies who, as *The Atlantic* put it in 2013, were paid to "be beautiful, and stand next to shiny new things."[7] I found that moniker demeaning. Almost all the women derided as "booth babes" had put in the time to genuinely learn about the products and services they were promoting and gave well-informed presentations to show attendees. That said, we ultimately made the decision to update our exhibitor guidelines and ban scantily clad models.

Those conversations were followed by a media frenzy in 2018, when our first three keynote speaker announcements featured men. While that year's full lineup included two featured female CEOs, the crisis certainly prompted us to pivot in the way we think about not just who we feature on our keynote stages, but how we announce it. I am not sure I got it or ever will get it entirely right. But I'm proud to be at the forefront of efforts in the trade show industry to make CES welcoming and comfortable for all our attendees, who represent many different countries and cultures.

Lead with Advocacy

It's important to identify the issues that really matter to you, either personally or professionally. Sometimes that perspective means pivoting to lead on contentious social issues. One area I'm particularly proud of is my advocacy as the head of CTA around LGBTQ equality and marriage. Same-sex marriage is a deeply personal issue that affects families and their decisions about where and how they live. But it's also a business issue. While a person's sexuality has nothing to do with their skills, ability, or work ethic, highly qualified and in-demand workers have a choice where they want to work—and they typically want to work at a place where they know they'll be valued and respected.

In the early 2010s, I recognized that keeping Virginia, the home of CTA's headquarters, competitive as a technology hub meant embracing equality for same-sex couples under the law. As a business leader, I felt the impact of regressive policies directly. I saw job recruits pass up offers at CTA and other businesses in the state because of efforts by then–attorney general Ken Cuccinelli and others to preserve Virginia's ban on same-sex marriage. A gay employee of mine could not take advantage of a CTA program to support local home ownership because he was unwilling to move his family into the state. (We ultimately granted him an exemption.)

Around that time, at a meeting of Virginia CEOs, university presidents, and then-governor Bob McDonnell, I raised my concern that Virginia's extreme anti-LGBTQ policies hurt the state's reputation and ability to attract and retain a strong workforce. I was surprised by his defensive response, denying that the state's policies were hostile to the LGBTQ community. That's especially true because my comments generated a huge outpouring of support following the meeting from the other business leaders and university presidents in the room. The CTA board had discussed the issue and supported my inclination to play a visible role on this issue.

Following that event, I was pleased to be invited to speak to the National Association of Manufacturers (NAM) board on CTA's position on LGBTQ issues as they impacted business and recruitment. I asked CEO Jay Timmons why NAM hadn't weighed in on the issue. After all, Jay had held important positions in the Republican Party and was not usually shy about sharing his views. Jay replied that I didn't yet know him very well, but that I'd soon get to know him better, and he showed me a family photo of himself, his kids . . . and his husband. Clearly, the issue was deeply personal. But in speaking with Jay, it was also clear that he felt his personal stake created a conflict of interest. I had no such conflict and urged the NAM board to take a public position on gay marriage that mirrored CTA's. That day, I'd like to think in large part thanks to my vocal advocacy, the board voted to change their position and get on the right side of history.

Lead with Action

If you're going to speak out, you have to believe in the cause. Too many CEOs fake concern that they don't actually feel, or wade into causes simply because they're making headlines. Sometimes, the wisest pivot is departing from conventional wisdom by choosing not to speak, or at the very least choosing your words wisely. In several decades as a CEO, I've observed that there are two types of people in the world: people who talk a lot and people who do a lot. Very often, there's not much overlap between those groups.

That principle was top-of-mind for me in mid-2020, amid the massive social justice movement that followed the killing of George Floyd. At the time, there was huge pressure on those of us in the business community to take an official position on behalf of our companies on racism, equality, and other social justice issues. In June of that year, CTA put out a statement calling the killing and other incidents "heartbreaking and abhorrent" and calling for the country to "move toward equal justice and equal opportunity [and recognize that] our diversity can and must be our national strength." But I also felt strongly that any statement should also recognize the enormous value and dedication of American police officers. I insisted on including the message that the great majority of officers are decent, well-trained, and hardworking, and emphasizing the importance of police to our public safety. I found it absurd that stating this simple fact could cause controversy, though I knew that it likely would. My convictions and the inane "Defund the Police" movement made me wish other business leaders (who I knew, from behind-closed-door conversations, shared my view) were willing to step up and lend their voice and credibility.

I received some criticism from staff I respect for my decision. But I felt—and still feel—that business leaders were acting irresponsibly in making major financial commitments or major declarations. As Fortune Media's Alan Murray said at the time, "Never have so many issued statements they do not believe." I often do a mental eye roll when I hear CEOs boast of grand plans around diversity, equity, and inclusion (DEI), because for so many it's merely lip service or a necessary mantra they must echo to stay in the C-suite. I am passionate about diversity but refuse to hire or promote any person who is not qualified for a position.

I also recognized that many of these commitments were more talk than action. In the limelight of 2020, American companies spent an estimated $3.4 billion on DEI programs and spoke often about DEI goals.[8] But despite this commitment, measurable progress has been disappointing. In a 2022 survey of chief diversity officers by the *Harvard Business Review*, participants broadly felt that "attempts to combat racial injustice had largely been performative, and had not fostered long-term organizational change."[9] In hundreds of top American companies, attrition rates for DEI-focused roles outpace those of non-DEI positions.[10] More, there's little evidence to suggest that workplace diversity trainings actually work—and some signs that they might actually be counterproductive for efforts to make companies fairer or more inclusive.[11]

That's not to suggest that we should ignore the goal of diversity in our workplaces. In fact, it's never been more critical. I have long believed that this country's diversity—continuously re-fueled by our immigrant population—contributes to our culture of hard work, new ideas, and leading innovation. As Dr. Richard Posner, the famous University of Chicago economist, argued, discrimination defies economic sense, as the companies discriminating lose out on opportunities that can be seized by competitors who embrace a diverse workforce. That idea is backed up in the data. Although there are mixed results, dozens of studies show that diverse teams produce better ideas, solutions, and results. In a report aptly named "Diversity Wins," published in 2020, McKinsey analysts found that companies in the top-quartile for ethnic diversity outperformed those in the fourth quartile by 36 percent in profitability. The same report showed similar performance benefits for companies with a gender-diverse workforce.[12]

Diversity has obvious advantages not only in problem-solving but in challenging the status quo, an especially important factor in the technology industry. That means coming up with new approaches and ideas, but also reducing the damage possible from a culture of followers kowtowing to a leader. So if diversity is important, but *talk* about diversity is cheap, where does that leave us?

Ultimately, I felt comfortable pushing back on the conventional wisdom that business leaders *must* announce new DEI initiatives back in 2020 because CTA already was walking the walk. In addition to highly successful efforts to promote diverse recruiting and retention in our own workplace, CTA is deeply invested in growing a diverse pipeline of technology founders and entrepreneurs. In 2019, CTA created a precedent-setting $10 million fund that contributes to VCs investing in startups created or headed by women, people of color, and other groups who historically lack access to venture capital funding. I'm grateful for the wise counsel of the CTA executive board—including serial entrepreneurs Denise Gibson and Mara Lewis, who independently conceived of and proposed similar ideas for the fund. Our beloved investment committee chair, Voxx founder and chairman John Shalam, showed true leadership by listening to their perspectives and ultimately becoming a vocal advocate for the fund. CTA senior vice president Tiffany Moore has been instrumental in spearheading our continued work with fund partners, and serves as a valued internal advocate on diversity issues, continually pushing me and other members of senior staff to engage in honest conversation and discuss institutionalized racism and other challenging topics. Thanks to the efforts of volunteers and staff, CTA was well positioned as an organization that was actually doing something to promote diversity, not just talking about it.

Our commitment to diversity wasn't just focused outward. As an event-hosting organization, we work to create platforms for diverse leaders, strictly upholding our commitment to develop diverse panels at CES and rejecting requests for CTA staff to participate in nondiverse panels at external events. Since the early 2000s, nominees for CTA's elected board seats have also been evaluated with a rubric that includes diversity as a major consideration. The results have been gratifying, driving greater representation by underrepresented entrepreneurs and innovators on our boards and in other volunteer leadership positions. I recognize that as a white guy, sibling to three white brothers, and father to four white sons, I'm not always the best spokesperson for diversity issues. As a rule of thumb, I also prefer to avoid talking about issues that divide people by individual attributes rather than bringing them together. But in surrounding myself with people who are deeply immersed in building more diverse, inclusive workplaces, I am proud of the role CTA has played as a leader in the space.

■ ■ ■

Find the Third Way

One lesser-known way that successful people pivot is by reframing decisions to look beyond a binary "this or that" choice and find alternative options. This concept isn't new. In fact, it dates back to biblical times and the story of King Solomon, who was wise enough to seek a third way in response to a nearly impossible decision: Two women came before him, each claiming she was the mother to the same baby. King Solomon suggested that rather than deciding in favor of one over the other, he would cut the baby down the middle and each mother would get half. He knew the actual mother would relinquish her rights so the baby would live—and he was right! Justice prevailed by creating a third choice.

President Barack Obama was famous for his mastery of this concept during his rise to the presidency and his subsequent eight years in office. When faced with two seemingly contrary alternatives he would often first describe each side's view, ensuring everyone felt heard. Then, he would label the differences a "false choice" and explain how the goals of both groups could be met with an alternative approach. In fact, the phrase "false choice" appears some seventy times in President Obama's public remarks as president.

It should be no surprise to see this philosophy embraced by some of tech's most impactful leaders. Bill Gates had a remarkable ability to cut through the noise and get to the crux of the issues to find a solution. AMD CEO Dr. Lisa Su abandoned the traditional "tick tock" development cycle—in which chipmakers choose to focus on either improving the manufacturing process for semiconductor chips or the design of the chips themselves—and went all-in to create an entirely new suite of products. Longtime Cisco CEO and executive chairman John Chambers displayed true leadership, empathy, and inclusiveness in growing Cisco's reach via many outside-the-box acquisitions across his multidecade career.

■ ■ ■

Ask Questions

Some people rarely if ever ask questions. They don't want to appear weak, stupid, or lacking in knowledge. Or, sometimes, they don't want new information that might force them to change an ingrained perspective. That's especially common for executives who have reached the upper echelons of the business world. I take the opposite approach. I believe (and even included in an early school yearbook) that choosing to ask a question may make you seem foolish for a minute, but not asking makes you a fool for life.

It's not just my opinion. Research shows that experts in various fields ask far more questions than they make arguments. According to University of Texas at Austin associate dean Gaylen Paulson, "experts are great at asking questions—sometimes three, four, five times as many questions as what average people ask."[13]

In an era of constant technology innovation and advancement, questions—and the flexibility to really listen to the answers and adapt accordingly—are even more critical. I'm not ashamed to admit that I am not an expert in the hundreds of technologies and dozens of technology fields that are covered by my team at the Consumer Technology Association. Like many in specialized fields, technology experts tend to use a host of niche terms and insider-only acronyms for keywords, key players, and key ideas. These terms serve as "secret handshakes" between industry players to show that they're part of the same in-the-know tribe. They allow for easy communication about sometimes complex issues, but perhaps more important, they build trust and cement relationships. They also determine status between individuals and identify outsiders. Asking questions ensures that I understand not only the work we do, but the larger implications of the technologies that are reshaping the industry and our world.

I ask questions to learn and get insights. Asking shows interest in another person. I have also learned that if I don't understand something, then most people in the room with me probably don't either. So I ask questions. That doesn't always mean I enjoy it. A few years ago, I attended a conference on blockchain with members of Congress and business leaders at the French Embassy in Washington, DC. During one session, a French mathematician explained how the binary yes/no checklist used by pilots for preflight safety checks led to bad decision-making, which could improve if pilots had more flexibility to focus on and resolve the unknown rather than just checking a box. As I listened to the talk, I wondered what in the world flight safety had to do with blockchain.

When the mathematician concluded, I raised my hand and thanked him for the decision-making insights, but said I didn't understand the blockchain connection. His response was dismissive and made me feel like an idiot. But later, several other attendees, including members of Congress, thanked me for asking and told me they couldn't understand the analogy either.

Questions are an invitation to knowledge, but it's also important to direct the questions wisely. I often ask my staff, "Did you ask the right question of the right person? You won't get the answer you need if you don't." Asking is my go-to behavior. It is who I am. I am usually rewarded for it with new information, insight, or another benefit. I also see asking questions as a sign of strength and confidence.

Make Conscious (and Ethical) Decisions

One special thing about humans is that we are the only species that can make conscious decisions. Only humans can imagine the future. Other species may appear to have a similar capacity for forethought: Squirrels bury nuts before winter. Dogs hide bones. Beavers build dams. Birds create nests and migrate. Bees swarm and pollinate. Bears hibernate. Cats seek stroking. Fish travel in schools. These all may seem thoughtful and deliberate, but scientists believe they are evolved instincts—that is, those individuals in each species with a stronger disposition to these instinctive actions were the ones more likely to survive and procreate. Their strong survival traits are passed on and strengthened with each generation of surviving offspring.

As humans, we are different. We have an unusual gift—a brain that, when developed, can envision future scenarios. We can plan, imagine the future, and be conscious in our decision-making. We can be self-aware. We can make conscious choices. We can make moral choices. Those choices define who we are and the arc of our individual lives. Unfortunately, we often fail to use this gift. We make poor or harmful choices despite this superpower. We speed in our cars. We commit crimes landing us in jail. We engage in unhealthy behavior. We drink alcohol. We do drugs. We smoke. We overeat. We underexercise.

Sometimes these behaviors are acts of rebellion, assertions of independence, or experiments. Many of us as teenagers made bad decisions. As a parent, I know from firsthand experience that most children naturally resist parentally imposed limitations. It's easy to simply give in to a child crying for a toy, arguing for a video game, or saying every other kid his or her age can do or get something. Parents must decide how to raise their children. If your goal is to raise a self-confident happy young adult working hard and making good decisions, then avoid giving your children everything they want. If you want an entitled, spoiled, and unhappy child who lacks resilience, then give the child everything he or she wants.

I believe there's a big reason even the best-parented among us go astray: We feel powerless and disconnected in today's world. We make bad choices because we don't feel in control of our lives. We escape into the moment because we feel we have little control of the future.

I am very aware that technology is part of the feeling of disconnection. Rapid advances in technology and science have enhanced and lengthened lives. Technology has empowered almost anyone to connect with information, knowledge, and entertainment in seconds. It only takes a connection, a device, and a voice command or a computer, table, notebook, or phone click. But it has come at a price. With technology, we risk losing human connection and social skills. While technology connected us and helped us maintain relationships during the uniquely challenging COVID-19 pandemic period, years of isolation took its toll. People lost the special indescribable feeling of being together, sharing laughter or even tears. The knowing touch, the hug of compassion and affection, the relationship-strengthening bond of a communal meal. We have created gaps in social skills and lost years of development. Perhaps worse, some people lost the sense that these things are even *important*. Being aware of these gaps is an important step in recovering and making conscious decisions.

There have been times in my career when I have been presented with a choice that, looking back, would point my life in one direction or another. Early in my career at CTA, the California legislature was ready to pass a bill that would hurt technology companies. One of our lobbyists, a well-known Democratic Party leader, went to California and returned triumphant, telling us he had taken care of the problem. "We just have to write a $100,000 check to the Democratic Party in California," he told us.

It would have been an "easy" fix, but I knew it wasn't the right, or ethical, or legal fix. I turned him down, and he got angry with me, calling me naïve. But I held firm.

I don't know if he ever made the payment, but our relationship chilled after that. Sometimes you have to stand up to people who may be older or more powerful or more "experienced" than you. But I never had to defend the payment. And I did not go to jail.

The US federal debt is another issue of principle for me. The rising federal debt is a huge threat to the health of the US economy and a theft of wealth from our children. I have been warning Americans about it for decades, cautioning Americans that the low interest rate economy would not last, and a normalized 5 percent interest on a $30 trillion debt would mean $1.5 trillion each year toward paying interest.

In 2008, CTA took a principled stand: we will not ask the federal government for money for our industry.

This doesn't always please some of our constituencies. We've sat on the sidelines as Congress gives billions of dollars to subsidize electric cars and helps chip plants relocate to the United States. Each year the situation gets more dire and the failure of both major parties to address the debt shakes my faith in the nation's two-party system. Our kids face a real challenge, which our generation has created. We need more leaders to make the decision to speak up against this.

When Things Seem Out of Control

The most difficult pivot is how we choose to respond to changes outside our control. I've learned from many years watching successful entrepreneurs that the key is knowing that we can control our efforts but not the outcome. It's also a lesson I've tried to teach my kids: they may not be able to control the actions of playground bullies, but they can control how they respond. What separates successful people from others is the ability to pivot when bad things happen.

The quarterback throwing the interception; the golfer hitting into a bunker; the business leader dealing with supply chain disruption, a failed product launch, a key employee loss, or a price-cutting competitor. Our pivot moment is how we respond. The best move on immediately and don't look around for who to blame.

I have seen time and time again that the most successful people are not defined by their family's income growing up, by their skin color, by their ethnicity, or by their circumstances. They refuse to see themselves as victims. I don't believe in getting anything just because of the circumstances you were born into—good or bad. I believe that big universities that set aside slots for "legacy" children of alumni should be barred from federal support if they don't eliminate the legacy benefits and allocate a fixed percentage of their endowment income for financial aid designated to support those who really need it. Similarly, I don't believe a student of a certain race or religion should be given preferential treatment based on that circumstance.

When I got to know Ivanka Trump during our work with apprenticeships, I was surprised and impressed by how hard she worked. She didn't believe she was "owed" anything because of her wealthy upbringing. She also appeared to be a quiet influence on her father against some of the crazy ideas people were urging him to act on. My invitation to her to speak at CES 2020 set off a predictable wave of criticism by the press, but her thoughtful, knowledgeable, and articulate keynote on the connection between apprenticeships and entrepreneurship wowed a skeptical crowd.

People Come First. Results Come Second.

This is the most important lesson I've learned over the course of my career: treat people like human beings, rather than like human capital.

I regret that it took me so long to understand that people matter. I focused on results, not realizing until midway through my career that results will come if you care about people. If I had to do it over, I would start with the important things: focusing on the people I worked with before anything else, and establishing those important relationships both personally and professionally.

At nineteen, I learned that everyone is the same. The summer after my freshman year in college, I found myself in charge of more than a hundred servers, busboys, and cooks at the Jones Beach Theater Restaurant. I asked my older brother, Ken, how he got along with everyone at the New York bakery he helped manage. He told me that everyone cares deeply about their family. If you recognize this, he said, you can treat people as loving fathers, mothers, children, or grandchildren. Ask about their families, and they will see you as a caring person rather than just a boss. I tried it. It works.

Some twenty years later, I learned that everyone is different. An industrial psychologist advised me that I would be a more effective executive if I put people before results. Care about the people and the results will follow. This means figuring out people's passions, desires, concerns, and fears, and then addressing these needs accordingly. Some people thrive on recognition, others want clear rules, others need incentives, others attention. I tried this. It works.

Applying this advice takes practice. Too often, I jump into the business at hand and then ease into more personal matters. But as a lifelong learner, I'm always working on being more empathetic. And the practice pays off: the more I genuinely care about people, the better they perform.

The bottom line: Everyone has other people (or pets) they care about. Showing real interest in them conveys care. It's a better way of living, and it's a better way of doing business.

One final word of caution: Ultimately, pivots should never mean fundamentally changing who you are. Moving away from your core beliefs or abandoning your ethical principles might be tempting, but it rarely leads to success in the long term.

Where Do We Go from Here?

When I was thirteen years old, I huddled around a tiny black-and-white TV set to watch Neil Armstrong be the first human to step onto and walk on the moon. That mission required massive facilities to house the computers that helped guide the team on Earth to get the astronauts to the moon and back. Yet today's smartphone has greater computing power, and it fits into your pocket! And today's TV sets are flat, five times as big with ten times the resolution, cost 98 percent less, and use a fraction of the energy. That's pretty incredible.

Today, humans live longer, with less physical pain, and in more comfort than ever in history. Products that were once astronomically expensive are available to the masses. But with all this growth in health and wealth, people still go to war, misuse drugs, drink too much alcohol, and eat too much food. Despite advances and knowledge in healthcare, we are hurting ourselves, fighting with each other, and becoming less happy, despite being more comfortable.

Can tech save us from ourselves? I think it can.

On a trip to New York in the summer of 2023, I sat down with Usha Rao-Monari, associate administrator for the United Nations Development Programme. Going into the meeting, I wasn't sure how much we would have to discuss. The UNDP funds the Trust Fund for Human Security, a partner of ours for CES 2023, and I assumed she would primarily be focused on fundraising—while I would be focused on fending off requests for money. But once we started talking, I changed my tune.

Technology, Rao-Monari told me, was critical as a force multiplier and accelerator to lift people out of poverty and support fundamental human rights. The UN was looking for opportunities to partner with and strengthen industry-led technology development that could make the world a better place—improving health, air and water quality, civic participation, education, accessibility, and more. As Rao-Monari explained her view that technology innovation can do more to improve human lives everywhere than nearly any other tool we have available, I thought hey— that's just what we've been saying!

At CES 2023, we launched a new partnership with the UN Trust Fund for Human Security and the World Academy of Art and Science (WAAS) to present our first "show with a purpose." While CES has been the platform for world-changing innovations for years, this CES added a special focus on showing technologies that are making the world better for millions of people through support of the Human Security for All (HS4A) campaign. From innovations in accessibility, healthcare, agriculture, public utilities, and much, much more, I was stunned by the incredible reaction from our exhibitors. In fact, the reaction was so overwhelmingly positive that we brought the partnership back for CES 2024! Our exhibitors have been enthusiastic and excited about the opportunity to show products that don't just entertain and delight us, but also solve real human problems in innovative ways.

Perhaps not coincidentally, it's also a philosophy that technology leaders have pivoted to publicly embrace. It's an obligation I feel strongly about myself. At a time when Americans' trust in elected officials is at an all-time low—just 38 percent in Pew polling from 2022—the opportunity and the need to change America is enormous for those of us in leadership positions.[1] I believe we ought to embrace the leadership role in society that business leaders are increasingly called upon to play.

I'm not alone. Technology leaders are focused on the good their companies can do. As Alphabet CEO Sundar Pichai put it in a speech at Stanford, "the desire for people to make their lives better by gaining access to technology is what compels me to go beyond."[2]

The demand for more tech for good has enabled startups like SOURCE Water, which debuted at CES in 2018 as Zero Mass Water, to get investments they might not have gotten a decade ago. Investors are understanding the newly blurred line between profitable businesses and doing good for the world. Engineering professor Cody Friesen invented a solar-powered device that captures vapor from the air and transforms it into drinking water. It's the world's first renewable drinking water solution, and highly effective. His family of four in Arizona can now generate enough water for their needs—six hundred bottles a month—from just two hydropanels.

SOURCE is now used in more than fifty countries worldwide, and that number is growing. Between 1 and 2 percent of the global carbon footprint (and 5 percent in the US) relates directly to bottled water. In many cases in developing countries, people rely on bottled water because they don't have a good municipal supply. Offsetting even a reasonable amount of dirty water fundamentally changes the trajectory on climate change.

In *Tomorrow's Capitalist*, Alan Murray argues that the core tenets of a capitalist system that dominated the world for more than a century are being challenged as never before. In the old model of capitalism, business existed to maximize shareholder value (profits). But in the new model, businesses have the potential to serve society in a greater way. Their success also depends on it. In the twentieth century, companies that controlled physical capital, like land, railroads, and oil, held the most power. But now the power lies in the intangibles—intellectual capital and brand reputation. And brand reputation is becoming increasingly associated with doing good for communities, consumers, the environment, and workers.

However, there is a cost to advocacy based on CEO personal views on divisive issues. Public-facing corporations getting involved in social issues far from their core function can risk alienating investors and consumers in an increasingly divided world.

Rethinking the Workforce

While demand for a tech savvy workforce is growing, the ranks of highly skilled workers isn't keeping pace. Our nation has an abundance of college graduates with choking debt, but not an abundance of people with the skills needed to actually do the jobs of the future. According to a 2023 survey of C-suite executives, even amid concerns about a recession, labor shortages and talent retention rank among the biggest challenges for business.

The situation is especially acute in the technology and manufacturing sectors. According to a 2021 survey by the National Association of Manufacturers, 80 percent of companies say their top challenge is the inability to attract and retain a quality workforce. If the current trend continues, there could be 2.1 million unfilled manufacturing jobs in the United States by 2030.[3]

At the same time, many teens who would have seen college as the automatic steppingstone between high school and a first job are skeptical about taking on tens of thousands, or even in some cases hundreds of thousands, of dollars of debt for a four-year college degree.

Alternative education models, like apprenticeships, will become more and more common in the coming years. Over the past decade, registered apprenticeships have risen 64 percent, according to the data from the US Department of Labor.[4] Apprenticeships make sense in view of the imbalance between open jobs and skills needed. They can also help companies resolve a fundamental internal contradiction: requiring bachelor's degrees for even those jobs that don't actually require them. According to a Harvard Business School study from 2017, in "nine out of 10 job postings that requested a bachelor's degree, the postings did not contain different duties or added responsibilities than postings with the same title that didn't require a bachelor's degree."[5] Job postings listing a college degree requirement have only grown over the last decade, reaching some 75 percent of job openings, according to Michelle Rhee, former chancellor of DC public schools. But 46 percent of job seekers lack that critical degree.[6]

Companies like IBM are stepping up to fill the gap. In partnership with CTA, then CEO of IBM Ginni Rometty launched an apprenticeship program at CES—part of what the company calls the "new-collar initiative"—that hires candidates with relevant skills but no college degree. American apprenticeships have traditionally centered on construction and the trades, but both Ginny and I recognized that the same model could translate to the tech sector. In fact, there's no reason they can't be expanded to nearly any willing employer. We recruited Jennifer Taylor (now head of the Northern Virginia Technology Council) as our first vice president of jobs; she stood out from scores of candidates with her can-do attitude, relevant experience, and thoughtfully written plan for the job. We also found a welcome ally in Ivanka Trump. Her passion for this issue and her knowledge of the world of apprenticeships were critical in helping us recruit companies to fill millions of open new-collar jobs in communities across the country. At our request, in 2019 she convinced President Trump to issue an executive order allowing qualified noncollege graduates to work on government IT contracts. State governors from both parties have since followed suit and made it easier for highly experienced nondegree-holding workers to take state jobs.

Many veterans, parents returning to the workforce, and inner-city and rural youth are technically proficient without degrees or are eager to learn technical skills getting them higher-paying jobs. Programs like IBM's could help get many of these talented people a foot in the door. Other companies have followed the lead; Accenture, Adobe, Airbnb, Boeing, Google, LinkedIn, Lyft, Microsoft, Pinterest, Salesforce, and many more have in recent years established apprenticeship programs that provide a pipeline for talent and opportunity for a broader cross-section of Americans. And under Rometty, IBM donated its IT apprenticeship program curricula and methodology so any other tech company could use IBM's model to create its own program.

The rise of apprenticeships has also spurred the creation of organizations designed to help nurture them. In early 2022, Michelle Rhee joined forces with entrepreneur Dr. Ximena Hartsock to launch BuildWithin. Born from the concept of "potential over credential," the consultancy helps companies launch and grow apprenticeship programs. Ximena served in the administration of Washington, DC, mayor Adrian Fenty, where she launched a tech apprenticeship program that eventually led to BuildWithin. Now the organization works closely with the Department of Labor to expand, modernize, and diversify apprenticeships.

Apprentices have proven to be super-loyal employees, with five-year retention rates exceeding 95 percent! Apprenticeships can also allow employers to tap diverse groups eager for training for higher-paying jobs. Requiring a bachelor's degree in hiring criteria excludes around 79 percent of Latino people and 72 percent of Black people from consideration for roles— a major barrier for tech companies seeking to diversify their workforce.[7]

Today, 75 percent of the jobs in Switzerland are apprenticeships. American apprenticeships are mostly in construction and trades, but technology apprenticeships are growing fast and there is no reason they can't be expanded to any willing employer.

A Diverse Workforce

The tech industry has made a lot of progress in diversity, but we still have a long way to go. Women make up just one third of the US tech workforce, as I previously mentioned, and hold just a quarter of tech leadership roles. Black employees make up 13 percent of the US workforce but hold just 4 percent of tech jobs. The situation is similar for Hispanic workers, who represent 17 percent of the workforce but have just 8 percent of STEM jobs.[8] Those statistics, while sobering, are certainly better than they were when I joined CTA four decades ago. In fact, they're significantly better than they were even a decade ago. (That's a credit to leaders in the tech industry—including many CTA members—who have focused on increasing diversity in their workforces through hiring and retention.)

Over the years, I've come to understand that inclusion doesn't just mean diversity in hiring. It means treating those you hire with warmth and empathy, so they feel part of the organization. Intentional inclusion naturally fosters employee engagement and leads to higher employee retention and better business results. Focusing on inclusion in this way can also help to inoculate organizations against groupthink.

I've worked hard to develop a culture in which our staff feel welcome to bring ideas to the table and have their voices heard. In fact, following a recent push internally focused on shoring up CTA culture in a newly hybrid work environment, this concept of mutual respect among all staff is literally written into our defining document, "The CTA Way." Having served on several boards and discussed the issue at length with dozens of CEOs, I hear broad consensus backed by research recognizing the link between employee engagement and retention. That's especially true for the younger generations, who tend both to have higher expectations for the workplace and to job hop more frequently. A recent Bank of America report found that 25 percent of Gen Z workers have switched jobs in the first six months of 2022 alone.[9]

From an ethical perspective, most hiring executives feel it is better, for our nation and for underrepresented groups, to cast a wide net and seek a diverse pool of candidates for recruitment and hiring. But perhaps more important, it is also a business imperative.

Comments by Jason Wright, a former NFL football player, McKinsey management consultant, and the first Black general manager of the Washington Commanders, Washington DC's pro football team, are especially compelling on this point. Speaking to the Northern Virginia Technology Council (NVTC) board of directors, he made the case against justifying DEI in terms of a "moral imperative." Emotion fades and cannot be the sole sustaining case behind lasting and impactful corporate DEI initiatives. Rather, he suggested, business leaders should proactively make the case for DEI as a business strategy. As GM of the Commanders, he noted that prioritizing diversity in the Commanders' three-hundred-some-person workforce helps the Commanders relate to, connect with, and grow a diverse fan base—an important consideration as the NFL works to shore up viewership and football participation. More, he went on, DEI is consistent with the aspirational team values and culture of honor, trust, and growth.

I see some interpretations of equity as a bit different from diversity and inclusion. People are not widgets; they are not readily interchangeable, especially in many white-collar workplaces. They have different skills and different years of experience, and work at different paces. In the real world, paying people in similar jobs the same wage or salary—devoid of their actual contributions—is demotivating and misses opportunities to incentivize high-performing employees.

As much as I support diversity and inclusion, I am concerned about our shift to a victimhood culture. I fear we hurt our children by shielding them from true discomfort. We give participation awards, make unreasonable demands on their teachers, and "helicopter in" to advocate for them. Success requires performance. High-quality performance requires hard work. Quality and skill rise to the top. We must be conscious as leaders—of both businesses and our families—and resist our desire for success; equality and diversity trump true performance and hard work.

My personal view of DEI continues to evolve. I feel we each must do our part to create opportunities for underrepresented groups. As a business leader, it's something I am committed to putting into practice. That starts by looking inward and acknowledging that progress toward greater diversity has been slow, despite the proven benefits.

What's at Stake

The arc of our lives is mostly about the pivots we make. Some are big, but most are small or somewhere in between. This doesn't make them any less important. The story of our lives is the story of the collective pivots we make or don't make.

What separates humans from other forms of life are the conscious decisions we make. And we need to make good decisions to survive, both as individuals and a species. Human pivots are often in response to—or in anticipation of—some kind of threat. The big disruptors, like weather shifts, earthquakes, volcanoes, or tidal waves, can suddenly make our environment deadly. But the biggest threats on Earth come from humans.

We overhunt, overfish, overeat, fight, and engage in destructive behavior. We also overuse energy, transportation, mining, and manufacturing.

We do better when we work together toward the same goals. The stakes are high—get it right and good things happen. Success means improving health, cleaning air and water, cutting fuel use, empowering the disabled, and enriching humanity. Innovation, especially in technology, can do more to improve human lives everywhere than nearly any other tool we have available.

We're already seeing this principle in action. Technology introduced at CES 2018 using solar power to create potable water out of the air is now deployed in communities around the globe. Agricultural tech helps farmers grow healthier, more abundant crops. Tech tracking food reduces waste and makes agricultural supply chains more sustainable. With access to the internet now almost ubiquitous, people are doing business around the world, sometimes from the phones in their pockets. In some countries, that same internet connection on your phone can be used to vote. Wearable medical devices are ushering in a world of more personalized medicine. Americans with hearing loss can now buy hearing aids over the counter at drugstores, just like reading glasses. More products may follow. In-home technology can activate devices with the wave of a hand or a spoken word. They can also predict falls and help prevent injuries. Self-driving vehicles can support people with mobility challenges and reduce traffic fatalities.

Most of these developments would have been impossible to imagine a century—or even a few decades—ago. The last half century has seen unprecedented and remarkable advances in technology especially in fields like robotics, self-driving vehicles, artificial intelligence, and quantum computing. Yet at the same time, the world faces unprecedented challenges that require urgent responses and new innovative solutions.

Technology isn't the only answer, but it offers a remarkable power to enhance what individual people can do and solve big human problems. Whether and how we improve the world and turn it over to the next generation is well within our control. It's our duty and our sacred obligation to harness technology that makes the world a better place. And after more than forty years of working in the technology industry, I'm confident that we're just scratching the surface of what's possible.

Acknowledgments

This book—my fourth—focuses on how to make big decisions in business and life. While I spent large portions of the book sharing my own views of this topic, they didn't come about in isolation. They're built on a lifetime of experiences and, perhaps more importantly, relationships. For previous books, I began my acknowledgments by recognizing colleagues and ended with family. For this one, I flip that order. My family members have fueled my mental and emotional growth and helped me make good decisions. Let's start with them.

My maternal grandparents, Max and Manie, emigrated from Eastern Europe to give their children a better life. After moving to Montreal, they raised my mother, Mildred, aunt Ida and uncle Nathan in a small apartment. It was a modest life, with my grandfather supporting the family by retouching photos.

My father's parents were also immigrants, Leonard hailing from Romania and Jane from Poland. They met in the New York City hat factory where they both worked. They married and had two boys: my dad, Jerome, and my uncle Albert. Like my mother's parents, they worked hard to earn a living, spending nearly every day running the tiny grocery store they owned on Ninety-First Street and Broadway in Manhattan.

The store closed in the early 1960s, after their kindness and generosity in offering groceries on credit became an unsustainable business model.

As the product of two families who understood the value of hard work, it's probably no surprise that the workplace—at least an early one—was where my parents first met, working as counselors at an upstate New York summer camp. My mom, Millie, loved reading and talk radio, and instilled in me the value of lifelong learning and striving to be my best self. My dad, Jerry, a World War II veteran and sixth-grade teacher, taught me to own the consequences and learn from my less-than-ideal decisions. A member of the NAACP, he had a clear sense of right and wrong and a strong desire to uplift all people. If the measure of parents is their ability to instill morals, give their kids the tools to make good choices, and eventually set them on the path to becoming confident and happy adults, my parents did a great job. Together, they raised me and my brothers, Eric, Ken, and Howie, to be curious, confident, and thoughtful about our life choices.

I take inspiration from each of my brothers, who share not only self-confidence but a hunger to creatively solve problems: personal, business, and societal. Our get-togethers often feature brainstorming sessions and political debates. We remain closely connected—not least through our friendly Wordle competition. I also appreciate my brothers' willingness to make time each January to travel to Las Vegas and help at CES.

My four sons each nourish me in different ways. With my first wife, Jan, I had two wonderful boys. Steve loves soccer, technology, history, writing and checking to ensure we know the facts on the various issues we discuss. Doug, occupied nonstop as a caregiver for his three young sons, is curious, thoughtful, and eager to ask questions as he delves into big projects. I have two younger boys with my second wife, Susan—my soulmate, best friend, and daily sounding board. As I worked on this book, I spent several hours teaching Mark to drive. He taught me that driving is a series of lifesaving decisions, and I am confident he will remain a careful decision-maker and driver (albeit a fast skier). His thoughtful questions and observations, and interest in logic and languages push me to learn more myself. My youngest son, Max, is a renaissance charmer, gifted in music, athletics, and academics. I hope he embraces the ninja decision-making this book envisions.

I have been blessed with many teachers, friends and mentors who made a mark on my life.

My former roommate and close friend Don Upson inspired me to take risks and be ambitious in efforts to change the world. He first convinced me to move in, train with him, and successfully complete the Marine Corps marathon. We double-dated, published a couple of joint commentaries, and worked together during Don's tenure as the state of Virginia's first Secretary of Technology to create and promote uniform laws facilitating commerce on the internet.

While in law school, I worked at a law firm with former Federal Trade Commissioner Jim Nicholson, who with his former FTC colleagues embraced me and taught me that law is about real people and their lives. They instilled in me a passion for our constitution and antitrust laws as the foundation for our national strategy, personal liberty, and vibrant business climate.

I first encountered Jack Wayman, a World War II veteran and Purple Heart recipient, head of the Consumer Technology Association's predecessor organization and creator of CES, when I was a student working at a law firm representing CTA. After I passed the bar, Jack brought me in-house, where he taught me that leadership means having a vision, seeing possibilities, and sometimes getting your hands dirty. He also emphasized the need to pivot quickly in response to opportunity—a lesson brought to life in the early 1980s, when he connected me to prospective partners to build a new structure for Las Vegas's biggest trade shows.

The partner we landed was Sheldon Adelson, owner and producer of COMDEX, then the nation's biggest trade show. Together, we built a

120,000 square-foot building. Working with the entrepreneurial Sheldon was a lesson in daily pivots as we rushed to start and finish amid strikes, change orders, and the hard deadline of a sold-out trade show.

I'm also grateful to other people in my life who, like Sheldon, inspired the kind of "coopetition" discussed in this book. While we may not always have agreed, they demonstrated an integrity that allowed us both to compete and to work together. These include the legendary and colorful MPAA head Jack Valenti and RIAA heads Hilary Rosen and Cary Sherman, who battled with us for decades over the legality of video and audio recording. It also includes Eddie Fritz, former Senator Gordon Smith, and David Rehr, all of whom headed the National Association of Broadcasters (NAB), with whom we often disagreed but also collaborated on successful projects like moving the United States to a world-class HDTV system.

They say if you want a friend in Washington, get a dog. But I recognize and honor the public service of all those elected officials—past and present—who have demonstrated leadership and a commitment to catalyzing American innovation. A special shoutout to our CTA Digital Patriots, members of the House Problem Solvers Caucus, and leaders of No Labels, who put their loyalty to the nation over their allegiance to political parties.

Beyond the United States, I see and learn from the leaders of other nations. Prince Constantijn van Oranje and the Netherlands' Ministry of Economic Affairs and Climate Policy have shown how a country can excel by encouraging entrepreneurs. Similarly, France's President Emmanuel Macron, French government officials, and leaders like Business France's Pascal Cagni, Ambassador Valerie Hoffenberg, and innovation expert and advocate Gilbert Réveillon have been instrumental in pushing French innovation forward. I have also been fortunate to work with business and government leaders in countries including Belgium, Israel, Italy, Japan, South Korea, Sweden, Switzerland, and Ukraine as they sought to expand innovation in their own countries.

Sitting on several boards taught me about big pivots, and the institutional leaders and thoughtful boards that are so often behind them. Serving on George Mason University's governing board under former Reagan Attorney General and Chief of Staff Ed Meese, I learned to question assumptions, think big, and use one-on-one talks strategically. The *Wall Street Journal* recognized our board for creating a teaching track to tenure. I still sit on the Focused Ultrasound Foundation board, as it transforms healthcare globally under the leadership of Dr. Neal Kassel, with board members including author John Grisham and investor and healthcare leader Michael Milken. Similarly, I sit on the Advisory Board for the CEO Forum Group, where founder Robert Reiss organizes events that convene both aspiring and established CEOs to share their pivoting successes and lessons learned.

Of course, the most important board to acknowledge and thank is CTA's Executive Board (EB). While many CEOs view their boards as challenges to be managed, the CTA board has served as a true partner in efforts to develop strategy and make big decisions. A particular thank-you to Austere founder and CEO and 2024 EB Chair Deena Ghazarian, an incredible industry advocate; Material Impact founder and Managing Partner and 2023 EB Chair Dr. Carmichael Roberts, whose quiet strength and thoughtful advice helped me become a better CEO; and Voxx International Director, President and CEO, and EB Industry Executive Advisor Pat Lavelle, who provides continuity, advice, and guidance on the biggest and most sensitive issues. And of course, my love, admiration, and gratitude to Voxx founder John Shalam, who has served for decades as a board member and our investment overseer. Other 2020–24 EB members making big and important decisions included: Ty Ahmad-Taylor, Alicia Abella, Melissa Andresko, Stephanie Dismore, Steve Downer, Mike Fasulo, David Hagan, Dr. Ximena Gates Hartsock, Bridget Karlin, Sally Lange, Megan Myungwon Lee, Neal Manowitz, Michael Mansuetti, Dr. James Mault, Debbie Taylor Moore, Michael Moskowitz, Luke Motschenbacher, John

Penney, Daniel Pidgeon, Drew Schiller, Fred Towns, Sonia Wadhawan, Michael Wise, and Gary Yacoubian.

CTA does well because of these amazing volunteers, and the many others who lend their time and expertise through the EB and our other volunteer boards in support of CTA and our mission to enable the technology that's improving lives around the globe. With hundreds of volunteers making up our divisional boards, councils and committees, standards efforts and more, there are too many people to name individually—but please know that I appreciate all you do. You are making the world better by ensuring technology will solve the world's biggest problems!

Of course, CTA would not be the incredible organization it is without our employees. They are creative, hardworking, smart, and passionate about innovation. I am beyond thrilled by Kinsey Fabrizio's success as the organization's new president. She is a fabulous leader with strategic, diplomatic, and communication skills I will never possess. A special thank-you to our retiring COO Glenda MacMullin, who ran huge portions of CTA for over twenty years. Thank you to Senior Vice President of Government and Regulatory Affairs Michael Petricone, who is a passionate advocate in Washington for innovation and startups. My gratitude to Senior Vice President of Political and Industry Affairs Tiffany Moore, who commands bipartisan respect and affection across Capitol Hill and opened my eyes to the value of diversity and inclusion. I also thank Senior Vice President of Research and Standards Brian Markwalter, whose equanimity, technical knowledge, and sense of right and wrong always help us make better decisions.

This book would not have happened without the contributions of many others. Director of Executive Communications Carolyn Posner expertly, patiently, deftly and diplomatically sifted through my writing to develop, edit, and fill in the gaps of early drafts. Carolyn and her supervisor, Vice President of Marketing and Communications Melissa Harrison, were my cheerleaders and task managers driving the project from beginning to end. Similarly, a special debt of gratitude to Vice President of CTA Marketing Michael Brown, who has been a constant guide throughout the process of both this and prior books, helping to navigate marketing, design, layout, and other requirements. My thanks to Senior Director of Innovation and Trends Brian Comiskey, the brains behind the chapter on technology trends. My enduring appreciation to Research Library Senior Manager Angela Titone and the library team for their support as fact checkers and reviewers. And of course, a huge thanks to the people who run my office: Director of Executive Office Kailey Adametz knows how I think, handles situations with wisdom and grace, is impeccably organized, and freed up my time to work on this book. She is backed up by Senior Coordinator Janine Rook, who ensures my schedule works and often knows better than I do where I am going next.

A special gratitude to the team at Pinkston, including David Fouse, Victoria Kelly, Nicole Tidei, and Melanie Wilcox, who not only helped to draft and edit the manuscript, but created the framework for marketing and promotion to help ensure that people actually read it.

It also takes a great publisher. HarperCollins and editor Nick Amphlett have been fantastic every step of the way. They are trustworthy, competent, fair, and willing to listen to our ideas. Thank you.

Finally, I wanted to note special friends who have made a difference in this process. Debbie Taylor Moore is not only an incredible quantum and cybersecurity expert, she is passionate about pivoting and has repeatedly stressed how important it is to share my views in a book. Kimberly Hardcastle Geddes is a great entrepreneur and business whiz, as well as a wonderful friend who is always sharing ideas and insights. David Leibowitz is an entrepreneurial strategist who always sees possibilities in the intersection of content and technology. Ted and Dr. Vilma Edgington are bright professionals and friends whose Friday night reprieves always encourage

Notes

CHAPTER 1: What Is Pivoting? The CES Story

1. Lippincott, Joaquin. "A Review of CES 2021." LinkedIn, 20 January 2021, https://www.linkedin.com/pulse/review-ces-2021-joaquin-lippincott/.

2. Best of CES 2021: Pandemic tech, green tech, air taxis and lots of robots." CNET.com, 15 Jan 2021, https://www.cnet.com/tech/computing/best-of-ces -2021-pandemic-tech-green-tech-air-taxis-and-lots-of-robots/.

3. Santoro, Phil. "Why Startups Fail | Lessons From 150 Founders." Wilbur Labs, 8 Nov 2023, https://www.wilburlabs.com/blueprints/why-startups-fail.

4. Wilding, Melody. "How to Stop Overthinking and Start Trusting Your Gut." *Harvard Business Review*, 10 March 2022, https://hbr.org/2022/03/how-to -stop-overthinking-and-start-trusting-your-gut.

5. Meyers, Josh. "New report finds almost 80% of active fund managers are falling behind the major indexes." CNBC.com, 27 March 2022, https://www.cnbc .com/2022/03/27/new-report-finds-almost-80percent-of-active-fund-managers -are-falling-behind.html.

6. "New Research: Immigrants Have Started More Than Half of America's Billion-Dollar Startup Companies." National Foundation for American Policy, 26 July 2022, https://nfap.com/wp-content/uploads/2022/07/Immigrant -Entrepreneurs-and-Billion-Dollar-Companies.DAY-OF-RELEASE.2022.pdf.

CHAPTER 2: Pivotal Shifts in the Tech Industry

1. Andreessen, Marc. "Why AI Won't Cause Unemployment." Substack, 4 March 2023, https://pmarca.substack.com/p/why-ai-wont-cause-unemployment?utm _source=substack&utm_medium=email.

2. Shiffman, Gary. "An Economist's View on Technology in the Future of BSA/ AML." Congressional testimony, 13 March 2019, https://www.congress .gov/116/meeting/house/109110/witnesses/HHRG-116-BA10-Wstate -ShiffmanG-20190313.pdf.

3. Kelly, Kevin. "We Are the Web." *Wired*, 5 August 2005, https://www.wired.com/2005/08/tech/.

4. Hesterberg, Karla. "A Brief History of Online Advertising." HubSpot, 29 November 2021, https://blog.hubspot.com/marketing/history-of-online-advertising.

5. Ries, Eric. *The Lean Startup: How Today's Entrepreneurs Use Continuous Innovation to Create Radically Successful Businesses*. New York: Crown Business, 2011.

6. "IMVU Is the World's Biggest Web3 Social Metaverse." Immutable.com, 21 July 2023, https://www.immutable.com/blog/immutable-games-spotlight-imvu-is-the-worlds-biggest-web3-social-metaverse.

7. Ries, Eric. "Pivot, don't jump to a new vision." Startup Lessons Learned, 22 June 2009, https://www.startuplessonslearned.com/2009/06/pivot-dont-jump-to-new-vision.html.

8. Ries, E. (2011). *The Lean Startup: How Today's Entrepreneurs Use Continuous Innovation to Create Radically Successful Businesses* [Kindle Android version].

9. Haque, Umair. "Fail Bigger Cheaper: A Three Word Manifesto." *Harvard Business Review*, 21 March 2011, https://hbr.org/2011/03/fail-bigger-cheaper-a-three-wo.

10. "A Brief History of Failure." *New York Times Magazine*, 12 November 2014, https://www.nytimes.com/interactive/2014/11/12/magazine/16innovationsfailures.html.

11. McCluskey, Mitchell, et al. "Ukrainians were 'ready to eliminate' Russian soldier before dramatic surrender, commander says." CNN.com, 15 June 2023, https://www.cnn.com/2023/06/15/europe/russian-soldier-surrenders-drone-bakhmut-ukraine-intl-hnk/index.html.

12. American Express. "American Express Digital Transformation Strategies Report." 21 November 2023.

13. Elmer-Dewitt, Philip. "Hazards Aloft." *Time*, 22 February 1993, https://content.time.com/time/subscriber/article/0,33009,977781,00.html.

14. Bilton, Nick. "It's Called 'Airplane Mode' for a Reason." *New York Times*, 28 November 2011, https://archive.nytimes.com/bits.blogs.nytimes.com/2011/11/28/its-called-airplane-mode-for-a-reason/.

15. Don Phillips, "Coffee or Tea or . . . Hey, Turn Off That Computer!" *Washington Post*, 20 June 1993, https://www.washingtonpost.com/archive/business/1993/06/20/coffee-tea-or-hey-turn-off-that-computer-airlines-authorities-wonder-whether-electronic-devices-are-safety-threat/fc1cfd02-e24b-47a7-a94f-fd8e406dc95a/.

16. Cushman, John H., Jr. "TRAVEL ADVISORY; Electronics Use Aboard Planes Debated in U.S." *New York Times*, 11 April 1993, https://www.nytimes.com/1993/04/11/travel/travel-advisory-electronics-use-aboard-planes-debated-in-us.html.

17. Olivetti, John. "Glitch's creator on the game's failure: 'Too foreign of a concept.'" Engadget, 30 November 2012, https://www.engadget.com/2012-11-30-glitchs-creator-on-the-games-failure-too-foreign-of-a-concep.html.

18. Lewis, Jared. "What Is the Average Profit Margin on Televisions?" Smallbusiness.com, accessed 15 February 2024, https://smallbusiness.chron.com/average-profit-margin-televisions-34457.html.

19. "New Law Will Expand TV Captions for the Deaf." *New York Times*, 16 October 1990, https://www.nytimes.com/1990/10/16/us/new-law-will-expand-tv-captions-for-the-deaf.html.

20. Markey, Edward. "Hearing on Innovation and Inclusion: The Americans with Disabilities Act at 20." Congressional remarks, 26 May 2010, https://www.commerce.senate.gov/services/files/B56C1D9F-B217-4E20-BDD4-8B1E8B2E21C7.

21. Mykhalevych, Nadia. "Survey: Why America is obsessed with subtitles." Preply.com, 13 October 2023, https://preply.com/en/blog/americas-subtitles-use/.

22. Shapiro, Gary. "Dems want to redesign your iPhone." *Washington Times*, 9 June 2010, https://www.washingtontimes.com/news/2010/jun/9/dems-want-to-redesign-your-iphone/.

CHAPTER 3: The Startup Pivot

1. Ransom, Diana. "The SBA After PPP: Inside Isabella Casillas Guzman's plan to remake the Small Business Administration, to better serve all entrepreneurs." *Inc.*, April 2023, https://www.inc.com/magazine/202304/diana-ransom/the-sba-after-ppp.html.

2. Graham, Jefferson. "How Ring's Founder Created a Doorbell Worth $1 Billion to Amazon." *Investor's Business Daily*, 11 October 2021, https://www.investors.com/news/management/leaders-and-success/jamie-siminoff-created-a-doorbell-worth-1-billion-to-amazon.

3. Adams, Susan. "The Exclusive Inside Story of Ring: From 'Shark Tank' Reject to Amazon's Latest Acquisition." *Forbes*, 27 February 2018, https://www.forbes.com/sites/susanadams/2018/02/27/amazon-is-buying-ring-the-pioneer-of-the-video-doorbell-for-1-billion/?sh=68a78240706c.

4. Zetlin, Minda. "5 Years Ago, He Was Rejected on 'Shark Tank.' Now He's Back as a Shark. Here's the Advice He'd Give His Younger Self." *Inc.*, 11 October 2018, https://www.inc.com/minda-zetlin/shark-tank-2018-premier-jamie-siminoff-ring-rejected-returns-as-shark.html.

5. Fisk, Peter. "The $3 trillion global start-up economy . . . where and how start-up ecosystems are driving new growth." Peterfisk.com, 18 October 2019, https://www.peterfisk.com/2019/10/the-3billion-global-start-up-economy-where-and-how-start-up-ecosystems-are-driving-new-growth/.

6. Chapman, Lizette. "Startups Raked in $621 Billion in 2021, Shattering Funding Records." Bloomberg.com, 12 January 2022, https://www.bloomberg.com/news/articles/2022-01-12/startups-raked-in-621-billion-in-2021-shattering-funding-records?.

7. "Frequently Asked Questions About Small Business." US Small Business Administration, March 2023, https://advocacy.sba.gov/wp-content/uploads/2023/03/Frequently-Asked-Questions-About-Small-Business-March-2023-508c.pdf.

8. Blankenship, Mary, et al. "How Technology-Based Start-Ups Support U.S. Economic Growth." Data Hub at Brookings Mountain West & Lincy Institute, 27 January 2020, https://digitalscholarship.unlv.edu/cgi/viewcontent.cgi?article=1011&context=bmw_lincy_econdev.

9. Akcigit, Ufuk, and William R. Kerr. "Growth Through Heterogeneous Innovations." National Bureau of Economic Research, 2018, https://www.nber.org/papers/w16443.

10. U.S. Small Business Administration. "Mentoring: the missing link to small business growth and survival." 4 February 2019, https://www.sba.gov/blog/mentoring-missing-link-small-business-growth-survival.

11. "The Complete List of Unicorn Companies." CB Insights, January 2024, https://www.cbinsights.com/research-unicorn-companies.

12. "Unicorn Companies Tracker." Pitchbook, February 2024, https://pitchbook.com/news/articles/unicorn-startups-list-trends.

13. Shoot, Brittany. "It's Like 23andMe . . . for Your Cat. A Look at CES's Strangest New Product." *Fortune*, 8 January 2019, https://fortune.com/2019/01/08/ces-2019-cat-dna-test-basepaws/.

14. "The State of Small Business Now." US Chamber of Commerce, 10 April 2023, https://www.uschamber.com/small-business/state-of-small-business-now.

CHAPTER 4: The Forced Pivot

1. Seftel, Joshua, dir. *The Steepest Climb: How Delta Air Lines Navigated the Global Pandemic.* Brooklyn, NY: Delta and SmartyPants Picture, 2023, https://steepestclimb.delta.com.

2. Miller, Ryan. "Small Businesses with Big Ambition: DroneUp." CoVaBIZ, 10 July 2018, https://covabizmag.com/small-businesses-with-big-ambition-droneup/.

3. El Koubi, Jason. "An Inside Look at Drone Innovation: A Conversation with Tom Walker." *Virginia Economic Review*, Fourth Quarter 2022, https://www.vedp.org/news/inside-look-drone-innovation-conversation-tom-walker.

4. Bursztynsky, Jessica. "DroneUp has partnered with Walmart to make home deliveries even faster." Fast Company, 19 November 2022, https://www.fastcompany.com/90810793/droneup-has-partnered-with-walmart-to-make-home-deliveries-even-faster.

5. Gaskell, Adi. "Are People Keen to Get Back to Their Commute?" 11 April 2020, *Forbes*, https://www.forbes.com/sites/adigaskell/2020/08/11/are-people-keen-to-get-back-to-their-commute/?sh=6d8139cb1786.

6. Del Rey, Jason. "The death of the department store and the American middle class." *Vox*, 30 November 2020, https://www.vox.com/recode/21717536/department-store-middle-class-amazon-online-shopping-covid-19.

7. Guillen, Mauro F. "How Businesses Have Successfully Pivoted During the Pandemic." *Harvard Business Review*, July 2020, https://hbr.org/2020/07/how-businesses-have-successfully-pivoted-during-the-pandemic.

8. From a keynote conversation at CES 2021, featuring BestBuy CEO Corie Barry and (then) Fortune CEO Alan Murray. No direct link available.

9. A Discussion with Corie Barry, CEO, Best Buy. Northern Virginia Technology Council. 29 July, 2020, https://www.youtube.com/watch?v=qt7HDNkBxMA.

10. Carson, Biz. "Uber's Secret Gold Mine: How Uber Eats Is Turning into a Billion-Dollar Business to Rival Grubhub." *Forbes*, 6 February 2019, https://www.forbes.com/sites/bizcarson/2019/02/06/ubers-secret-gold-mine-how-uber-eats-is-turning-into-a-billion-dollar-business-to-rival-grubhub/?sh=525451411fa9.

11. Richter, Felix. "Uber's Pandemic Pivot." Statista, 17 February 2022, https://www.statista.com/chart/21651/uber-gross-booking/.

12. Hale, Conor. "Tracking not just data, but individual symptoms, like vomiting: BioIntelliSense exits stealth with FDA-cleared wearable." Fierce Biotech, 28 January 2020, https://www.fiercebiotech.com/medtech/biointellisense-exits-stealth-fda-cleared-wearable-tracks-individual-symptomatic-episodes.

13. Siddiqui, Faiz. "Coronavirus is forcing Uber to return to its start-up roots." *Washington Post*, 26 May 2020, https://www.washingtonpost.com/technology/2020/05/26/uber-coronavirus-pivot/.

14. Turi, Janice Bitters. "Pandemic Pivot: These 3 Health Tech Startups Are Case Studies." Crunchbase, 13 October 2021, https://news.crunchbase.com/startups/pandemic-pivot-health-tech-startups-case-studies/.

15. Bernstein, Lenny, and Meryl Kornfield. "To curb drug deaths, communities turn to Reddit, texts and wastewater." *Washington Post*, 5 February 2023, https://www.washingtonpost.com/health/2023/02/05/drug-deaths-prevention/.

16. Pifer, Rebecca. "Digital health funding reaches record $29.1B in 2021." Healthcare Dive, 11 January 2022, https://www.healthcaredive.com/news/digital-health-funding-record-291b-2021-rock-health-bubble-2022/616980/.

17. Speakes, Larry M. "Statement by Deputy Press Secretary Speakes on the Soviet Attack on a Korean Civilian Airliner." Ronald Reagan Library, 16 September 1983, https://www.reaganlibrary.gov/archives/speech/statement-deputy-press-secretary-speakes-soviet-attack-korean-civilian-airliner-1.

18. Goode, Lauren. "Ukraine's Startups Kept Innovating Through 1 Year of War." *Wired*, 25 February 2023, https://www.wired.com/story/ukraines-startups-kept-innovating-through-1-year-of-war/.

19. Sato, Mia. "Working Through It." The Verge, 13 January 2023, https://www.theverge.com/c/23546117/ukraine-tech-workers-russia-war.

20. Anant, Venky, et al. "The consumer-data opportunity and the privacy imperative." McKinsey, 27 April 2020, https://www.mckinsey.com/capabilities/risk-and-resilience/our-insights/the-consumer-data-opportunity-and-the-privacy-imperative.

21. Hughes, Michael D., and Emilia Hull. "Want business growth tomorrow? Act on climate today." Accenture, 2023, https://www.accenture.com/us-en/insights/sustainability/ungc.

22. "The State of Fashion." McKinsey, 2020, https://www.mckinsey.com/industries/retail/our-insights/state-of-fashion-archive#section-header-2020.

23. The Economist Intelligence Unit. "An eco-wakening: Measuring awareness, engagement, and action for nature." World Wildlife Fund, 17 May 2021, https://

www.worldwildlife.org/publications/an-eco-wakening-measuring-awareness
-engagement-and-action-for-nature.

24. "Consumer passion for the environment grows as a result of the pandemic."
Mastercard, 12 April 2021, https://www.mastercard.com/news/insights/2021
/consumer-attitudes-environment/.

25. "Unilever reveals influencers can switch people on to sustainable living." Uni-
lever.com. 9 March 2023, https://www.unilever.com/news/press-and-media
/press-releases/2023/unilever-reveals-influencers-can-switch-people-on-to
-sustainable-living/.

26. "Industry Initiative Saves Consumers $2.5 Billion in Annual Energy Costs."
Consumer Technology Association, 12 April 2021, https://www.cta.tech
/Resources/Newsroom/Media-Releases/2022/October/Industry-Initiative
-Saves-Consumers-Energy-Costs.

27. "CTA U.S. Adult Emergency Alert Survey 2023." Consumer Technology
Association, 2023, https://cdn.cta.tech/cta/media/media/pdfs/cta-u-s-adult
-emergency-alert-survey-2023.pdf?_ga=2.16593910.1392573447.1697740373
-1137150322.1665511700.

CHAPTER 5: The Failure Pivot

1. Whitaker, Sterling. "Remember When Elvis Presley Bombed in Las Vegas?"
Taste of Country, 23 April 2022, https://tasteofcountry.com/elvis-presley
-bombed-las-vegas/.

2. Thompson, Gayle. "67 Years Ago: Elvis Presley Bombs in Las Vegas Debut." The
Boot, 23 April 2023, https://theboot.com/elvis-presley-las-vegas-debut/.

3. Simmonds, Ross. "Don't Stop Believin: A Look at the Founder Failures That
Came Before Unicorn Status." Medium, 6 April 2016, https://medium.com
/@thecoolestcool/don-t-stop-believin-a-look-at-the-founder-failures-that-came
-before-unicorn-status-6498ce4ef374.

4. "Las Vegas ranks first as 'most popular city to visit in America,' study finds."
KTNV.com, 3 May 2023, https://www.ktnv.com/news/las-vegas-searched-by
-americans-1-9-million-times-annually-for-vacation-study-shows.

5. Hupfer, Suzanne, et al. "Women in the tech industry: Gaining ground, but
facing new headwinds." Deloitte, 1 December 2021, https://www2.deloitte
.com/us/en/insights/industry/technology/technology-media-and-telecom
-predictions/2022/statistics-show-women-in-technology-are-facing-new
-headwinds.html.

6. Bajwa, Rumzz. "5 Reasons Why Women Are Better and More Successful Entrepreneurs Than Men." Addicted2Success, 14 September 2020, https:// addicted2success.com/entrepreneur-profile/5-reasons-why-women-are-better -more-successful-entrepreneurs-than-men/.

7. Abouzahr, Katie, et al. "Why Women-Owned Startups Are a Better Bet." BCG, 6 June 2018, https://www.bcg.com/publications/2018/why-women-owned -startups-are-better-bet.

8. "Diversity and Inclusion: Driving Sustainable Change in the Workplace." Consumer Technology Association, 21 September 2021, https://shop.cta.tech /collections/research/products/diversity-and-inclusion-driving-sustainable -change-in-the-workplace.

9. Hupfer, Suzanne, et al. "Women in tech are cracking the industry's glass ceiling, achieving double-digit gains in leadership roles." Deloitte, 21 April 2022, https:// www2.deloitte.com/us/en/insights/industry/technology/women-tech-leadership .html.

10. Foster, Tom. "The Untold Story of How Massive Success Made GoPro's CEO Lose His Way. Can He Recover?" *Inc.* Winter 2017/2018 edition, https://www .inc.com/magazine/201802/tom-foster/gopro-camera-drone-challenges.html.

11. Cheshire, Tom. "How Rovio made Angry Birds a winner (and what's next)." Wired, 3 July 2011, https://www.wired.co.uk/article/how-rovio-made-angry -birds-a-winner.

12. Liu, Christina, and Yanting Li. "Rovio and Angry Birds." UCLA, 2011, http:// www.econ.ucla.edu/sboard/teaching/tech/Rovio.pdf.

13. Batchelor, James. "How Angry Birds broke the limits for mobile games." GamesIndustry.biz, 11 December 2019, https://www.gamesindustry.biz/how -angry-birds-broke-the-limits-for-mobile-games.

CHAPTER 6: The Success Pivot

1. Colvin, Geoff. "How Amazon grew an awkward side project into AWS, a behe-moth that's now 4 times bigger than its original shopping business." Fortune, 30 November 2022, https://fortune.com/longform/amazon-web-services-ceo -adam-selipsky-cloud-computing/.

2. *Ibid.*

3. "How It Started." Sonos.com, accessed 25 February 2024, https://www.sonos .com/en-us/how-it-started.

4. May, Steve. "20 years on: How Sonos invented the future of wireless audio." Tech Radar, 25 October 2022, https://www.techradar.com/news/20-years-on-how-sonos-invented-the-future-of-wireless-audio.

5. Dredge, Stuart. "Music listening in 2019: 10 takeaways from the IFPI's new report." Musically, 24 September 2019, https://musically.com/2019/09/24/music-listening-2019-ifpi-report/.

6. Masters of Leadership: A Discussion with Michael Chasen, CEO, Class Technologies. Northern Virginia Technology Council. 11 March, 2021, https://www.youtube.com/watch?v=GEQqvcGx8KU.

7. Berger, Rod. "Blackboard's Founder Breaking New Ground with Class Technologies." *Forbes*, 17 June 2022, https://www.forbes.com/sites/rodberger/2022/06/17/blackboards-founder-breaking-new-ground-with-class-technologies/.

8. Chuang, Tamara. "The future of cable TV, an industry once driven by Colorado, may be in its past." *Colorado Sun*, 23 December 2019, https://coloradosun.com/2019/12/23/cable-tv-future-colorado-history/.

9. Famojure, Erica. "HubSpot Releases the State of Partner Ops and Programs Report, Detailing the Business Impact of Partner Ecosystems." HubSpot, 8 November 2022, https://www.hubspot.com/company-news/the-state-of-partner-ops-and-programs-report-2022.

10. Reinhard, Beth, et al. "NRA money flowed to board members amid allegedly lavish spending by top officials and vendors." *Washington Post*, 9 June 2019, https://www.washingtonpost.com/investigations/nra-money-flowed-to-board-members-amid-allegedly-lavish-spending-by-top-officials-and-vendors/2019/06/09/3eafe160-8186-11e9-9a67-a687ca99fb3d_story.html.

11. Mullins, Brody. "Chamber CEO's Rare Washington Perk: Private Jet Service, Even for Vacations." *Wall Street Journal*, 6 June 2019, https://www.wsj.com/articles/chamber-ceos-rare-washington-perk-private-jet-service-even-for-vacations-11559825503.

12. "Energy Star Impacts." Energy Star, 2022, https://www.energystar.gov/about/impacts.

CHAPTER 7: The Emerging Technologies Reshaping Our World

1. Andreessen, Marc. "Why Software Is Eating the World." Andreessen Horowitz blog post, https://a16z.com/why-software-is-eating-the-world/.

2. "Gartner Forecasts Worldwide Public Cloud End-User Spending to Reach Nearly $600 Billion in 2023." Gartner, 31 October 2022, https://www.gartner

.com/en/newsroom/press-releases/2022-10-31-gartner-forecasts-worldwide
-public-cloud-end-user-spending-to-reach-nearly-600-billion-in-2023.

3. Morgan, Steve. "The World Will Store 200 Zettabytes of Data by 2025." Cyber-
    crime Magazine, 1 February 2023, https://cybersecurityventures.com/the
    -world-will-store-200-zettabytes-of-data-by-2025/.

4. Roth, Bill. "Using Cloud Economics to Model the Value of Multi-Cloud."
    Forbes, 21 January 2022, https://www.forbes.com/sites/vmware/2022/01/21
    /using-cloud-economics-to-model-the-value-of-multi-cloud/?sh=3459116c2875.

5. Pratt, Mary K. "Cloud computing's real-world environmental impact." Tech-
    Target, 7 June 2023, https://www.techtarget.com/sustainability/feature/Cloud
    -computings-real-world-environmental-impact.

6. Sinha, Satyajit. "IoT connections market update." IoT Analytics, May 2023,
    https://iot-analytics.com/number-connected-iot-devices/.

7. "Key Takeaways from S&P Global Market Intelligence Discovery Report: The
    Impact of Continuous Security Validation." SafeBreach, 13 April 2023, https://
    www.safebreach.com/blog/key-takeaways-from-sp-global-market-intelligence
    -discovery-report-the-impact-of-continuous-security-validation/.

8. "2023 Official Cybercrime Report." eSentire, 2023, https://www.esentire.com
    /resources/library/2023-official-cybercrime-report.

9. McCurdy, Chris, et al. "Prosper in the cyber economy." IBM, 2023, https://
    www.ibm.com/thought-leadership/institute-business-value/en-us/report
    /security-cyber-economy.

10. "The state of generative AI in 7 charts." CB Insights, 2 August 2023, https://
    www.cbinsights.com/research/generative-ai-funding-top-startups-investors/.

11. "Worldwide Spending on AI-Centric Systems Forecast to Reach $154 Billion in
    2023, According to IDC." IDC, 7 March 2023, https://www.idc.com/getdoc
    .jsp?containerId=prUS50454123.

12. Spiegel, Jeff. "Investing in robotics: Why now could be the right time." Black-
    rock, 25 January 2023, https://www.blackrock.com/americas-offshore/en
    /insights/investing-in-robotics.

13. "China overtakes USA in robot density." International Federation of Robotics,
    5 December 2022, https://ifr.org/ifr-press-releases/news/china-overtakes-usa
    -in-robot-density:~:text=%E2%80%9CThe%20speed%20of%20robotics%20
    adoption,measured%20only%20six%20years%20ago.%E2%80%9D

14. Ajewole, Femi, et al. "Unlocking the industrial potential of robotics and automation." McKinsey, 6 January 2023, https://www.mckinsey.com/industries/industrials-and-electronics/our-insights/unlocking-the-industrial-potential-of-robotics-and-automation#/.

15. Hair, Corbin. "Global emissions targets spell growth for CO2 tech sector." E&E News by Politico, 20 September 2022, https://www.eenews.net/articles/global-emissions-targets-spell-growth-for-co2-tech-sector/.

16. "Green Buildings." World Bank Group, 2019, https://documents1.worldbank.org/curated/en/586841576523330833/pdf/Green-Buildings-A-Finance-and-Policy-Blueprint-for-Emerging-Markets.pdf.

17. "Natural disasters caused $313 bln economic loss in 2022—Aon." Reuters, 2 January 2023, https://www.reuters.com/business/environment/natural-disasters-caused-313-bln-economic-loss-2022-aon-2023-01-25/.

18. "Foodtech." Dealroom.co, accessed 15 February 2024, https://dealroom.co/guides/foodtech.

19. "Digital Health Market Size." *Fortune Business Insights*, October 2023, https://www.fortunebusinessinsights.com/industry-reports/digital-health-market-100227.

20. Boersma, Peter, et al. "Prevalence of Multiple Chronic Conditions Among US Adults." CDC, 2018, https://www.cdc.gov/pcd/issues/2020/20_0130.htm.

21. "Chronic diseases taking 'immense and increasing toll on lives,' warns WHO." United Nations, 19 May 2023, https://news.un.org/en/story/2023/05/1136832.

CHAPTER 8: How the US Must Pivot

1. Zitner, Aaron. "America Pulls Back from Values That Once Defined It, WSJ-NORC Poll Finds." *Wall Street Journal*, 27 March 2023, https://www.wsj.com/articles/americans-pull-back-from-values-that-once-defined-u-s-wsj-norc-poll-finds-df8534cd.

2. Gaida, Jamie, et al. "ASPI's Critical Technology Tracker." ASPI, March 2023, https://ad-aspi.s3.ap-southeast-2.amazonaws.com/2023-03/ASPIs%20Critical%20Technology%20Tracker_0.pdf?VersionId=ndm5v4DRMfpLvu.x69Bi_VUdMVLp07jw.

3. Nietzel, Michael T. "U.S. Universities Fall Further Behind China in Production of STEM PhDs." *Forbes*, 7 August 2021, https://www.forbes.com/sites/michaeltnietzel/2021/08/07/us-universities-fall-behind-china-in-production-of-stem-phds/?sh=6eb0ff234606.

4. Marcus, Jon. "Americans have poor math skills. It's a threat to US standing in the global economy, employers says." Associated Press, 27 September 2023, https://apnews.com/article/math-scores-china-security-b60b740c480270d552d750c15ed287b6.

5. Han, Zoe. "China outnumbers the U.S. for the first time in this ranking of the world's 'best' universities." MarketWatch, 31 October 2022, https://www.marketwatch.com/story/for-the-first-time-china-outnumbers-the-u-s-on-this-ranking-of-the-worlds-best-universities-11666729011.

6. Zakrzewski, Cat. "Sinking FTC workplace rankings threaten Chair Lina Khan's agenda." *Washington Post* 13 July 2022, https://www.washingtonpost.com/technology/2022/07/13/ftc-lina-khan-rankings/.

7. Ponciano, Jonathan. "The World's Largest Technology Companies in 2023: A New Leader Emerges." *Forbes*, 8 June 2023, https://www.forbes.com/sites/jonathanponciano/2023/06/08/the-worlds-largest-technology-companies-in-2023-a-new-leader-emerges/?sh=4721b5995d1d.

8. Garver, Rob. "US National Debt Tops $30 Trillion for First Time in History." Voice of America, 3 February 2022, https://www.voanews.com/a/us-national-debt-tops-30-trillion-for-first-time-in-history-/6424498.html.

9. "Amazon CEO Andy Jassy Speaks with CNBC's Andrew Ross Sorkin on 'Squawk Box' Today." CNBC, 11 April 2024, https://www.cnbc.com/2024/04/11/cnbc-exclusive-cnbc-transcript-amazon-ceo-andy-jassy-speaks-with-cnbcs-andrew-ross-sorkin-on-squawk-box-today.html.

10. Anderson, Stuart. "Immigrant Entrepreneurs and U.S. Billion-Dollar Companies." National Foundation for American Policy, July 2022, https://nfap.com/research/new-nfap-policy-brief-immigrant-entrepreneurs-and-u-s-billion-dollar-companies/.

11. Anderson, Stuart. "AI and Immigrants." National Foundation for American Policy, June 2023, https://nfap.com/studies/ai-and-immigrants/.

12. Vogels, Emily A. "Digital divide persists even as Americans with lower incomes make gains in tech adoption." Pew Research, 22 June 2022, https://www.pewresearch.org/short-reads/2021/06/22/digital-divide-persists-even-as-americans-with-lower-incomes-make-gains-in-tech-adoption/.

13. Allen, Mike. "Record number of Americans say they're politically independent." *Axios*, 17 April 2023, https://www.axios.com/2023/04/17/poll-americans -independent-republican-democrat.

14. Basuroy, Tanushree. "Number of internet users in India 2010–2050." *Statista*, 18 July 2024, https://www.statista.com/statistics/255146/number-of-internet -users-in-india/.

15. "North Koreans are at growing risk of starvation." *The Economist*, 21 March 2023, https://www.economist.com/asia/2023/03/21/north-koreans-are-at -growing-risk-of-starvation.

CHAPTER 9: The Personal Pivot

1. Bastian, Ed. "A note from Ed: Thank you for your feedback on the SkyMiles Program." Delta News Hub, 18 October 2023, https://news.delta.com/note-ed -thank-you-your-feedback-skymiles-program.

2. Genovese, Daniella. "Delta CEO says airline will modify SkyMiles changes: 'Probably went too far.'" Fox5 Atlanta, 29 September 2023, https://www .fox5atlanta.com/news/delta-ceo-says-airline-will-modify-skymiles-changes -probably-went-too-far.

3. Dhingra, Naina, et al. "Help your employees find purpose—or watch them leave." McKinsey, 5 April 2021, https://www.mckinsey.com/capabilities /people-and-organizational-performance/our-insights/help-your-employees -find-purpose-or-watch-them-leave.

4. Achor, Shawn, et al. "9 Out of 10 People Are Willing to Earn Less Money to Do More-Meaningful Work." *Harvard Business Review*, 6 November 2018, https://hbr.org/2018/11/9-out-of-10-people-are-willing-to-earn-less-money-to -do-more-meaningful-work.

5. Liveris, Andrew. *Leading through Disruption: A Changemaker's Guide to Twenty-First Century Leadership*. HarperCollins Leadership. 2023.

6. Gordon, Nicholas and Murray, Alan. "CEO lessons from the Jack Welches of the world are 'mostly obsolete' now, ex-Dow Chemical chief executive says." *Fortune*. 31 July 2023, https://fortune.com/2023/07/31/dow-chemical-ceo -andrew-liveris-book-jack-welch-lessons/.

7. Greenfield, Rebecca. "A Brief History of CES Booth Babes." *The Atlantic*, 7 January 2013, https://www.theatlantic.com/technology/archive/2013/01/ces -booth-babes-history/319817/.

8. "Global Diversity and Inclusion (D&I) Industry." Global Industry Analysts, February 2024, https://www.reportlinker.com/p06219616/Global-Diversity -and-Inclusion-D-I-Industry.html?utm_source=GNW.

9. Corley, Todd, et al. "What Has (and Hasn't) Changed About Being a Chief Diversity Officer." *Harvard Business Review*, 23 September 2022, https://hbr .org/2022/09/what-has-and-hasnt-changed-about-being-a-chief-diversity -officer.

10. Telford, Taylor. "Critics of corporate diversity efforts emerge, even as initia-tives falter." *Washington Post*, 1 April 2023, https://www.washingtonpost.com /business/2023/04/01/woke-capitalism-esg-dei-climate-investment/.

11. Singal, Jesse. "What If Diversity Training Is Doing More Harm Than Good?" *New York Times*, 17 January 2023, https://www.nytimes.com/2023/01/17 /opinion/dei-trainings-effective.html.

12. Dixon-Fyle, Sundiatu, et al. "Diversity wins: How inclusion matters." McKinsey, 19 May 2020, https://www.mckinsey.com/featured-insights/diversity-and -inclusion/diversity-wins-how-inclusion-matters.

13. Gale, Casey. "The Power of Asking Questions." PCMA Convene. 28 June 2023, https://www.pcma.org/power-asking-questions-career-strategy/.

CONCLUSION: Where Do We Go from Here?

1. "How Americans See Problems of Trust." Pew Research, 22 July 2022, https:// www.pewresearch.org/politics/2019/07/22/how-americans-see-problems-of -trust/.

2. "Sundar Pichai: 'Reward Effort, Not Outcomes.'" Stanford Graduate School of Business View from the Top speaker series. Season 5, Episode 8. 17 June, 2021. https://www.gsb.stanford.edu/insights/sundar-pichai-reward-effort-not-outcomes.

3. NAM News Room. "2.1 Million Manufacturing Jobs Could Go Unfilled by 2030." National Association of Manufacturers, 4 May 2021, https://nam.org /2-1-million-manufacturing-jobs-could-go-unfilled-by-2030-13743/.

4. "Registered Apprenticeship National Results Fiscal Year 2021." U.S. Department of Labor, https://www.dol.gov/agencies/eta/apprenticeship/about/statistics/2021.

5. Fuller, Joseph B., and Manjari Raman. "Dismissed by Degrees." Harvard Busi-ness School, 13 December 2017, https://www.hbs.edu/managing-the-future-of -work/Documents/dismissed-by-degrees.pdf.

6. Fuller, Joseph B., and Manjari Raman. "Dismissed by Degrees."

7. "Second & Third Quarters 2022 Report." Washington State Apprenticeship & Training Council, 20 October 2022, https://lni.wa.gov/licensing-permits/apprenticeship/agenda-docs/JulyOctober2022QuarterlyReport.pdf.

8. Carlton, Genevieve. "Why the Tech Diversity Gap Continues to Persist." Bestcolleges.com, 18 April 2023, https://www.bestcolleges.com/bootcamps/guides/tech-diversity-gap-persists/.

9. Staglin, Garin. "The Future of Work Depends on Supporting Gen Z." *Forbes*, 22 July 2022, https://www.forbes.com/sites/onemind/2022/07/22/the-future-of-work-depends-on-supporting-gen-z/?sh=39a5ad30447a.

Index

commercialization of the internet, 30–32

commitment, 56

Committee for a Responsible Federal Budget, 160

Communications Decency Act of 1966, Section 230, 158–59

Compaq, 121–22

Comprehensive and Progressive Agreement for Trans-Pacific Partnership (CPTPP), 169–70

conscious (and ethical) decisions, 197–200

Constantijn of the Netherlands, 172–73

Consumer Electronics Show. *See* CES

Consumer Technology Association. *See* CTA

Consumer Technology Association Foundation, 40

continuous glucose monitoring (CGM), 141–42

cooperation, 117–21, 125

coopetition, 121–25

Co-opetition (Brandenburger and Nalebuff), 121

copyright, 98, 179

"cost threshold," 160

COVID-19 masks, 13

COVID-19 pandemic, ix–x, 1–3, 5

    Best Buy and curbside pickup, 64–66

    CES pivot, 9–16

    digital health, 142

federal spending, 159

food delivery services, 66–67

Forced Pivots during, 21, 59–71

    as pivot point, 127–28

    remote access to healthcare, 166–67

    Walker and DroneUp, 61–63

COVID-19 tests, 15, 69

COVID-19 vaccines, 2, 10, 60, 123

creativity, 22

cross-licensing, 118

CrowdStrike, 131

Crunchbase News, 68

Crutchfield, Bill, 104

CTA (Consumer Technology Association), 2, 3, 8–9. *See also* CES

    closed captioning, 41–43

    coopetition, 122

    diversity, 193–94, 209–11

    energy efficiency, 82

    Innovation House, 22

    Innovation Scorecard, 57

    step trackers and privacy, 78–80

    tech mandates, 44–45

    US Cyber Trust Mark, 126, 131–32

    women in tech, 91–92

Cuban, Mark, 47–48

Cuccinelli, Ken, 190

Cullen, Tom, 108–10

curbside pickup, 64–66

curiosity, 4, 55

cyberattacks, 8, 117, 176

cybersecurity, 8, 125–26, 130–32

243

Motion Picture Association of America
(MPAA), 97–98, 122

Motorola, 96

Movano Health, Evie Ring, 142

MTV, 116

Murray, Alan, 102–3, 185, 186, 192,
205–6

Musk, Elon, 107, 121

Mynd Immersive, 142–43

Nadella, Satya, 129

Nalebuff, Barry, 121, 207

Nanoleaf, 139

Nasdaq, 27, 132

National Association of Home Builders,
122

National Association of Manufacturers
(NAM), 122, 191, 206

National Association of Realtors, 122

National Bureau of Economic Research,
49

National Institute of Allergy and Infectious Diseases, 9–10

National Institute of Standards and
Technology (NIST), 126

National Music Publishers Association
(NMPA), 98

National Rifle Association (NRA), 122

National Science Foundation (NSF), 30

natural selection, 7–8

Nazi Germany, 152–53

Near Field Communication (NFC), 74

Nemo's Garden, 119, 141

Netflix, 29, 107

Netherlands, 172–73

Netscape, 30, 32

Netscape Navigator, 30

Newsweek, 88

New York Stock Exchange, 68

New York Times, 38

Nike, 186–87

Ninja Future (Shapiro), 45, 56

"ninja mindset," 53, 188

ninjas, 4–5

Nintendo, 28–29, 37

Nixon, Richard, 24

Nokia, 28, 96

No Labels, 171

Northern Virginia Technology Council
(NVTC), 65, 70–71, 112, 210

North Korea, 157, 173

Northwest Airlines, ix

Nuance Audio, 144

Nuguna, 55

Nuheara, 144

NuraLogix, 142

Nuvilab, 140

NVIDIA, 133–34

Oakland University, 68

Obama, Barack, 195

Obrecht, Cliff, 99–100

Ocean Reef Group, 141

O'Connor, Dan, 143

offsetting, 205

Oh Se-hoon, 174

O'Leary, Kevin, 52

OpenAI, 165